Wisconsin's Lost Towns

W0038202

Wisconsin's Lost Towns

Rhonda Fochs

NORTH STAR PRESS OF ST. CLOUD, INC.
St. Cloud, Minnesota

DEDICATION

To the Holbrooks.
You gave me family, love, laughter, and a wealth of stories, tales, and memories. I thank God everyday for the gift of you. There isn't a day that goes by that I don't think of you, that I don't miss you.

Copyright © 2017 Rhonda Fochs
Cover map © Andrea Hill, iStock/Getty Images

All rights reserved.

ISBN 978-1-68201-058-7

Printed in the United States of America.

Published by:
    North Star Press of St. Cloud, Inc.
    Saint Cloud, Minnesota

www.northstarpress.com

ACKNOWLEDGMENTS

Without the assistance, help, and support of many, many people and organizations, this book would not have been possible. Early historians, known and unknown, wrote local and family histories and left them for later generations. Those early records and memoirs have proven to be an invaluable record of the times and people of the past. Their memories, letters, oral and written histories are a treasure trove of memories, tales, anecdotes, and facts that would be lost without their foresight and their efforts to record them. Without their contributions we would be severely limited in our knowledge and rich details of the past. It is a great debt, that I, that *we*, owe to those early historians.

I can't stress enough the importance of local historical societies and museums. These local repositories are true gems right in the midst of our local communities. With limited funds and resources, the staff and volunteers of these organizations preserve our past and ensure our future. I urge you to visit them, support them, and perhaps even volunteer. Without them, and the people involved with them, we would be sorely lacking in our historical knowledge and legacy. Libraries are equally important. This book could not have been written without them.

To my family and friends, I thank you for your belief, support, and your help in so many ways.

To all those that I missed, my apologies and thanks.

Please pass your own family and local memories on!

ORGANIZATIONS

Adams County Historical Society
Buck-A-Neer
Clark County Historical Internet Library
Iron County Historical Society
Langlade County Historical Society
Manitowoc County Historical Society
Marathon County Historical Society
Mellen Area Chamber of Commerce
Mid-Continent Railway
Milwaukee County Historical Society
Oconto County Historical Society
Pepin County Historical Society
Portage County Historical Society
Price County Historical Society
Richland County Historical Society
Sauk County Historical Society
Sawyer County Historical Society
Shawano County Historical Society
Sheboygan County Historical Society
Trempealeau County Historical Society
Vernon County Historical Society
Walworth County Historical Society
Winter Area Chamber of Commerce

INDIVIDUALS

Kevin Abing
Ruth Anderson
Joyce Bant
Gail Barrenco
Jodie Bednar- Clemens
Joyce Bednar Young
Nick Benard
Nancy Bergman
Jesse Borlen
Pat Blackman
Beverly Brayton
Harry Davis
Martha Degner
Linda Deith
David Engel
Crystal Foley
Jill Gondeck
Barb and John Grek
Joseph Hermolin
Virginia Feld Johnson
Sue Johnston
Mary Lee Klaus
Carol Krogan
Margaret Kropp
A.K. Lallas

Jeffery Lentz
Linda Levenhagen
LuAnne Lind
Jodie Fobes Livingston
Michael Meier
Terry Mesch
Carol Pearson
Gary Peterson
Larry Reed
Kate Reily
Tammie Renel
Melinda Roberts
Jerry Rohlinger
Marion Scharfnagel
Janet and Stan Schwarze
Anne Seubert
Elaine Spindler
Gordon and Toni Stevenson
Pastor Sylvia Lee-Thompson
Catherine Techtmann
Norbert Vissers
Dave Walters
Kitty Werner
Matthew Wykle
Barb and Mark Zimmerman

TABLE OF CONTENTS

INTRODUCTION

A few years back my grandmother's former house (also my aunt and uncle's former house) was up for sale. I hadn't been inside the house for decades, so my cousin Caryl gave me a final tour.

Just driving up to the house brought back memories. I could almost see my aunts and uncles and grandmother coming out to greet me. Going into the house intensified the feeling. Everywhere I looked I saw the people of my past. All of us at the kitchen table, eating, laughing and telling the stories of the past and our lives.

Oh, how I wish I had listened better. How I wish I had paid more attention to the banter around the table. But I was young, and the people and places didn't mean much to me. As I grew older and could listen and observe better, they too were older. My time listening to their stories was growing short and then was over all too soon. Now they live in my memories and in my heart. Tears fall as I write this. Walking through that house brought it all back as it does when I think of them.

With time and thought, I realized that, even though it was home to loved ones, it was only a house. A house filled with memories, but the people who lived there, the people who brought it to life are gone, except from the heart. Their stories are special and they matter.

Such it is with all lost towns. Each and every one is special, as were the people who lived there and brought them to life. By sharing their stories, we keep the people and the towns alive.

My Aunt Charlotte once wrote, "Land is land. It is the people who are the history makers."

Journey to the past, as we visit the people and places of *Wisconsin's Lost Towns*.

WHAT IS A GHOST TOWN?

With no clear-cut definition, determining what constitutes a ghost town is highly subjective, often a matter of degree and opinion.

Purists will define a ghost town—a true ghost town—as a town that has been completely abandoned. Others argue that a ghost town is any community that is a semblance, shadow—or "ghost"—of what it used to be.

At its core, on a basic level, the most agreed upon definition would be that of a human settlement that has been abandoned. With an arbitrary definition in place it is possible to further classify ghost towns into categories or classes based on definitive characteristics.

The most common breakdowns and classes are: **

CLASS A - Barren site, nature has reclaimed the land, no visible signs of former inhabitation;

CLASS B - Rubble, foundations, roofless buildings;

CLASS C - Standing abandoned buildings, no/rural population, hamlet, no viable organized community;

CLASS D - Semi/Near Ghost town. Many abandoned buildings, small resident population;

CLASS E - Busy historic community—smaller than in boom days;

CLASS F - Restored town, historically preserved status.

A seventh category could also be included:

CLASS G - town joined to or was absorbed by neighboring/thriving city.

Many communities, whatever their class, did leave behind tangible remains in the form of cemeteries. The hallowed grounds are a visible record of the times and lives of the town's inhabitants. Many areas also carry the town's name.

**Modified from Gary Speck's *Classes of Ghost Towns*

Note: Classification is subjective into more than one class, or may not completely fit in any class.

LIFE-CYCLE OF A GHOST TOWN

Wisconsin, with its abundance of natural resources, has a multitude of used-to-be-towns—ghost towns. Generally based on a one-resource, one-industry economy, the population and all town activity would be heavily dependent on that one factor. The town survived as long as the resource did. Once it was depleted, the industry/owners moved workers and equipment to new locations and new opportunities.

The Michigan Chronoscope E-press describes the process simply and effectively. After the owners/industry moved on, soon the supporting businesses (retail, banks, saloons, brothels, hotels) failed, and the owners closed shop. Residents moved on to new lives, new jobs, homes, and communities. Some towns were dismantled, packed up and shipped out, to be reassembled in new locations. Others were abandoned and reclaimed by nature. Most left no physical remains except a cemetery or place name.

The earliest settlements first appeared along major transportation routes, primarily rivers. As time would progress, other transportation routes provided prime locations for a town, along tote roads or railroad lines. Others grew in haphazard patterns, when and where there was an opportunity. Native American villages were among the first communities. Though many were seasonal, they had some permanent villages. As settlers moved in, the communities became more permanent.

While each town or community was unique and had its own personality, there was a definite pattern to their life-cycles. The only variable being the rate of progression or pace at which a town moves(ed) through the cycle. Depending on the commodity or resource, this time frame could vary greatly.

Economists, sociologists, and historians have labeled this a "boom-and-bust" economy. Models have been created that include definitive characteristics and stages of such an economy. Mining towns, particularly Western mining towns, were the examples most often used in setting the model. In large part, mining towns moved through the progression at a rapid pace. Moving at such an accelerated pace, it was possible to make observations that fit most of the towns that were products of a "boom and bust" economy. Michael Conlin, a business professor in Canada concisely lists the six stages of a "boom and bust" cycle in his book *Mining Heritage and Tourism*. The following are simplified modifications of his model as well as the process described by E-Press:

Stage One – Discovery and Growth
Resource is discovered and developed.
Size of the workforce is capped by workforce required to exploit the resource, often dictated by size and type of resource

Stage Two – Production
Highest level of activity

Stage Three – Decline
Production begins to decline—can be depletion of the resource or a decline in demand.
Can also be that costs have escalated making it unprofitable.
Decline may be rapid.

Stage Four – Abandonment
Owners move equipment and workers to new locations, closing down current production.
Supporting businesses fail/close shop.
Residents move on.

Stage Five – Decay
Town is either packed up or moved on, or buildings are left to decay.

Stage Six – Disappearance of Evidence of Occupation
Everything moved on or reclaimed by nature.

As the E-Press states, towns built on this model were doomed from the beginning to be ghost towns.

LIFE CYCLE BIBLIOGRAPHY

Conlin, Michael V., Lee Joliffe, ed. *Mining Heritage and Tourism: A Global Synthesis.*, UK, Routledge, 2010.
"Ghost Towns of Newaygo." E-Press Chronograph Number II. Big Prairie Press. Winter 2007. Web. 16, November 2012.

GHOST TOWN CODE OF ETHICS

By their very nature, ghost towns are subject to the ravages of time and the elements. Harsh winter weather and humid summers in Wisconsin take their toll on the remnants of abandoned communities. Vandalism as well as accidental or unintentional damage adds to the ultimate deterioration of the sites. It is our duty and responsibility to treat these historic sites with respect and to do all we can to preserve the integrity of ghost towns. Use common sense and follow a code of ethics.

RESPECT PRIVATE PROPERTY.

Many former town sites are now located on private property. Please respect all private property.

Do not trespass—Do not enter private property without permission from the owner.

OBEY ALL POSTED SIGNS

Do not destroy, damage or deface any remains, buildings, or structures.

Do not remove anything from the sites.

Do not cause any disturbance to the foundations, vegetation, or land.

Do not litter. Remove and properly dispose of any trash you take into the area.

Always be courteous, respectful and SAFE.

TREAD LIGHTLY—TAKE ONLY PHOTOS—LEAVE ONLY FOOTPRINTS

Make as little impact on the environment as possible.

Honor the past and preserve it for the future.

Adams County

Big Flats vintage postcard (Author's Collection)

Big Flats stage stop (Courtesy of Adams County Historical Society)

BARNUM

1865 – 1883

CLASS A

APPROXIMATE LOCATION:
Highway 131 north of Steuben, Town of Rome

Company towns had a brief and limited lifespan. Built to accommodate the company and its employees, the towns lasted only as long as the company, the business, and the resources did. In Barnum's case, as long as the timber did.

Barnum proved to be a readily accessible and convenient location for logs to be floated over the rapids. One report tells that, at its peak, the Barnum mill sawed over 100,000 feet of lumber daily.

Operations began in the mid-1860s and lasted until the late 1870s, when disaster struck. In 1876 fire destroyed the mill and, along with it, most of Barnum itself. An early resident wrote that arson was considered the cause. Sawing had been completed for the season, and the mill had been shut down for weeks. The fire was sudden and unexpected, and arson seemed to be the only logical reason.

The mill was not rebuilt; the houses were torn down or moved. The post office was discontinued in 1883, with services being relocated to New Rome.

BIG FLATS

1862 – 1924

CLASS C

APPROXIMATE LOCATION:
Highway 13, Town of Big Flats

Boys will be boys. Because of that, only male teachers were hired for the winter term of school classes in Big Flats. Most of the boys in the district attended school only in the winter and their minds were more interested in pranks and causing disruptions than in getting an education. People thought a male teacher could better handle the shenanigans and the unruly lads. Perhaps so, but many a time,

the male teacher was found locked out of the schoolhouse. Female teachers were hired for the fall and spring terms, at a discounted salary.

First called Brownsville, the community also included a hotel, a tavern, a large dance hall, and a nearby Woodsman Hall. A post office operated from 1862 until 1924. The early post office was considered a fourth-class post office, as it did not issue money orders. Later, when the post offices in Roche a Cri and Beatrice closed, the Big Flats post office was upgraded to a third-class facility and was able to sell money orders.

Prone to frequent fires in the early 1900s, the burned-over land was ideal for blueberries. Bumper crops were reported. The dance hall had to be converted to a blueberry warehouse in the summer to hold the bounty. The blueberries were packed in baskets, covered with mosquito netting and hauled by teams to Grand Rapids, Wisconsin, for rail shipment to further points.

Several travelers overnighted in Big Flats. The New Big Flats store offered six bedrooms and a living room on the upper floor. Hot meals were served, and a livery barn were available. The stage coach made stops from 1895 to 1900. The building was later moved and converted to a bed and breakfast.

A 1992 tornado wreaked havoc on the area. Two people were killed, twenty-two injured, and twelve buildings were flattened. Damage was estimated at 5.6 million dollars (in 1992 dollars). Rebuilding was slower than hoped.

A 1971 *LaCrosse Tribune* article featured the Big Flats village. At that time, a handful of families lived there.

BIG SPRING

1854 – 1904

CLASS C

APPROXIMATE LOCATION:
7 miles east/northeast of Wisconsin Dells

Begun as a settlement around the sawmill, Big Spring evolved into a village. The sawmill was later converted to a flour- and feedmill. Big Spring prospered and with time included a general store, a post office, a blacksmith, a physician, a tobacco/sweet shop, a cobbler, a creamery, a cheese factory, and two churches. Other entities included a foundry and machine shop as well as a carding mill.

Big Spring's heavy clay soil was found to be ideal for growing hops, one of the main ingredients in beer. Much of the

Big Spring Cheese Factory, as shown on this vintage postcard. (Courtesy of www.vintagewisconsindells.com)

area's farmland was put into growing the prized crop, which artificially inflated the region's property and land values. Some reports state that hop-producing land sold for as much as one thousand dollars an acre. When the bottom fell out of the hop market, the region's economy collapsed as well. Only the up-and-coming dairy industry staved off disaster. The region remained agriculturally based with a wide European ethnicity.

DELLWOOD

1915

CLASS A/B

APPROXIMATE LOCATION:
County Z and County J, Town of Strong's Prairie

Developed as a summer recreational resort area in the early twentieth century, Dellwood is, according to the Adams County Historical Society, a "phoenix." At its inception, over 3,000 acres of land along the Wisconsin River were purchased by the Badgerland Development Corporation. The land was divided into twenty-five-foot-by-one-hundred-thirty-foot lots. Thirty-three-foot and sixty-six-foot-wide roads were constructed and paved with cinders. Originally the lots

sold for $47.50 each, but buyers had to purchase a minimum of two lots. River frontage land was not subdivided but was designated a community property for all land owners to enjoy. Three large public areas were set aside as "parks": Dellwood and Roche a Cri parks were along the Little Roche a Cri Creek, while Fidelity Park was along the Wisconsin River. The development corporation offered landowners the option of having a cabin, available in four styles, built at cost. Model homes were built, as was a community house.

An aggressive marketing and advertising program was targeted at Chicago-area residents in 1926. A sales letter invited prospective buyers to Dellwood to visit the resort. Reports state that over 300 people came to the area over Memorial Day weekend in 1926. Hugely successful, over 4,500 lots were sold. The next year saw even more growth, with a 150-unit hotel being built. Electricity came to Dellwood that same year. Far from advanced, electricity was supplied by a car motor running two hours a day.

A dance hall and "soft-drink" parlor were also new in 1927. Dubbed the Dellwood Pavilion, it quickly became the entertainment center for the region. The Adams County Historical Society writes that big-name bands from as far away as Milwaukee and Chicago played at the Pavilion. Ahead of its days, a mirrored ball splashed glittering lights around the dance floor. It is said the Pavilion had a back room that offered slot machines and bootleg alcohol.

The 1929 stock market crash put an end to the prosperity and the project. Many lot owners lost everything and the property was sold for back taxes. Businesses were forced to close their doors, including the Pavilion and the hotel.

Following World War II, Dellwood continued its decline and was all but abandoned.

In the 1940s, the Consolidated Water Power and Paper Company of the Wisconsin River began to buy up river frontage land. Plans were underway to build two dams. The dams created Castle Rock and Petenwell Flowage. Once again, the area promised recreational opportunities, and once again, people flocked to the area. With the lake and all it offered, Dellwood was once again bustling. The burgeoning automobile traffic offered travelers easy access to the area and the region boomed with tourists, visitors, sportsmen, and year-round residents. Once again, Dellwood was booming.

The community house still stands and is now private property. The hotel was dismantled, and the site is now under Castle Rock Lake, as are Dellwood's three former parks. The Pavilion was operated under a succession of owners and underwent several renovations. It is still in operation. Tourism is big business in the region and once again Dellwood is at the heart of it.

EASTON

1866 - 1920

CLASS C/D

APPROXIMATE LOCATION:
East of Highway 13 on County Road A near intersection of A and 11th Drive

As with the majority of early settlements, it all began with the mill, and oftentimes ended with the mill. Easton's mill was built in the early 1850s, and the village was born. Easton is also the township name and the two are often interchanged in the records and histories.

Easton came to life in the Civil War years. In the beginning, things looked promising. A 1868 news article predicted prosperity and great things for the village.

In addition to providing water power for the mill, the creek also provided power to the local blacksmith, who dammed up the creek and used his own water wheel for power.

Records tell that in 1925, Easton village was home to fifty people. An early industry was the carding mill. The mill

Colby's Mill, Easton (Author's Collection)

processed wool from local sheep producers. After the wool was spun into yarn, it was sent to Baraboo to be "fulled," after which it was used to make men's pants. The carding mill was gone by the 1870s.

The mill lasted until the 1930s and stood until 1940. The cheese factory operated until the 1920s or 1930s, and the building was later used as a tavern. A local landmark was the "Stone House," built in the 1870s.

The town of Easton (township) celebrated its 150th anniversary in 2006.

Above: A river scene from Easton (Author's Collection)
Below: Colby's store, Easton (Author's Collection)

Easton's Stone House (Author's Collection)

HOLLIDAY (FLIGHT'S) MILL

1900 – 1904

CLASS A/B

APPROXIMATE LOCATION:
East of Highway 13 on Aspen Avenue

First called Flight's Mill, the settlement was renamed when a new owner took possession of the mill. Situated on the Big Roche a Cri Creek, the mill was later converted to a flour and grist mill. The settlement included a large, two-story hotel with a basement kitchen. The stage coach ran from Grand Rapids, Wisconsin, to Portage, Wisconsin, along the Pinery Road and made stops at the hotel. The hotel burned to the ground in 1938 or 1939 and was not rebuilt. A tavern and school were also part of the settlement. A post office operated just four years, from 1900 to 1904.

Atcherson's Resort, Plainville. (Author's Collection)

NEW ROME

1858 – 1951

CLASS A

APPROXIMATE LOCATION:
Town of New Rome

As with many early villages, New Rome developed around a mill, in this case Fordham's Mill. The post office lasted nearly one hundred years. The village itself lasted well into the 1970s, although little written documentation of the village was found.

After Friendship was designated the county seat, the mill moved to Arkdale, the post office was discontinued, and New Rome diminished.

NIEBULL

1888 – 1913

CLASS A/B

APPROXIMATE LOCATION:
Big Flats area

While the village of Niebull is long gone, a part of the community lives on.

In 2002, the school was moved to the grounds of the Adams County Historical Society in Friendship and was rededicated. The building was constructed to replace the original log school. According to the Adams County Historical Society, the school was one of the last one-room schools to close, and did so in 1961.

Today, the school is still in the business of education. It is used for meetings, exhibits, and other events.

PLAINVILLE

1856 - 1942

CLASS A

APPROXIMATE LOCATION:
Near the intersection of County K and Highway 13

Plainville's 1938 flood. (Courtesy of www.vintagewisconsindells.com)

No one was immune. The scourge traveled fast, as rampant as a wildfire. Everyone was afflicted or knew someone who was. Students, families, friends, and even the teacher suffered the symptoms, chief of which was itching. It is said the teacher experienced great difficulty in trying to fight the urge to scratch in front of the class. Things got so bad the school was known to the locals as "The Scratching School." Treatment ran a course of three months.

Centered by a sawmill on Plainville Creek, the community was Adams County's first platted village. A mill was built in 1840 by James Edson of New York. Edson stayed just a short time, but the mill gave rise to a bustling community that lasted nearly ninety years.

Plainville was established at a meeting in 1851. Just a few short years later the settlement included thirty homes, a blacksmith, a tavern, a furniture shop, and a church. In 1856, a post office was established. Mail was delivered by horseback three times a week.

An early resident reported that by the 1870s, most of Plainville was gone. The post office was discontinued in 1942.

ROCHE A CREE (CRI)

1856 - 1905
CLASS C/D

APPROXIMATE LOCATION:
Highway 13, 6 miles north of Friendship

Oftentimes settlements and communities took on the name of early settlers and prominent citizens. Thus it was with Cottonville, or, as it was officially known, Roche a Cri.

Emulous P. Cotton, a former delegate to the 1884 Wisconsin Constitutional Convention, and his brother were the first to settle in the Adams County area. Their first order of business was to build and operate a mill along the Roche a Cri Creek. That they did in 1856. That same year, E.P.'s son built and operated a general store. Officially platted in 1856, things looked promising for the fledgling community. Lots were selling well, a school was built, a post office was established, and a tavern was operating. Main Street ran across the dam, providing easy access to Grand Rapids (now Wisconsin Rapids). The Civil War would put an end to all the progress.

According to the Adams County Historical Society, many area men were away fighting the war and the county's population dropped from over 7,000 residents to just 6,000 in the five years of the war. A railroad survey crew came to Cottonville but no railroad line was realized, at least for Cottonville.

After the war, a major flood destroyed the mill, and it was determined to not be worth rebuilding. The post office was discontinued in 1905 or 1906. In the 1920s, a power dam was built on the old mill site creating Cottonville Lake. Today the area is a popular recreation area for area residents and vacationers.

A card postmarked from White Creek. (Author's Collection)

Marker in Roche a Cri (Courtesy of Wisconsin Roots/Hintz)

Above and below: Postcards from Strong's Prairie. (Author's Collection)

Strong's Prairie Cemetery.
(Courtesy of Karen Nelson, www.findagrave.com)

STRONG'S PRAIRIE

1857 - 1952

CLASS C

APPROXIMATE LOCATION:
Chicago Drive and 21st Avenue, Town of Strong's Prairie

How times have changed. A period news article written in 1872 that read "M.F. Hammond, dealer in drugs and medicines is doing a lively business" would certainly be interpreted differently in today's world. Yes, the world was a different place in the nineteenth century.

Strong's Prairie, the village, can be easily confused with the town (township), and often historical records and documents interchange the two. Records are clear the post office operated nearly one hundred years, from 1857 until 1952. Still, written resources are hard to locate. The village also had a dance hall, a nearby Methodist church and a general store said to have the biggest ice cream cones in the world.

WHITE CREEK (CASCADE)

1855 - 1945

CLASS D

APPROXIMATE LOCATION:
9½ miles from Adams, County H, 1 mile from Highway 13

Location, location, location! Any real estate agent will tell you that location is the number one predictor of success. So when Adams County's Cascade was founded in an "ideal location" because it was situated on a reliable water source and was equidistant between Friendship and Kilbourne (Wisconsin Dells), big things were expected.

Key to the new mill site was White Creek, with its natural twelve-foot waterfall. There was more than enough water to power the mill. A mill was often the precursor to an adjacent settlement, and thus Cascade was established. The mill was built in 1850 and the lumber milled at the site was used to build the village. The settlement was platted in 1851 and dubbed Cascade. That name was short-lived as the Postal Service informed the citizens that a Cascade, Wisconsin, already existed, so an alternative name had to be chosen. Though the area was known as and referred to as Cascade, its official name was White Creek and the area is still known as White Creek today.

As the mill's success continued, settlement of the village hastened. Early settlers encouraged family and friends to relocate to the rapidly growing community. Soon White Creek included a blacksmith, a general store, two hotels, a dance hall, a church, a school, a lawyer's office, and a post office. Main Street was lined with board sidewalks. The post office had an exceptionally long lifespan, nearly one hundred years, from 1855 until 1945. The hotel was at one time the largest in the county. The dance hall was later moved to Easton and was part of the Easton Town Hall. A Congregational church was established in 1870. It was still active in recent years.

Growth of the community was credited, in part, to its location along the stagecoach line. As trains became the transportation mode of choice, a rail line was platted in the area, bypassing White Creek by ten miles. The new station town of Adams benefitted from the rail line as White Creek was impacted by the loss of both the stage and railroad. Further impacting White Creek was the fact that when automobiles became the norm, a new highway was built, again bypassing White Creek. The new Highway 13 was constructed just one mile from the village. Growth was at a standstill and White Creek's demise was on a roll.

Decline for White Creek was gradual. White Creek's former Main Street became County Highway H. In 1938, a tavern was built, and in 1940, a dance hall was added. It remained a popular spot for years, both for residents and the new influx of summer and recreational visitors.

In 1945, the postmistress resigned due to health concerns. She was not replaced, and the post office was discontinued.

Mobile homes, Castle Rock Elementary School, two taverns, the church, new homes, and remnants of former buildings occupy the village today. Referred to as a "bedroom" community, many live in the White Creek area and work in neighboring communities.

The Greenwood Store in White Creek. (Author's Collection)

White Creek. (Author's Collection)

White Creek Tavern. (Courtesy of Ralph Sabroff)

White Creek's business district. (Author's Collection)

The hotel in White Creek shortly before demolition. (Courtesy of Teresa Heitman)

The interior of the hotel shortly before demolition. (Courtesy of Ralph Sabroff)

Ashland County

Cuyuga Hotel and Saloon today. (Courtesy of Cuyuga Hotel and Saloon)

One of the eleven hotel rooms available for visitors at the Cuyuga Hotel and Saloon. (Courtesy of Cuyuga Hotel and Saloon)

The interior of the saloon. (Courtesy of Cuyuga Hotel and Saloon)

CAYUGA

1906 – 1956

CLASS C/D

APPROXIMATE LOCATION:
10 miles north of Glidden

It's not often we can learn the history of a long-ago town from someone who lived there. Richard Evanson was born in Cayuga in 1924. In 1990, he retired back to his hometown. With the help of the Carol at the Mellen Chamber of Commerce, Richard shared his memories of Cayuga. Always a history lover, luckily for us, Richard told us of Cayuga. The following is a summary of his recollections.

Cayuga was first known as Cornell Siding. A New York company associated with Cornell University chose the name. However, when a post office application was submitted, it turned out that Wisconsin already had a Cornell, so it was named Cayuga after New York State's Cayuga Lake. Wisconsin's Cayuga is on Highway 13 and the Bad River runs through the town (good thing we aren't superstitious).

Richard says the folklore legend behind the village's name was Cayuga because Model Ts would go through town and blow their horns, "OOOga, OOOga."

At its peak, Cayuga had a post office (which lasted until 1956), a grocery store, a shingle factory, a school, a Chevrolet dealership, a boarding house, and lumbering activities. The population was three hundred.

As the timber resources dwindled, after about seventeen years, the village faded. Approximately twenty-five area residents call Cayuga home. The only business still in operation is the Cayuga Hotel and Saloon, which occupies the former boarding house. The eleven upstairs rooms are available for rent, perfect for hunters and snowmobilers. The saloon offers great food and bar drinks.

MORSE

1890 – 1958

CLASS B/C

APPROXIMATE LOCATION:
7½ miles south/southeast of Mellen

Living a rollercoaster existence of boom and bust, Morse had a series of name changes, as well.

Beginning in 1881, workers began improving a branch of the Bad River for logging and began clearing a forty-acre site for the logging settlement. The Wisconsin Central Railroad agreed to construct a siding to the site, first known as Jacob's Station. When it was said and done, a boarding house, a warehouse, stores, a blacksmith, and number of timber sheds were on the site. Twelve miles of the Bad River had been improved. Plans were to bring in fifty families (German), but the mill owner William Jacobi died unexpectedly. His successor dropped the plans for the German settlement.

In 1883, mill operations were wildly successful. Randall Rohe, in his book *Ghosts of the Forest: Vanished Lumber Towns of Wisconsin, Volume I*, wrote that the mill produced an average of 50,000 feet per day, six million for the season. During October alone, ninety-six car loads of lumber were shipped out.

By 1884, a thriving settlement grew up around the mill. In 1887, the Penokee Lumber Company was established and according to Rohe, this would impact the Bad River as extensive improvements on the Bad changed the dynamics of logging and milling in the area. One of the lumber company's founding partners took charge of local operations and Jacob's Station was renamed Morse in 1889. The company added an electrical light plant that provided lighting.

Records from insurance inspectors tell that the yard was the cleanest of any mill of the time. Morse officials believed, and rightly so, that the greatest fire danger came from the refuse lying around a mill. The company never suffered a single dollar's worth of damage due to fire. Large water barrels bearing the words "Keep Me Full" in red were placed every few feet and around all the buildings.

Approximately 225 men were employed by the mill. For men with families, the company built neat little residences, all of them painted Morse red. The company also built a church that could seat one hundred people. When the mills closed down for the winter, most of the men went to work in the company's logging camps. Seventy-five Clydesdales were kept as working draft horses. Rohe wrote that in October of 1891, as a bandsaw cut through a thirty-two-inch diameter log (can you imagine such a large log today?) it uncovered an iron tomahawk, six inches long with a two-and-a-half-inch blade.

During the summer of 1891, the company constructed sidewalks, graded roads, and dug ditches to carry off the refuse. A two-story meat market was built. Morse at the time had a population of 400 to 500 and a school enrollment of thirty.

Baseball was popular and games with neighboring communities (Butternut, Glidden, Ashland, Park Falls, and Washburn) were well-attended. The company constructed a clubhouse at the edge of the village, which included a coat room, a smoking room, a dance hall, and dressing rooms, complete with electric lights. Gymnastic equipment was added in the fall of 1891.

Being in Wisconsin's snowbelt, Morse got an average of 140 inches of snow a year. Winter activities were also popular.

The population of Morse reached six hundred in 1895. That year was also the end of the Penokee Lumber Company, and with that, Morse quickly resembled a ghost town. Company houses were moved to vacant lots in Ashland. Before many houses were moved, a Boston company purchased all the property, except for the school. Their plans were to build a tannery. They tore down Morse's buildings and moved them to Mellen in 1896.

Morse wasn't vacant for long. An Oshkosh lumberman set up a new mill operation. Morse came alive again as a house-building boom began. Fifteen homes were built for the newly arrived Russian families.

Short-lived, the revival lasted until the fall of 1903. Fire destroyed the mill, the store, and approximately six million feet of lumber. The cause of the fire was determined to be arson, set by a recently discharged employee. The loss put the Chase Company in bankruptcy. Morse's population dropped to twenty-five. The post office was discontinued. New owners dismantled the mill and Morse was once again just a side track.

Logging operations in the area sometimes used Morse as a base. One owner did manage to get the post office reestablished. Hanging on, new owners took over in 1917 and brought Morse back to life, albeit briefly. Houses were built, the population soared to four hundred and a boarding house, a large store, and a restaurant were added.

The swell in population increased school enrollment numbers so much so that the old school became too small. Town officials appropriated $5,000 for a new school with a library, washrooms, and a furnace.

Morse today. (Courtesy of "Jeff the Quiet," Wikimedia Commons, http://commons.wikimedia.org/w/index.php?curid=31594151)

Things were busy and thriving until 1926, when operations stopped. A 1927 fire destroyed the store, meat market, and ice house. Flames spread so rapidly, any efforts to quell them were useless.

It was decided in 1929 to run out the timber supply. The sawmill ran day and night. Smaller mills operated in the area and Morse was still a village. The company pulled out in 1933. Company houses sold for seventy-five dollars and were moved to nearby communities and some as far away as Phillips. The Great Depression was Morse's final death knell

In the 1940s, the old dry kilns made cedar shingles. In 1946, a company made hampers and ladders. The post office was discontinued in 1958. Morse is still on some maps, but only a few buildings remain.

The sign welcoming visitors to Shanagolden. (Courtesy of "Shanagolden," http://www.naish.50megs.com/)

SHANAGOLDEN

1903 - 1912

CLASS B/C

APPROXIMATE LOCATION:
3½ miles west of Glidden

Shanagolden is one of those lyrical places whose memories former residents cherish and whose tales today's historian's treasure. Thanks to the efforts of Wisconsin historians Randall Rohe and Dave Engel, much is known about Shanagolden, and through their words we can revisit its history. Written memoirs also aid our journey, and Judge Herbert Bunde left us a remarkable recollection in Dave Engel's book on Shanagolden. Herein lies the tale of Shanagolden.

Right after the turn of the twentieth century, 1901 to be exact, the Nash Lumber Company purchased 40,000 acres in southern Ashland County and adjoining Sawyer County, and set about building a logging village. The east branch of the Chippewa River divided the sawmill and the planing mill from the office, store, boarding houses, and homes. A foot-and-wagon bridge connected the two.

Shanagolden was different than other logging towns in that it helped its workers build homes of their own. The company furnished the lots and the lumber and offered payment plans. With private ownership, the homes were nice and neat and the village looked more like a village than a logging settlement. In 1905, the population of Shanagolden was 400 to 500 people.

Judge Bunde lived in Shanagolden as a young boy. He fondly remembered the things of youth: Christmas, friends, and family. He recalled that there was one street along the river with another set back but running parallel to the first. There were three or four connecting streets. "Downtown," according to Bunde, was small and consisted of only three buildings: the general store with the Nash Lumber Company office in the rear, a boarding house with long tables and a lounge for card-playing (the second floor consisted of rooms for the boarders), and a bunkhouse with two floors of rooms. A community hall that hosted lots of social events was across the street from the store.

The school was located on a back street. It was a frame building with a front entrance, two rooms, and two teachers. One teacher taught the first four grades, the other the upper four grades.

A Modern Woodmen of America hall (with a glee club) also hosted many a social event. Fifteen to twenty homes made up the residential district. But the prize of all Shanagolden was the Nash House in the Woods. Located on the northeast edge of the village, the frame building was said to be magnificent in every way.

Shanagolden never had a church, so residents traveled to Glidden for services. If an itinerant preacher happened by, makeshift services were offered in the school or any available building.

A Ladies' Aid Society was established in 1905. The ladies hoped to raise enough money to build a reading room and lecture hall. Ice cream socials, dances, and suppers were hosted to raise funds. The hall was called the Shanagolden Improvement Club. The hall had a fireplace at each end and kitchen in the rear.

Nash Lumber never allowed alcohol in the village, although a "blind pig" (alcohol sold illegally) was suspected.

A wagon wheel, overgrown by brush in Shanagolden. (Courtesy of "Shanagolden," http://www.naish.50megs.com/)

Fishing and hunting were popular activities and most men had a gun. There was even a Shanagolden Gun Club with a trap-shooting range. Competitions with each other and neighboring communities were popular. The mill pond was the town swimming hole until the sandy-bottomed pond was filled in to make a baseball diamond. Card games, especially cinch, were popular. Nearby Glidden hosted concerts and other events.

A fire broke out in 1907 and the mill burned to the ground. Workers and residents tried to put out the fire with buckets of water, but the water spread hot ashes through the mill and within minutes the entire mill was an inferno. They could do little other than stand by and watch. The loss of the mill put most of the employees out of work, and no work meant no pay. Many men found work in nearby communities and some left the region. Nash sold out in 1910 and new owners put in a shingle mill, but that only employed a fraction of the mill's workforce.

At one point, the Mellon Lumber Company bought logging rights, but the base of business was in Glidden. It was only logical that since the work was in Glidden, so should be the homes. Many houses were moved. Glidden was considered a rough-and-tough town, with most of the businesses being saloons.

The Ashland Farm Company was formed and purchased Shanagolden's store, boarding house, sawmill site, the majority of the remaining residences, and 40,000 acres of cutover land. With a purchase price of $800,000, Rohe wrote that it was the largest deal in cutover land in Wisconsin up to that time.

Extensive plans to develop an agricultural community were laid. A church, an orphanage, pure-bred cattle, and hybrid vegetables and grain were part of the plan. Repairs of the remaining structures were undertaken and a small demonstration plot was planted. Agriculture never replaced logging. The short growing season and the rocky soil hampered efforts from the beginning. Things didn't go well and in October of 1916, 4,000 acres of land were put up for sale at five to seven dollars an acre. Nearly everyone who looked bought at least forty acres, with most buying 160 acres.

Today Shanagolden is, as Rohe wrote, one of the more interesting ghost towns to visit. Some of the houses now stand on Park Street in Glidden. Most of the railroad grade that led to the mill still stands. Portions of the brick wall of the boiler still stand. Crumbling foundations of the company office, the store, and the boarding house are still visible in the weeds. A lone hydrant stands sentinel. The former community club building was the Shanagolden Town Hall, and is now dedicated to the pioneers of Shanagolden.

Part of the ruins of Shanagolden's lumber mill. (Courtesy of "Shanagolden," http://www.naish.50megs.com/)

Shanagolden Town Hall. (Courtesy of "Shanagolden," http://www.naish.50megs.com/)

Barron County

Our Lady of Lourdes in Dobie, Wisconsin. (Courtesty of the St. Joseph's Church Cluster)

DOBIE

1893 – 1903

CLASS A/C

APPROXIMATE LOCATION:
Northeast of Rice Lake near 24th Avenue and 23rd Street

Coming from Canada, the first immigrants to the region were the French (from Quebec) and Irish (from Eastern Ontario). The French settled to the south while the Irish settled in the north. Though of differing ethnic backgrounds, the two groups shared the Catholic faith. Early services were held in a settler's cabin. In the late 1860s, a priest laid out the location of the first church building, Barron County's first Roman Catholic church. That first church was a fourteen-by-seventy-foot building just north and east of the present church.

After construction of the church and parsonage, a school and convent was built in 1881. The Sisters of Notre Dame managed the school until 1968. Students often boarded with the sisters. The convent and school closed in 1970.

The first church burned in 1895, and the present building was constructed in 1904.

In 1976, the church celebrated its centennial and in 2001, the church building was designated a Wisconsin Historic Place. In 2014, Our Lady of Lourdes clustered with four other churches near Rice Lake.

REEVE

1898 – 1913

CLASS C/D

APPROXIMATE LOCATION:
County Roads A and K

Though much smaller and quieter now than in its heyday, Reeve is home to a handful of homes, the Vance Town Garage, and Reeve's Evangelical Free Church. Back in its prime, the crossroads community included a general store/post office, a couple of gas stations, a meat locker, a creamery, and until recently, a bar and grill. A small-gauge railroad connected the logging camps to the community. The Reeve Evangelical Free Church is still active and fosters a welcoming community spirit to residents and visitors.

Reeve Evangelical Free Church. (Courtesyof the Reeve Evangelical Free Church and Pastor Todd)

Bayfield County

Today's Delta Diner (above) and the Delta Diner Store (below). (Courtesy of the Delta Diner)

BIBON

1899 - 1909

CLASS A

APPROXIMATE LOCATION:
Intersection of Highway 63 and County E, between Mason and Grand View, now known as Bibon Swamp

Boom-and-bust towns were settlements based on one resource, and thus one industry. Everything in the community was dependent on that industry, that resource. As long as the resource lasted, so did the settlement. When the logs were gone, the mines mined out, whatever the resource, so went the settlement. Railroads also played a major role in the establishment of the boom-and-bust settlements.

According to an article posted on the Marengo Valley History Association Facebook page, Bibon was one of those boom-and-bust locations. The vast northern forests provided logs for the Chicago Lumber and Coal Company's mills. The railroad shipped the timber to points north (Ashland, to be loaded on Great Lakes freighters), south to Chicago, and west to Minneapolis and St. Paul. The settlement provided support services and businesses.

Once home to over seven hundred people Bibon had all the necessary amenities for the workers and crews, even a high school. Things in Bibon were booming indeed—until 1903, when the mill was destroyed by fire. Since the timber had nearly been logged off, the company chose not to rebuild the mill and the end was in sight.

The history recounts that in 1906, Bibon still had 600 residents, but by the next year it was down to just seventy-five. Today the area is known as Bibon Swamp.

DELTA

1924 - 1965

CLASS A/C

APPROXIMATE LOCATION:
County Highway H near FR223 and Camp I Road

For nearly thirty years, the old site sat vacant. What had once been the heart of Delta, the former Delta Store site, was unused and forlorn. All of that changed in 2002, when an old "Silk City" dining car, in need of restoration, was found in New York and moved to the northern woods of Wisconsin. With a lot of heart and hard work, owners Todd and Nina established the Delta Diner and the Delta Diner Store. Today the diner is known for its classic diner fare, its own unique delectable specials, and its down-home atmosphere, as well as its special events, such as vintage and classic car shows, their "Blueplate Special Lecture" series and more, including an in-house bakery.

Begun by logging interests in the late 1800s, the community along Highway H in Bayfield County was also a station stop along the Duluth, South Shore and Atlantic Railroad. Delta was along its route from Duluth to Nestoria, Michigan.

The Delta Store was established in 1923, one year before the town of Delta was officially organized. A post office was commissioned in 1924 under the name of Buhl or Buol. At that time the post office didn't accept the name Delta as there were already too many "Deltas" in existence. The store was a multi-purposed business and included the general store, the

The original Delta Store. (Courtesy of the Delta Diner)

Above: An early view of the Delta Store and post office. (Courtesy of the Delta Diner)
Below: The Delta Store in 1928. (Courtesy of the Delta Diner)

Above: Delta's "Little Brown Church in the Woods," the St. Paul United Church of Christ. (Courtesy of St. Paul's United Church of Christ, Delta, Wisconsin)
Below: The sign welcoming visitors to the Delta Diner today. (Courtesy of the Delta Diner)

post office, an icehouse, the rail station, a bar and restaurant, and a gas station. When the store burned in 1972, the heart of the surrounding area was gone.

The region had many early schools and later consolidated with Ondossagon Schools in 1954. In the 1930s, a Civilian Conservation Corps Camp operated in the Delta area. For several years a church was active and still is. In 1935, a new church building was constructed. That building is today's St. Paul United Church of Christ, known as the "Little Brown Church in the Woods."

Today's Delta Diner is open seven days a week, year round. That adjacent store offers an in-house bakery, coffee, cold drinks, and Delta Diner apparel and gifts. Stop by when you are in the area, as the food and friendliness can't be beat. Learn more at www.deltadiner.com.

INO

1908

CLASS C

APPROXIMATE LOCATION:
U.S. 2 and County E, 15 miles west/southwest of Ashland

Never amounting to a full-fledged village or community, the post office lasted less than one year. Lasting a bit longer are the roadside taverns at the crossroads.

A view of Moquah today. (Courtesy of Creative Commons)

Above and below: Scenes from Ino today. (Courtesy of "Royalbroil," Wikimedia Commons, https://en.wikipedia.org/wiki/File:Ino_Wisconsin_Sign_US2.jpg and https://en.wikipedia.org/wiki/File:Ino_Wisconsin_Buildings.jpg)

MOQUAH

1903 – 1967

CLASS C/D

APPROXIMATE LOCATION:
9½ miles south/southwest of Ashland

Everyday activity has slowed down in Moquah since the post–World War II years. Where in 1946 there were seventy-two dairy farmers along the milk route, today there is only one. The grade school burned down in 1957, and was followed by the closing of the post office in 1967. Increased automobile traffic and changing lifestyles have quieted the crossroads community.

Moquah's early business district included a general store, a cheese factory, the school, the post office, a tavern or two, and a few area churches. One of the churches, Saints Peter and Paul Church, with declining membership, just celebrated its 100th anniversary.

The population and activity may have slowed down, but the community is full of community spirit and pride. In 1987, several area residents formed the Moquah Heritage Society, renamed the Moquah Historical Society. Originally, cultural events with song and dance were part of the society. Today the focus is on preserving and displaying the area's rich heritage and history. An impressive website has been created and is in the process of being organized and expanded.

Recently, I had the privilege of visiting with a few area residents key to the formation of the historical society, Dave Walters and Barb and John Grek. I learned that the area was settled in the early 1900s by Czech and Slovak immigrants. The land was cutover land. Several crops had been tried and hay seemed to be the most successful, so dairy farming became the area's mainstay. Nearly every forty-acre plot had cows.

One of today's establishments of repute is the Plywood Palace, built out of scraps and particle board. The original building had been an auto repair garage and had burned in the 1980s. The building requires winter outerwear as there is no glass or plastic on the windows. Summertime offers one-hundred percent natural air.

According to the history, Moquah is an Ojibwe word meaning "bear." It seems that when the surveyors were in the area, they set up camp and went about their work. When they returned to their camp, it was torn to shreds by a bear. The Native guide simply said, "Moquah." The term was noted in the journals and the name stuck.

Moquah's Plywood Palace, made of scraps of lumber and particle board. (Courtesy of Joyce Bickford)

Brown County

Kropps Supper Club today. (Courtesy of Kropps Supper Club)

MILLS CENTER

1867 - 1906

CLASS C

APPROXIMATE LOCATION:
5 miles northwest of Green Bay on Shawano Road

Aptly named, Mills Center was named for the ten sawmills centered in the settlement. Sources state that the ten mills with all of the logging activity was the "greatest mill section in the state, perhaps the entire Northwest."

Settled by Civil War veterans, the bustling community also included a general store, a blacksmith, a cheese factory, other business staples, a post office, a Methodist church, a boarding house, and a school. At one time, school enrollment was over one hundred students, all taught by one teacher!

In 1904, a businessman by the name of Lawler built a saloon. Because of its location along the plank road, the saloon, with rooms for rent on the second floor, was a busy place. That same building is still feeding folks today. In fact, it is Mills Center's only current business.

Kropps Supper Club is that lone surviving business. It became Kropps in 1946. Originally selling only ham sandwiches, chili, and homemade pies, today the restaurant is known far and wide for its supper club fare, most especially the Friday night fish fry. People flock to Kropps and often wait in line for the tasty, just-right fish and fries. All agree it is well worth the wait.

An early photo of Mills Center. (Courtesy of Kropps Supper Club and Margaret Kropp)

Burnett County

The furniture factory's mill in Trade River. (Courtesy of Gary Peterson)

Trade River's church at Christmas. (Courtesy of Gary Peterson)

Trade River school prior to 1907 (Courtesy of Gary Peterson)

RANDALL (BENSON)

1885 - 1951

CLASS A/C

APPROXIMATE LOCATION:
Town of Anderson

Residents knew the community as Benson, but since Wisconsin already had a Benson, the official post office name was Randall. The St. Paul and Duluth Railroad line connected Grantsburg, with its depot at Rush City.

TRADE RIVER

1879 - 1907

CLASS C

APPROXIMATE LOCATION:
Highway 87

Even though Burnett County is in Wisconsin's timber region, Trade River began with a flour and feed mill. The exact date of the first mill's establishment isn't known, but in 1886, C.E. Peterson of St. Paul bought the mill. Later that fall, he moved his family to Trade River. The Peterson family has long been connected with and an influencing factor in Trade River history. Gary Peterson's history proved to be a valuable resource in this summary, as are his photos.

Gary's uncle was a photographer and Gary has over 300 of his uncle's glass negatives.

C.E. operated the mill using water power for ten years, until the river was too low to garner any power. Moving the mill up the hill to his house, he added steam power and a sawmill and planer.

Trade River was home to two churches, one a mile east of Trade River. Many Native Americans worshipped at that church. In 1890, the Trade River Free Church was constructed using donated lumber and labor. The sanctuary still stands, albeit with several additions. A new church was built in 2000, overlooking today's Trade River. The church and congregation recently celebrated their 125th anniversary.

An important part of Trade River was the general store, built in 1891. A post office was located in the store and it operated until Rural Free Delivery (RFD) came to the area. The store operated until the mid-1960s. Other businesses included a furniture factory, which opened in 1902. They crafted beds, dressers, desks, bookcases, and other wooden items. According to Gary Peterson, the shipping costs proved to be unprofitable.

There was also a co-op creamery, a blacksmith, and a woodworking shop that could build or repair anything. A log school was built and used until 1907, when a new frame building was constructed. A garage operated in the 1940s.

Early Trade River. (Courtesy of Gary Peterson)

Taking an early Harley Davidson for a spin in Trade River. (Courtesy of Gary Peterson)

Clark County

Tioga once boasted a depot (above) and an inn (below). (Courtesy of the Clark County Historical Internet Library, http://www.wiclarkcountyhistory.org/)

Clark today. (Courtesy of Creative Commons)

The Hemlock Creamery. (Courtesy of the Clark County Historical Internet Library, http://www.wiclarkcountyhistory.org/)

Clark County Historical Internet Library

www.wiclarkcountyhistory.org/

Finding some lost towns can be difficult at times. Sometimes the only information we have is the name, the township, and the post office operation dates. Occasionally they are located on old railroad maps. Every now and then its possible to find a reference on a genealogical website. Often, that's it, that's all there is to tell us of a lost and long-ago town. With no place to look and records few and far between, these elusive lost towns stay that way: lost.

I'd hit that brick wall many times in researching lost towns. With no place to look or turn to, I've had to suspend and abandon many lost towns. Clark County, Wisconsin, was one of those places for me, until I happened upon the Clark County Historical Internet Library. It was my lucky day. At their site I found not only the names of the county's lost towns, but I found personal stories, photos, information, and so much more.

The award-winning site (2009 Governor's Archive Award for Archival Information, the Heritage Award, the Genealogical Sleuth Award) was created by and is maintained by a host of hard-working, dedicated, and knowledgeable history buffs. The website is a virtual bookshelf of all things historic in Clark County. Furthermore, the site and its keepers believe in sharing that information. Unique photos and history not found anywhere else can be found here. Visit the site yourself.

CHRISTIE

Located on Highway 73 between Neillsville and Greenwood, the settlement included a store, two churches, a school, and a post office (from 1875 until 1903). During the 1950s, a popular drive-in movie theater was in the community.

CLARK

Short-lived, the community had a post office from 1855 to 1856

EIDSVOLD

1884 - 1906

Eidsvold was on the Soo Line between Thorp and Stanley. It included a sawmill, shingle and hoop mill, a blacksmith shop, a boarding house, a post office, a general store, and a cheese factory.

GLOBE

1890 - 1908

APPROXIMATE LOCATION:
Ten miles northwest of Neillsville

The farming community included a creamery, German Lutheran church, a school, and a store.

HEMLOCK

1883 - 1901

Hemlock was nearly destroyed by one of Clark County's greatest disasters, the 1914 flood. The four-story grist mill, two-story sawmill and other buildings were washed downriver, as was the bridge over the Black River.

Hemlock before (top) and after (bottom) the 1914 flood. (Courtesy of the Clark County Historical Internet Library, http://www.wiclarkcounty history.org/)

LONE OAK

Four logging camps were in the Lone Oak area in 1901, and a cheese factory operated in 1916. The town was also known as Horn's Corner. The school closed in 1952, and students went to Withee. The school building was later a Kingdom Hall.

LONGWOOD

1873 - 1905

Active until Rural Free Delivery (RFD) came into existence, the settlement included a store, a blacksmith, a cheese factory, a town hall, a church, and a school.

MAPLEWORKS

1860 - 1892

CLASS A

APPROXIMATE LOCATION:
½ mile northeast of Granton

Just one-half mile northeast of Granton was an early stage stop. Originally slated to be called Maplewoods, a reading error by Washington, D.C., postal officials resulted in the community being called Mapleworks.

The area was first settled by Nelson Marsh in 1857. From Sparta, Wisconsin, Marsh was building a temporary road through the woods. He established a farm and tavern and soon the location became a stopping place on the stagecoach route from Neillsville to Steven's Point.

In 1877, Charles Cornelius built the tavern and store and persuaded others to join the community. Soon a blacksmith, a wagon maker, a furniture maker, and a physician were part of the settlement. It was a busy rural trade center and continued to grow until 1890. At that time, Granton was established and businesses moved to the new location.

SPOKEVILLE

1885 - 1905

Spokeville was one of Clark County's earliest communities. Located between Loyal and Sherman, it included a large sawmill, a store, a cheese factory, a boarding house, and a church.

TIOGA

1898 - 1953

VEEFKIND

1892 - 1911

WESTON RAPIDS

1858 - 1868

Once one of the locations hotly contested in the county seat designation, Weston Rapids lost the election by just seventeen votes. "Free Whiskey" was offered at the competition's polling place.

WINDFALL

One of Clark County's earliest settlements, Windfall was named for the large number of trees that had blown down during an early wind storm. There was a schoolhouse at the crossroads, but it was later moved to Granton.

Columbia County

Keyeser today. Gilbertson's Store, on the left, is still in operation. Gullickson's, on the right, has been closed for some years. (Courtesy of Pastor Sylvia Lee-Thompson)

Spring Prairie Lutheran Church, February 2016. (Courtesy of Pastor Sylvia Lee-Thompson)

KEYESER

1877 - 1908

CLASS C/D

APPROXIMATE LOCATION:
County DM and C near DeForest

Early Keyeser. (Author's Collection)

Generals stores were a staple of nearly every long-ago community. Keyeser was home to two, Gullickson's and Gilbertson's. One was located on the southwest corner of the intersection, the other on the southeast corner. Both are considered among Wisconsin's longest-lasting general stores. The two buildings still stand; however, Gullickson's Store has been closed for years while Gilbertson's is still operating.

Early Norwegian settlers were primarily dairy farmers and tobacco growers (at that time tobacco was a government-subsidized cash crop). A post office operated for over thirty years. An active church and congregation, Spring Prairie Lutheran, is also at the intersection.

NEWPORT

1852 - 1868

CLASS A/C/F

APPROXIMATE LOCATION:
2 miles from Wisconsin Dells

Sometimes you don't have to search for lost towns, they find you. So it was for Newport.

Not thinking of lost towns at all, we were on a family trip to Madison, Wisconsin. Our relatives Ray and Sandy were celebrating their fiftieth wedding anniversary so two of my sisters, a brother-in-law, and I met up and made the drive together. Deciding we needed a pit stop, we chose Wisconsin Dells to take our break. The big question was what one thing we would do while in the Dells. Debating all the options—and there are many—we all agreed it would be the Original Wisconsin Ducks (a World War II–era amphibious vehicle) since we had never done them before. It was a great choice, with land, water, scenic beauty and no walking; a casual boat ride. Then about midway through the trip the duck driver (the man

driving the duck, not actually a duck driving) told us to look to our right and we would see the lost village of Newport. Coincidence? I think not. So there I was doing the one tourist thing we chose and a lost town was involved. Well, I did a double-take and my family all stared at me, saying, "Really, a lost town on a duck ride?" So it was. Trying to snap photos from both sides all the while listening to the guide, I found another lost town, or it found me.

Newport was a true boom town, built on speculation, rampant with rumors and undercover goings-on, done in by political maneuvering, bribes, and other not-so-nice happenings. Here is her story.

Prospects looked bright and promising in 1849. Rumor was that Newport would be the site of the Milwaukee and La Crosse Railroad bridge that would span the Wisconsin River. That's all it took and the rush was on. Settlers, promotors, and land speculators rushed in. Lots sold for exorbitant prices.

The site of Newport today, as seen from a Wisconsin Duck. (Courtesy of Diane Lewis)

Soon thirteen large stores, three hotels, a brewery, a private school for girls (Mary Lyon Female Seminary, patterned after Mt. Holyoke in Massachusetts) and at least fifty smaller businesses sprang up. The population went from two to over two thousand in just five years. To say Newport was booming would be an understatement.

The dam was actually begun, but so were the shenanigans, and they were much further along than any construction. Under cover of night, the railroad line was surveyed, but not at Newport—instead, it was surveyed two miles upstream. In a twisted tangle of finagling, the end result was that Byron Kilbourn controlled the railroad, where it would run, and where it would cross the river. He had permissions to build the dam at any one of three sites (one of which he owned and had platted as Kilbourn). Surprisingly, or not, he chose to locate the dam on his property. Newport's fate was sealed.

Residents left the village in droves. Lots that had sold for $1,000 now couldn't fetch $100. The land later went for back taxes. Later records show that Byron Kilbourn paid out over $900,000 dollars in bribes. Scandal became his legacy, and he moved to Florida. The scandal also ended the career of a Milwaukee mayor and a Wisconsin governor.

Though little remains of Newport today, an impressive antebellum home, Dawn Manor, preserves the legacy. Dawn Manor stands at the western end of Newport on the northeast shore of Lake Delton. In 1855, Captain Vanderpoel, a close friend of Abraham Lincoln, built Dawn Manor to house his large family. Later a Chicago millionaire purchased the manor and added elaborate stables and a carriage house. After his death, the mansion was purchased by W.J. Newman, who wanted the house to overlook a lake. So he spent $1.2 million dollars to dam up Dell Creek, creating Lake Delton. He didn't

enjoy the house and lake view for long. He lost his fortune in the 1929 stock market crash and died penniless.

Helen Raab bought the mansion in 1942, and she was the premier caretaker of the manor. Following the advice of her good friend, Frank Lloyd Wright, she lovingly restored the manor, adding her own touches. She was a world traveler and spent time and money adding great works of art, porcelain, antiques, prints, and other treasures to the manor. She also purchased six hundred acres of land, preserving the wilderness. That preserve is now the Lower Dells Scenic Park.

The Dells ducks pass by the manor on their journey. Who would have thought all of this history in information would come alive riding a duck? Next time you take a drive, a trip, or a vacation, be on the lookout for the unexpected. You might just find a lost town, or it might find you.

A marker at the site of Dawn Manor. (Courtesy of Laura Aguilar)

Dawn Manor, as seen from a Wisconsin Duck. (Courtesy of Laura Aguilar)

Crawford County

The post office/store in Rising Sun. (Courtesy of Bruce Wicks)

St. James Church in Rising Sun. (Courtesy of Friends of St. James of Rising Sun)

MT. ZION

CLASS A/C

APPROXIMATE LOCATION:
U.S. 61 and County W

It's not often a community gets a starring role in a Hollywood movie with A-list actors such as Academy Award–winner Sissy Spacek. Titled *The Straight Story*, the movie told the story of Alvin Straight and his journey from Laurens, Iowa, to Mt. Zion, Wisconsin.

After years of estrangement, Alvin Straight knew he wanted to—needed to—mend fences with his brother. His brother's recent stroke made it all the more imperative. Trouble was, Alvin, a World War II veteran, also had many health concerns. Because of issues with his legs (he walked with two canes) and his poor eyesight, Alvin didn't have a driver's license. He didn't like or trust public transit, so his usual mode of travel was his riding lawn mower. Alvin often drove his lawnmower to town or to the tavern. Sometimes his wife would join him on the journey, driving her own riding lawn mower. Off they would go, at the maximum speed of five miles per hour.

But this was different than a short trip to town. Alvin lived in Laurens, Iowa, and his brother lived in Mt. Zion, Wisconsin, a distance of 240 miles. Alvin bought a new John Deere 110 model lawn mower, hooked up a trailer filled with necessities and supplies, and off he went to Mt. Zion. The trip took six weeks. The movie details the journey and all its happenings.

One of the locations used in the filming of the movie was the Mt. Zion Pub. In 2016, the pub was for sale.

The Mt. Zion Pub. (Courtesy of United Country Marshall Real Estate)

RISING SUN

1856 – 1904

CLASS C/D

APPROXIMATE LOCATION:
Near County B and Highway 27

Folklore has it that Rising Sun was named after a prolonged rainy spell. Folks were so happy to finally see the sun come up that they named the community Rising Sun.

Located along the stage line between Prairie du Chien and Black River Falls, the community had a post office/store, which was built in 1876. Rising Sun is the highest point (the ridge behind the store/post office building) in Crawford County. By the late 1800s, Rising Sun was also home to two hotels and a few saloons. The church (St. James) began as a log building. An annual summer service is hosted by the church, as are special events. The Friends of the St. James Church maintains the church and hosts many special events. The former store/post office is currently being restored.

Interior, St. James Church. (Courtesy of Friends of St. James of Rising Sun)

STAR VALLEY

Mid-1800s

CLASS A/C

APPROXIMATE LOCATION:
County C and Zehrer Drive

Above: The sign at Star Valley. (Courtesy of Star Valley Flowers)
Below: Star Valley today. (Courtesy of Star Valley Flowers)

Some of the most beautiful flowers in the Midwest are grown at Star Valley Flowers, said by many to be the "prettiest farm in Wisconsin." Star Valley Flower's two hundred acres produce primarily woody ornamentals and perennials and is the largest entirely field-grown (no greenhouses) source of cut flowers in the Midwest. Not open to the public, the flowers are primarily wholesale and are shipped via Chicago to points as far west as Honolulu and as far east as Boston.

Star Valley, the region and the former small hamlet, is at the apex of five valleys in an area referred to as "Driftless Wisconsin" because it is an area that was never touched by glacial activity.

The village once had a co-op creamery known as the Star Valley Creamery, which was built in 1893. An early home was converted to a store and was used until a new store was built in 1916. Today the area is rural farmland.

TOWERVILLE

1857 – 1903

CLASS C

APPROXIMATE LOCATION:
County Highway B and Tainter Creek,
6 miles west of Soldier's Grove

Today a roadside hamlet, Towerville was once the trade and mill center for a large area. Everyone from miles around came to Towerville for business and socialization. The mill was built in 1854 and was Crawford County's first mill outside of Prairie Du Chien. The settlement that grew around the grist mill was named for an early settlement family, the Towers. A post office was established in 1857, and soon a sawmill, a school, a woolen mill, a large boarding house, and a hotel were part of the community. The store, built of cement blocks, also doubled as a cream receiving station. The building was later used as a tavern, which closed several years ago, though the building is still standing.

Dane County

DOVER

Mid-1800s

CLASS A

APPROXIMATE LOCATION:
20 miles west of Madison on Highway 14

Things don't always go according to plan. The idea sounded good when the British Temperance Emigration Society laid the plans out in 1842 in Liverpool, England. They were going to purchase land in Wisconsin. The land would be divided up into eighty-acre parcels and each parcel would be improved with a fourteen-by-twenty-foot cabin, the farmland cultivated, and the first year's crops already planted. The parcels would then be sold to investors.

The first eleven families arrived in Wisconsin in 1844. By 1847, the society had 9,600 acres set aside for their investors. They first called the area Gorstville. However, they didn't plan for the fact that their investors were not farmers. In fact, they knew little to nothing about farming. The settlers also had few provisions and little money. So when it came time for the society leaders to collect rent, there wasn't any to be had. Still, the settlers continued on.

Soon a population of 250 necessitated a post office, several stores, a blacksmith, a cooper, a hotel, a school, and a ferry across the Wisconsin River. The Milwaukee and Mississippi Railroad wanted to purchase land in the settlement for a depot. Culver, the owner of the desired property, didn't much want to sell any land to the railroad so he put a ridiculously high price on the property. Not willing to pay the exorbitant price, railroad officials made plans to build a depot two miles east (one consideration for that location might have been the fact that one railroad official already owned the property they would need). That new location became known as Mazomanie.

After the Civil War, a Dover resident, John Appleby, returned home. Appleby was quite the tinkerer. He even had a patent for an improved magazine and automatic feeder for rifles. His newest invention was for a twine knotter, which could revolutionize farm machinery. In a field in Dover, across from his home and adjacent to today's roadside park and Dover historical marker, he demonstrated his knotter. A large crowd was assembled but as it usually goes, the device didn't work properly and repeatedly broke down. Appleby didn't give up and by 1870 had the knotter perfected. William Deering, a major farm equipment manufacturer, and Appleby negotiated a deal and the twine knotter became a common component on all binding machines. But, as William Stark, a Wisconsin historian, wrote, it was too late for Dover. By that time nearly all of Dover's businesses and residents had relocated to the bustling village of Mazomanie.

POKERVILLE

1830s – 1880s

CLASS A

APPROXIMATE LOCATION:
2 miles west of Blue Mounds

For centuries, the Native Americans considered the area sacred. The blueish haze that surrounds the top of the mound on clear days was thought to be smoke from the Great Spirit's pipe. Records show that the Winnebago Indians mined surface iron ore as early as the 1700s. Most likely it was that ore that attracted the first white settlers to the region a century later. The first settlers arrived sometime in the early nineteenth century.

Ebenezer Brigham is considered the first white settler in all of Dane County. Arriving in 1828, his nearest white neighbors were more than one hundred miles away. Brigham, a life-long bachelor, found a rich vein of ore and immediately laid claim to 1,400 acres. With new settlers arriving almost daily, Brigham converted his substantial cabin to a store, a boarding house, and a tavern. Known as "Brigham's Place," it became a well-known stop along the new military road.

Things were peaceful until the outbreak of the Black Hawk War in 1832 between Native Americans and the US government. Lying in the path of the hostilities, settlers feared attack and so a fort was built a mile from Brigham's Place. Nearly all the residents moved to the fort for safety. Area men also formed a garrison of fifty. Though two soldiers were killed in sight of the fort, the fort itself was never attacked.

Pokerville, also known as West Blue Mounds, Moundsville, and Harrisville, was the site of Dane County's first school. Life was rowdy in the settlement during the 1840s and 1850s, Pokerville's peak. Brawls, fisticuffs, shootings, and lots of alcohol consumption were common. Gambling was so prevalent that folks called the settlement "Pokerville." After the Civil War, the mining of ore was in decline and many residents turned to farming.

In 1881, the railroad extended its line west of Madison and a new community was established, Blue Mounds.

An interesting note is that when Barnum brought his circus to Pokerville, the train didn't run to the settlement so the circus unloaded in Madison. The elephants walked from Madison to Pokerville, many carrying packs on their backs. What a sight it must have been. Also an early storekeeper, John Adams, had two sons who later became governors of Colorado.

Dodge County

Dodge County

NASBRO

1913 - 1916

CLASS A

APPROXIMATE LOCATION:
3 miles west of Lomira

Primarily a company town rather than a village, a settlement did grow up around the quarry operations. Several different owners mined and processed lime at the location. The first were the Nast Brothers, thus the name Nasbro. At its peak the settlement included a boarding house, a store, a tavern, and a population of fifty. A post office operated for three years.

Although the quarry operated for many years, even recently, the site no longer has any buildings or residents. Joel Valle, an historian, writes that some foundations remain, but, except for the recent quarry, the site of the town is being reclaimed by nature.

Door County

Viking boathouse built by Charles Thordarson at Rock Island State Park. (Courtesy of Mark Ludwig, Grafton, Wisconsin)

The site of the Native American camps on Rock Island. (Courtesy of National Register of Historic Places, Thordarson Estate Historic District, Rock Island State Park, Door, Wisconsin, #85000641)

ROCK ISLAND

1600s – early 1900s

CLASS A/F

APPROXIMATE LOCATION:
½ mile from Washington Island, now Rock Island State Park

Rock Island Lighthouse and grounds. (Courtesy of Mark Ludwig, Grafton, Wisconsin)

Throughout its long history, Rock Island could be categorized as a lost town several times over. Archeological evidence dates a Native American settlement on the island as early as 600 BCE (Before Common Era). Evidence also supports the existence of a Potawatomi palisaded (walled) settlement in the 1600s. Fifty years later, a Huron settlement was located at the site. When the Europeans arrived, a fishing village was there and, lastly, in the early 1900s, Icelander Charles Thordarson established his estate on the island.

Rock Island is one-half mile off the north shore of Washington Island in Lake Superior. Encompassing nine hundred wooded acres, the island today is uninhabited and is a Wisconsin state park. The terrain is both rugged and stunningly beautiful.

It is believed that French explorer Sieur de La Salle wintered on the island, when their ship, the *Griffin*, was lost (the Great Lake's first). Remains found include a wood plank from the palisade wall, a French officer's army button, and a British clay pipe.

In the mid-1830s, there was a colony of fishermen on the southeast shore of the island. Approximately one hundred people occupied the one-square-mile village.

Great Lakes shipping began in earnest in the early 1830s. Desperately needing a lighthouse, over thirty different ship owners and captains petitioned the U.S. Congress to authorize the construction of one. Four years later, a government crew came to the island and built the lighthouse as well as a house for the keeper. Rock Island's lighthouse was Wisconsin's first. With the completion of the lighthouse, several part-time residents settled on the island. Fishing was especially good in the 1840s and 1850s, so much so that fishing was considered to be the basis of the island's economy at the time.

As other parts of Door County began to be organized, Rock Island's population declined. Always at the mercy of the weather, the isolation, and the lack of a good harbor, residents chose to leave the island.

A school was built in 1863, but it was a too late to make a difference. As William Stark, Wisconsin historian, wrote, only seven families with school-aged children were still on the

island by then. The last permanent resident left the island in 1890. Afterward, the only resident was the lighthouse keeper, and he would remain the only islander until 1910.

That is when Icelandic multi-millionaire Charles Thordarson and his wife visited the island. Charles was extremely poor in his childhood. According to Stark, Charles's father died when he was a young boy. He didn't attend school much as a child. When Charles was eighteen, he went to live with a married sister in Chicago. In two years, Charles completed the fourth through seventh grades. He got a job winding armatures in an electrical firm. Charles was a hard worker and a quick learner. At the age of twenty-seven, he took his entire life savings of seventy-five dollars and stated his own electrical repair shop. He also began manufacturing his own inventions and soon he was rich and famous.

When Charles and his wife visited the island in 1910, they fell in love with it, so they bought the entire island except for the lighthouse. They had the old frame fishing houses rebuilt, as well as a stone water tower.

Charles then decided that the southwest side of the island was the best place to build their home. Sparing no expense, Charles built a magnificent boathouse and great hall. Many say the structures resemble ancient Viking halls. It took twenty stonemasons three years and over a quarter of a million dollars to build the complex. And that is in 1920 dollars. Several stone cottages and a grand log lodge were also constructed. The Thordarsons hosted many celebrity guests, including Clarence Darrow, Earle Stanley Gardner, and Chicago's notorious Prohibition-era mayor Big Bill Thompson, a very close friend.

Botany was a special interest of Thordarson, and he could be considered an early environmentalist in ways. He preserved the island's wilderness. He died in 1945, and is buried in one of the islands two cemeteries.

Thordarson willed the property to his family, who in turn sold it to the state of Wisconsin in the 1960s for $175,000. The state created Rock Island State Park. The park/island maintains the ruggedness of the terrain. No vehicles are allowed on the island. There is a campground, but it is primitive camping with no electricity or water. It is also a hike to the campsite. The boathouse and hall are open to the public. Many special events are hosted on the island each year. The great hall displays historical artifacts from all of the island's history.

The Thordarsons' estate is now on the National Register of Historic Places.

See for yourself just how spectacular and beautiful the state park is.

Rock Island State Park. (Courtesy of Mark Ludwig, Grafton, Wisconsin)

Thordarson historic district. (Courtesy of National Register of Historic Places, Thordarson Estate Historic District, Rock Island State Park, Door, Wisconsin, #85000641)

Thordarson historic estate. (Courtesy of National Register of Historic Places, Thordarson Estate Historic District, Rock Island State Park, Door, Wisconsin, #85000641)

Douglas County

CLEVEDON (COLONY)

1896 - 1897

CLASS A

APPROXIMATE LOCATION:
Clevedon Road and Highway 13

Samuel Budgett of Bristol, England, envisioned a self-supporting, bustling, and prosperous settlement. He imagined that the members of his group, to be known as Clevedon Colony, would fish, make their own barrels to pack the fish in and then would ship the fish to points eastward. In the pursuit of his vision, he purchased just over 3,300 acres surrounding the Percival Mine on the Copper Range, which also included three miles of Lake Superior shoreline.

According to a history by Nan Wisherd on the early Brule area history, thirty people from England made the journey by ship. The property was divided into forty-acre plots, and settlers set about farming. Supposedly apple orchards were planted, and a sawmill and several houses built. To make extra money, the men worked in logging camps over the winter.

Things looked so promising that the overseer of the colony went to Superior to petition for a road from the railroad depot (in today's Brule) to the settlement. The principal form of transportation for the region was Lake Superior, but that was shut down for months once the winter freeze arrived.

An 1885 Bayfield newspaper reported that Douglas County had approved the new road. The road was eventually built and is still maintained by the Village of Brule.

Harsh winter weather, isolation, blizzards, and weeks of below-zero temperatures took their toll on the community and eventually the colony was abandoned.

Others believed it was the members' and the overseer's fault the colony failed. Records indicate that the colonists often burned hay for heat instead of using the plentiful wood resources available. The sawmill was underused at best. Lumber for all construction was sawn in Duluth and floated to the colony. Some say that as long as the colonists had money, it was easier to buy supplies than to produce their own.

The overseer moved to Superior after the colony failed and eventually returned to England. Of the original 3,300 acres purchased, only a little over 2,100 were sold. Budgett had paid $15,000 for the land, and sold it for $6,000. The remaining acreage was tax delinquent.

Bernard Doherty purchased some of the land and built his own sawmill. Log rafts were constructed and then floated to Ashland and Superior. When the logging drives ended in 1899, Dougherty also abandoned Clevedon.

CLOVERLAND

Late 1880s - 1900s

CLASS A/B/C

APPROXIMATE LOCATION:
East of Superior on Highway 13

According to a recent news article, the school in Cloverland closed in 1948 and was converted to use as a Community Center Club.

Early residents recalled that dances were held at the center at least once a month. An annual rummage and bake sale took place during the Bayfield Apple Festival.

As area residents aged and retired, moving out of the area, the clubs activities declined and the group disbanded.

The school sat empty for decades. Nature and weather took its toll and vandals further destroyed the building. At the time of this writing, efforts were being made as to the preservation of the building.

Cloverland Garage today. (Courtesy of Edward Marek)

MARTINSON

1905 – 1916

CLASS A/C

APPROXIMATE LOCATION:
8 miles north of Waino

Mail was delivered in Martinson once a week from Waino, eight miles to the south. Waino itself is a very small unincorporated community. The village took its name from the postmaster, E. Martinson. The settlement included a school, a sawmill, and a dock on the lake. Most, if not all, supplies came by boat, including catalog orders filled by Sears, Roebuck, and Company and the Montgomery Ward Company. Flour came in one-hundred-pound sacks with "Pillsbury" stamped on them. Supplies generally came from Duluth or Superior.

The school term was three months long and in 1896, enrollment was fourteen pupils. The school closed in 1897.

In 1899, a telephone line connected Waino and Martinson. After the timber had been harvested, the settlement was abandoned.

Dunn County

A marker at the Woodlawn farmhouse. (Courtesy of LeAnne Holden)

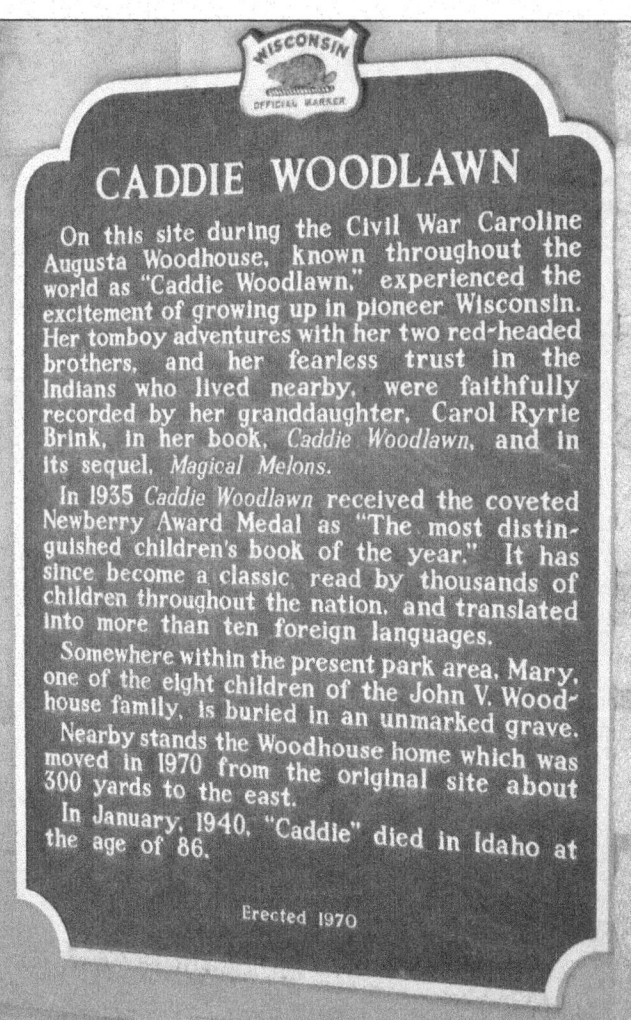

CADDIE WOODLAWN

On this site during the Civil War Caroline Augusta Woodhouse, known throughout the world as "Caddie Woodlawn," experienced the excitement of growing up in pioneer Wisconsin. Her tomboy adventures with her two red-headed brothers, and her fearless trust in the Indians who lived nearby, were faithfully recorded by her granddaughter, Carol Ryrie Brink, in her book, *Caddie Woodlawn*, and in its sequel, *Magical Melons*.

In 1935 *Caddie Woodlawn* received the coveted Newberry Award Medal as "The most distinguished children's book of the year." It has since become a classic read by thousands of children throughout the nation, and translated into more than ten foreign languages.

Somewhere within the present park area, Mary, one of the eight children of the John V. Woodhouse family, is buried in an unmarked grave.

Nearby stands the Woodhouse home which was moved in 1970 from the original site about 300 yards to the east.

In January, 1940, "Caddie" died in Idaho at the age of 86.

Erected 1970

Above: Dunnville schoolhouse, now in Dunnville Park. (Courtesy of LeAnne Holden)
Below: Caddie Woodlawn's childhood home. (Courtesy of Doug Connell)

DUNNVILLE

1856 - 1907

CLASS A

APPROXIMATE LOCATION:
County Road Y

Logging was the region's livelihood, but Dunnville's first settler, Samuel Lamb, wasn't in the logging business, per se. He was a tavern owner, which many could argue put him in the business of loggers and lumberjacks.

Knapp, Stout and Company, a major logging company, controlled over 48,000 acres of the region's virgin timber. As such, Dunnville was a company town, built because of and for their logging interests and their employees' needs. A few businesses, including the creamery, the quarry, and the stone mill, were not owned by the company but most certainly were influenced by the company. Without the company, there would be no customers nor any need of the auxiliary businesses.

Life in Dunnville was often rowdy and boisterous. After two years, Lamb sold his tavern to his brother-in-law, McCann. According to Wisconsin historian William Stark, McCann was the area's first murder victim. Apparently a temporary employee, Sawyer, stopped by the tavern to pick up his pay. He stayed a while, played cards and drank heavily with McCann. Somewhere along the line, a heated argument ensued, and McCann was so angry he threw a scale weight at Sawyer. Sawyer then left but returned a short time later with a loaded gun. He called McCann out into the street. When McCann stepped out the door, Sawyer shot him point blank, killing him on the spot. A large reward was offered, but Sawyer was never heard from again.

William Stark wrote of another incident in Dunnville. One day a group of approximately forty Native Americans showed up at the Colburn House, the hotel. (Dunnville was first called Colburn but was later renamed in honor of Wisconsin Territory's first chief justice, Charles Dunn). The Native Americans wanted food and overnight lodging. They were Minnesota Sioux on their way back home when hostilities with the Chippewa broke out. They insisted that the windows be covered with blankets so the Chippewa couldn't see them and shoot them. Leaving the next morning, they didn't pay their bill, but all were happy to see them leave.

Dunnville reached its peak period of activity in the 1850s. A large company store was built in 1854, with the top floor

Sandstone marker in Dunnville. (Courtesy of LeAnne Holden)

serving as a dance hall. In 1858, the Tainter House, a large hotel, was constructed. Warehouses lined the banks on both sides of the river. The Knapp Stout Company at one time owned six shipping vessels, making Dunnville a river port. The company also owned and operated a four-horse stage.

Designated the Dunn County seat in 1854, a large wooden courthouse was built. The courthouse burned in 1858. In a double whammy, a portion of Dunn County was reapportioned to form Pierce County. No longer located at the center of the newly drawn Dunn County, the county seat designation was awarded to the better located and larger community of Menominee.

The increasing use of railroad traffic made river towns obsolete. With timber resources also dwindling, Dunnville was on the decline. In the 1880s, the discovery of high-quality sandstone nearby, said to be some of the best in the United States, provided a bit of a revival. The sandstone quarried near Dunnville was used in many prominent buildings across the United States, including St. Thomas's Cathedral in New York.

Though it continued on for several decades, each year saw the loss of businesses and population. The school closed and nature started to reclaim parts of Dunnville.

Today, Dunnville Park on Highway 25 is one remnant of the village. The five-acre park features a restored 1856 farmhouse relocated to the park from Dunnville. The Woodlawn family, with seven children, lived in the home from 1857 to 1867. One of the children was young Augusta, nicknamed Caddie. If the name sounds familiar, Caddie Woodlawn was and is a popular children's literature classic series. Written by Carol Ryrie Brink, the books tell of Brink's grandmother's childhood.

HATCHVILLE

1889 - 1903

CLASS A

APPROXIMATE LOCATION:
County P and PP

St. John's Church in Hatchville. (Courtesy of Bev Fuhrman)

Hatchville is noted as having been located in three counties (Dunn, St. Croix, and Pierce) and in four townships. In 1883, the Seventh Day Adventists purchased one acre of land for one dollar. They built a church that stood until 1889, when it was moved off-site.

In 1896, the small settlement included a lumber mill and a broom handle factory. Two years later, in 1898, brothers Frank and Ed purchased the church land. They built a general store with an upstairs hall that hosted dances, shows, community activities, and church services. Two years later, in 1900, a farmer's co-op creamery, a blacksmith shop, and another store joined the settlement. A cheese factory began operating in 1917 and did so until the mid 1970s. St. John's Church is still active.

Eau Claire County

PORTER'S MILLS (PORTERVILLE)

1873 - 1903

CLASS A

APPROXIMATE LOCATION:
4 miles south of Eau Claire on the left bank of the Chippewa River

As far as logging towns went, Porter's Mills (Porterville) was a cut above the rest. Randall Rohe, author of *Ghosts of the Forest: Vanished Lumber Towns of Wisconsin, Volume I*, wrote that by 1873, Porter's Mills was a thriving settlement with named streets, numbered houses, and thirty-two homes for married employees. The rent on the homes was seventy-five dollars a month, and that included firewood delivered to the door. Many residents also built and owned their own homes. Nearly every household owned a cow.

Everything was well-maintained. Rohe wrote that the good living conditions allowed the Northwest Company to hire more married employees than other logging camps. Married men with families were more desirable than single men. They were deemed more stable, as well as more permanent. The company did all they could to keep all their employees happy, married or single. There was a large dining hall and sleeping apartments for the single men. A general store adjoined the company office. Porter's Mills also included a post office, blacksmith shop, a shoe shop, a hotel, two candy stores, and for a while an independently owned store. The company offered a five-hundred-acre farm plot for those that wanted to grow their own produce.

Floods were a common springtime event, but the flood of 1884 was historic. The Chippewa River rose twenty-seven feet in just a few hours. Water reached the second stories of many homes. Heavy rain and the opening of the Little Falls dam only made things worse. At one point, the river was rising six to nine inches an hour. Warnings were sent to the company agent saying that the Dells Dam north of Eau Claire was ready to give out and some bridges had already been washed away. By the time the agent hung up, water was waist high in the store. The sawmill and planing mill suffered no damage, but over 350,00 board feet of lumber was swept away. Residents took shelter at the Methodist church, the school, or nearby farms. Nearly the entire town was swept away.

Porter's Mills rebuilt. In November of 1885, a steam cylinder exploded, tearing off the roof and blowing out one wall of the mill. No one was injured, as most of the employees were off for dinner. The mill was again rebuilt.

Several fires struck the village in 1887, including one in May that destroyed the company store and mill office.

Porter's Mills was at its peak in the late 1880s. There was even talk of the village becoming a city. The 1890 population was nearly 1,200, and some records say 1,500, with a melting pot of ethnicities, primarily Scandinavian.

As with most company towns, Porter's Mills was dry, no saloons or alcohol. However, Eau Claire was only three miles away and plenty of alcohol was available there.

Two churches were built, Lutheran and Methodist. The company strongly supported the churches, as they attracted families. There was a lack of English-speaking ministers but folks attended the Norwegian services anyway. As Rohe wrote, they couldn't understand a word, but they liked the singing!

Social events were common. Picnics, church socials, and the community-wide Fourth of July celebration were popular events. The Modern Woodmen of America sponsored dances, concerts, and other activities. Porter's Mills even had its own eighteen-member brass band.

Unusual for most settlements, Porter's Mills had a community library with nearly five hundred books. Residents could check out a book for two months for a fee of five cents.

Skating and hockey were popular activities in the winter, as were sleighing parties. There were four sleighs and as many as fifty people participated in the rides. Afterward there were oyster dinners, dancing, and music.

Porter's Mills schools had eight grades, two teachers, and at one time had an enrollment of 225 students. A diphtheria epidemic closed schools in 1882. Porter's Mills didn't have a doctor of its own but with Eau Claire just a few miles away, people could see doctors there.

As with all logging settlements and camps, fire was common. The year 1896 had been exceptionally dry. In April, lightning hit the planing mill. The mill and a substantial amount of lumber was lost. Rohe wrote that the heat was so intense the railroad tracks warped.

Ever-decreasing timber resources coupled with the slowly declining population forced the closure of the mill in early 1899. Once the closing was announced, the population declined rapidly. By the early 1900s, fewer than fifty people were left. Most had moved to Eau Claire. Houses sold for little to nothing. What didn't sell was moved or torn down. The Methodist church was moved to County Z and Highway 37 and was known as Mount Hope Episcopal Church. The school was disassembled and sold for the lumber.

In 1902, the last building in Porter's Mills, the Modern Woodman of America hall, was put on large sleds, and fifteen teams of horses pulled it to Mount Hope.

A town reunion was held in 1919. Estimates state that between three hundred and five hundred former residents and their families attended. Many walked from Stanley to the old town site.

Florence County

TIPLER

1918 - 1954

CLASS C/D

APPROXIMATE LOCATION:
Highway 70 near intersection with Highway 139

Gaining vast timber tracts in the early 1900s, the Tipler-Grossman Lumber Company owned or held options on sixty-three sections of timber. Their timber rights ran for miles in all directions.

With the sawmill, workers came and soon a settlement developed. A boarding house was built, as well as other "company" buildings: a horse barn, a blacksmith shop, a tool shed, and a company office, as well as housing for married workers and their families. Soon a grocery and clothing store and a doctor's office joined the community. A one-room school burned in 1922. Classes were held in a small movie theater until a four-room school building was constructed in 1923.

Many other businesses, including a saloon or two, operated in Tipler through the years. The post office was discontinued in 1954, but it did not signal the end of the small settlement. The mill closed in 1928, and the town faded in population and activity. Today the Tipler Bar and Grill is still operating and is a popular local destination.

The sign for Tipler on Highway 70. (Courtesy of Creative Commons)

Fond du Lac County

CERESCO

1844 – 1856

CLASS C/F

APPROXIMATE LOCATION:
Now part of Ripon

Above: A Ceresco long house. (Author's Collection)
Below: One of the long houses after being converted to apartments. (Courtesy of National Register of Historic Places, Ripon, Fond du Lac, Wisconsin, #75000064)

Called by many a great northwoods experiment, Ceresco was established in 1844. Also known as the Wisconsin Phalanx, followers of Charles Fournier settled and established the community. At its peak, 180 people farmed the 2,000 acres. Described as a Utopian community, a three-story grist mill, a hotel, and post office made up the commercial portion of the community. Three "long" houses were constructed as boarding/apartments for the followers.

The experimental community dissolved in the 1850s for a combination of reasons, one being that communal living was not generally accepted. One history tells that when the community dissolved, it was unique in the fact that the group had more assets than liabilities.

Several of the historic buildings stood for years and, in fact, some are still standing and functional. Now a part of the City of Ripon, the Ceresco buildings are listed as the Ceresco Historic District on the National Register of Historic Places. One of the long houses was converted to five apartment buildings.

Though the experiment was not considered a success, the group and its members were instrumental in forming Ripon and many of its institutions, including Ripon College and the city's Republican Party.

Forest County

BLACKWELL

1905 – 1961

CLASS C

APPROXIMATE LOCATION:
County T near Goodman Park Road, now part of Nicolet
National Forest

Going, going, gone. The July 1932 *Milwaukee Journal* article (found at www.laonahistory.com) told the tale of the entire village of Blackwell being on the auction block. Blackwell was not an abandoned village at the time—quite the contrary. It had a population of 250 and only two of the fifty company houses were unoccupied. True, the Flanner Mill had been shut down for over a year. Still, the residents looked to the auction as hope for the future. They had hopes that a buyer would step up, buy the village, and reopen the mill.

Blackwell was a company town, built up around the mill established in 1904. Financial difficulties ensued and in 1930, a large bond issue failed and the property was court-ordered to be sold.

Blackwell the village faded away, however, the town of Blackwell (the township entity) still exists.

Today Blackwell is home to the Blackwell Job Corps Center. The center is housed in a former 1930s-era CCC (Civilian Conservation Corps) facility. Established in 1965, the center offers a no-cost educational and career tech training program for at-risk students aged sixteen to twenty-four.

Grant County

Above: Pleasant Ridge cemetery. (Courtesy of www.schoepski.com)

Below: Pleasant Ridge today. (Courtesy of www.schoepski.com)

FAIR PLAY

1841 – 1907

CLASS A

APPROXIMATE LOCATION:
Highway 11 and Sandy Hook Road

Duels seemed to be a fairly popular way of settling disagreements in the mid-1800s. At least they were in some Wisconsin locations. Grant County's last threatened duel took place in 1846 in Fair Play, but more on that later.

The area's first settler wasn't a farmer or a logger, he was a prospector. Arriving in 1838, it took him two years to hit his first strike. But once it hit, other prospectors flocked to the area. With the influx came claim jumpers, fisticuffs, brawls, and threatened bloodshed. One such fight had the crowd chanting, "Fair play," "Fair play." Thus the community formerly known as Hard Town had a new moniker, Fair Play. As for that fight, it was amicably resolved.

By the mid-1840s, Fair Play was home to a number of stores, a combination church/school, and a population estimated between five hundred and eight hundred. The large population did nothing to refine the community. All reports tell that Fair Play was a frontier town filled with rowdy taverns, drinking, gambling, and knock-down, drag-out fights. Such shenanigans led to a threatened duel in 1846. It was averted and said to be Grant County's last threatened duel.

Dwindling mineral resources, a drop in ore prices, and the discovery of gold in California all combined to deplete Fair Play's population. You could say Fair Play played out. Thomas Lundeen, in a 1981 presentation, said at that time the only remnant of Fair Play was a limestone town hall, which at that time was the oldest town hall in Wisconsin. It was later converted to a house.

PARIS

1838 – 1843

CLASS A

APPROXIMATE LOCATION:
⅛ mile south of Dickeyville near Highway 151/61

Wisconsin has had a French influence and connection from its earliest days to the present. Early French explorer Martial Detantabaritz came to the region in 1835 with the intention of establishing a settlement. Historians note that Detantabaritz was known as "La Jaune," "The Yellow," for his yellowish complexion (malaria?). At the confluence of the Platte River, he laid out his settlement and built a store, a furnace for ore smelting, and many years later, a tavern. True to his French origins, he named the settlement Paris.

In 1839, he built a toll bridge across the river, Grant County's first. Now that it was more accessible, settlers came to the area. Thomas Lundeen, in a 1981 presentation, stated that with more settlers came trouble. Detantabaritz experienced financial problems. One creditor was especially problematic and soon things escalated into a duel. Detantabaritz chose swords as his weapon of choice. Most certainly he chose swords because as a former French dragoon he had great skill with them. The creditor, with no experience, withdrew from the duel. Detantabaritz hung himself in 1842 and Paris died, as well.

Lundeen said that in the 1970s, just one remnant of Paris remained, that being a tavern an eighth of a mile from Dickeyville called the Paris Tavern. It later operated as a rib establishment.

PLEASANT RIDGE

1848 – 1961

CLASS A/F

APPROXIMATE LOCATION:
5 miles west of Lancaster

Unique! That would be the one word that best describes Pleasant Ridge. The community was unique in that it was strictly a farming settlement. There was no trade center, no commercial district, and no retail. There was a church and a school and still it was in every sense a community. Perhaps most unique was the fact that Pleasant Ridge's residents were black, all of them ex-slaves or descendants of slaves.

William Horner, a white plantation owner, left his home state of Virginia to settle in Wisconsin. The lure of the land and a life free of slavery issues were the prime motivations behind his move. Horner sold his plantation, freed his slaves, and headed north. The trip in 1848 was arduous, taking a riverboat to Illinois and from there a wagon and oxen team to Wisconsin, his former slaves traveling with him. Upon arriving in the region, Horner sold land to his newly freed slaves for $1.50 an acre. He firmly believed in building responsibility and character and as such did not "gift" the land but gave them the added honor of being landowners on their own. Building a life was hard work. First the forest had to be cleared of the thick pines, cabins had to be built and the fields cultivated.

With time and uneasy tensions over the slavery issue and the onset of the Civil War, other former slaves (many from Missouri) joined Horner's community. John Greene, one of the recent residents, was unique in that he could read and write. Many slaves were forbidden to do so. Greene became a leader in the community and at times the settlement was referred to as "Greene's Colony."

After the war, Pleasant Ridge continued to grow and prosper. By 1900, the population was over two hundred. Together, blacks and whites built a log school, which all students attended. Wisconsin historian William Stark wrote that it was probably the first integrated school in the United States. Teachers were also of both races. The education provided was superb, and many students graduated and even continued on to college. The Autumn Leaf Club was another community success. It brought former residents and families of the area together in social settings.

Annual events included a fall barbecue and dance. Whole pigs and sides of beef were prepared while dancing continued into the wee hours of the morning. Estimates were that over eight hundred attended the events. The group went strong until the World War II years. Lasting over one hundred years, the community came to an end when the last black landowner died.

William Stark offered an explanation for the demise of the community, citing education as the cause—not the lack of it, but the excess of it—behind the hastening decline. In many very small communities, children and students go off to college or the big city, leaving a hometown behind. In the early 1900s, a high school education was not common and a college degree rare. As the Pleasant Ridge students graduated they returned home, but not for long. They found their way to large

Markers at the site of Pleasant Ridge. (Courtesy of www.schoepski.com)

cities where jobs and opportunities were available. They were simply too educated to remain in Pleasant Ridge. Today a historical marker and the Pleasant Ridge Cemetery mark the former community.

SINIPEE

1838 – 1841

CLASS A

APPROXIMATE LOCATION:
3 miles east of East Dubuque

Shining brightly but briefly, Sinipee ("lead ore" in the area Native American dialect) left a lot of tales to tell.
Totally dependent on Dubuque and Galena for shipping the lead ore mined in the region, local businessmen formed the Sinipee Company in 1836. Its purpose was to develop a settlement with a port and shipping point. That same year a town was platted and included stores, a post office, a mill, a blacksmith shop, and a church. Paper currency was even printed in the community. A magnificent hotel, said to have the finest fixtures, was built. Guests of note stayed at the hotel, called the Stone House, including two presidents: Zachary Taylor, later President of the United States, and Jefferson Davis, later President of the Confederate States.

Business was good, and Sinipee prospered. Talk was the river community would one day surpass Dubuque, maybe even Chicago or St. Louis. At one time, sixteen steamboats and forty teams of oxen were unloading and loading at one time. Choice building lots were commanding two thousand dollars and more.

One Sinipee businessman was also of note: John Plumbe Jr. Plumbe had immigrated from Wales to America at the age of twelve. He was a hard worker and had big ideas and even bigger plans. His passion was the idea of a transcontinental railroad from Milwaukee across to Dubuque and west on to the Oregon Territory. He even lobbied officials in Washington, D.C. While in Washington, Plumbe learned of a new French device, the daguerreotype. The new mode of photography became an obsession of his. Selling his business, Plumbe went to the West Coast to pursue his dream of a transcontinental railroad. Little is known about his time there, but he returned to Sinipee in 1856 a broken man. He later committed suicide.

An interesting twist to the Plumbe story was told by Thomas Lundeen in a 1981 historical presentation. At a San Francisco Flea Market in 1972, a daguerreotype of the U.S. Capitol was sold for eight dollars. Six years later, in 1978, that photo was authenticated as being taken by Plumbe and it then sold for $14,000. It is one of the two earliest known photographs taken of the U.S. Capitol.

Eight years after Sinipee's inception, 1939, there was an early spring thaw followed by heavy rains. There was massive flooding. While the flood did no great property damage, it left stagnant pools of slimy water behind. The slime was perfect for breeding mosquitos, and mosquitos carried malaria. Early medicine didn't know the cause of the disease nor did it have any treatment for it. Many residents fell ill and died. Seemingly, the only way to avoid the disease was to leave, and that the remaining residents did in droves. One early founder and his family did stay in the community. Sinipee was by all accounts a ghost town. One traveler visited the now nearly abandoned community and found it eerie and surreal. Most the buildings were abandoned, yet looked new and pristine. They showed no decay and no deterioration. The streets were void of life, human or animal.

In 1934, Lock and Dam #11 raised the water level, putting most of Sinipee underwater. High on a bluff stands the Sinipee Cemetery, with about seventy-five graves, most of them from the malaria outbreak.

Green County

The Attica church today. (Courtesy of Karl Baumeister)

A postcard of the dam and early Attica. (Author's Collection)

ATTICA

1849 - 1911

CLASS C/D

APPROXIMATE LOCATION:
County C and X

After lightning destroyed the first church, a new one was built in 1906 or 1907. Services were conducted until 1953, when the congregation disbanded. Two years later, nineteen area families banded together, each contributing twenty-five dollars toward the purchase price. Plans were to use it as a community center. The community maintains the building today and hosts cemetery walks and historical events.

Early Attica's blacksmith had a substantially large building with an upstairs used as a hall for the Modern Woodmen of America.

Kim Tschudy knows Green County history better than anyone. In talking with Kim, he told me that Attica was once home to between 500 and 700 people. Two community buildings are still standing: the church and the blacksmith shop. Recently a "knock your socks off" restaurant was found in the village.

MARTINTOWN

1892 - 1938

CLASS C

APPROXIMATE LOCATION:
South of Brownton on Wisconsin/Illinois border

Living the life of most mill towns, Martintown developed around a mill that was established in 1854 by Nathanial Martin. When the Illinois Central Railroad arrived the mid 1880s, Martintown became a busy trade center.

Spring floods in 1911 caused the abutments of the railroad bridge to collapse into the Pecatonica River. Crews were brought in to pull the engine from the river. A diver had to do the underwater rigging.

The dam at Martintown was converted from water power to powering electrical generators. Because of the size of the river at Martintown, that plant was the largest along the Pecatonica.

The community had all the usual businesses of a mill town. The school had two doors, one for the boys and one for the girls.

When the railroad left, the town died. In recent years, a handful of homes, the railroad depot (converted to a home), and a few other vintage buildings still stood. The Martintown Community Church is in the roadside hamlet.

Martintown Community Church. (Courtesy of Martintown Community Church)

Iowa County

Above: The view from the lead shot tower in Helena. (Courtesy of "McGhiever," Wikimedia Commons, http://en.wikipedia.org/wiki/File:Tower_Hill_State_Park_1.JPG)

Right: The lead shot tower. (Courtesy of "Free-kee," Wikimedia Commons, https://en.wikipedia.org/wiki/File:Tower_Hill_Park_WI_May10.jpg)

HELENA

1831 – 1894

CLASS C/F

APPROXIMATE LOCATION:
Tower Hill State Park

Just a small crude community in 1830, Helena soon became a boom town. The discovery of lead ore in the region and becoming primarily a river port town changed all that. A Green Bay businessman thought the settlement's geographical landscape and its location at the spot where the river makes a dramatic turn were perfect for his plans. The sandstone, pine-covered bluffs would be ideal for the construction of a lead shot tower. *Just what is a lead shot tower?* I wondered.

Seems it is a long, vertical shaft, which in this case rose from the base of the cliff to a ledge 120 feet above. From the ledge, the lead shot tower rose another sixty feet to the top of the cliff. A horizontal tunnel runs into the shaft. William Stark, Wisconsin historian, wrote that the builder of the tower did not have a compass, so he "eyeballed" the shaft with stakes and lit candles. He hit the perpendicular vertical shaft dead center. It took two men 187 days to build the apparatus. T.B. Shance, the builder, took some time to serve in the militia during the Black Hawk War.

The process is detailed, but to summarize, lead was melted in two large kettles at the top. It was then strained in a series sieves of various sizes. The molten metal then fell down the shaft into a cistern of cold water. As the lead fell, it took on a spherical shape and pellets were formed. They were cooled when they hit the cold water. The pellets continued on for sorting, polishing, and shipping. Green Bay businessman Whitney sold the tower in the late 1830s.

A marker in Helena. (Courtesy of "McGhiever," Wikimedia Commons, http://en.wikipedia.org/wiki/File:Helena_Marker.JPG)

A gazebo built by the Tower Hill Pleasure Company, now a park in Helena, Wisconsin. (Courtesy of "McGhiever," Wikimedia Commons, https://commons.wikimedia.org/w/index.php?curid=24039710)

In the 1850s Helena was at its peak. By then, it boasted a hotel with a ballroom, a post office, a five-story warehouse, and a 120-foot wharf. Helena's prosperity was short-lived, however. The ferry was replaced by a bridge, but the bridge was located several miles upstream. Stark wrote that the bridge location dictated where the railroad line would run, and Helena was bypassed. New towns sprang up along the new railroad line and Helena fell into decay. The financial panic of 1857 finished Helena off. The shot tower didn't last much longer. Houses were moved to other communities, the shot tower machinery was sold and moved out, and the land went for back taxes, which in 1864 were $46.85.

Frank Lloyd Wright's uncle, Jenkin Lloyd Jones, purchased the property in 1889 for sixty dollars. He formed a religious and educational retreat known as the Tower Hill Pleasure Company. The complex included a pavilion, dining hall, ice house, stables, and three "long" houses. After Jones's death in 1922, his widow donated the property to the state of Wisconsin for use as a park.

Jones's pavilion became the park shelter. A massive restoration project rebuilt the tower. Today park visitors can walk into the tunnel and look down from the top of the vertical shaft. The old Helena Cemetery lies across the road and within the park.

Iron County

Above: Logging in Emerson's early days. (Courtesy of Audrey Holbrook Clark)
Below: A marker on Pinery Road. (Author's Collection)

PINERY ROAD

THE LEGEND

IRON COUNTY

HERITAGE AREA

In 1904, a tornado ripped through this area, toppling the last great stand of virgin pine. The "windfall" in salvagable timber attracted brothers John and David Emerson to the vicinity of Bearskull Lake.

Hauling sawmill machinery, supplies, and logging equipment 25 miles through swamps and forest from Park Falls, they established a sawmill town here in 1905. Work to salvage wind blown timber had just begun when a fast moving forest fire destroyed the mill and new community of "Emerson".

Come spring, the brothers hauled in larger, more modern sawmill equipment. Emerson was rebuilt. Wood frame homes, to house lumberjacks and their families, lined both sides of Emerson's half mile long main street.

Emerson boasted, a school, post office, store, and town hall-- but there was no saloon. The Emersons were pious prohibitionists. Intoxicating liquor was not allowed in their town!

Was it curse or coincidence when lightening struck and killed brother John and three members of the Emerson family, while they were fishing near Bearskull Lake in 1908?

The family never recovered from the tragedy. The mill and town were soon abandoned and logging operations moved away from Bearskull Lake.

Wisconsin
You're Among Friends

EMERSON

1906 – 1920

CLASS A/B

APPROXIMATE LOCATION:
Town of Sherman, off Highway 182

Photos of Emerson's school. The top photo is from 1910; the bottom is undated. (Courtesy of Audrey Holbrook Clark)

For me, it all started with Emerson. As a young child—even now—I marveled at the stories my aunts told me about the town that used to be near their homes. As I walked the back woods and clearing of Aunt Jean's place, I wondered, how a town could have existed there, where now there is nothing? The photos of Emerson in its heyday my Aunt Audrey showed me spurred my imagination, and I never got over the sense of awe and wonder. Those tales and that location sparked my curiosity and still stir my imagination. It led to a lifelong interest and research into lost towns that has led to four Minnesota's Lost Towns books and now this *Wisconsin's Lost Towns*. Yes, for me, Emerson started it all.

The best resource on Emerson history available is a memoir written by Hugh Emerson in 1966. Hugh was the son of one of the Emerson founders, and he grew up and attended school in the long-ago settlement. He wrote the manuscript to preserve the history, as he knew it, for generations to come. Combined with my family stories, we can visit Emerson in their words.

In 1904, a tornado touched down in southern Iron County, deep in the Wisconsin woods, leaving a three-mile swath of downed timber. Lots of it. The Emersons built a sawmill half a mile from Ferry Lake with the sole purpose of cleaning up the timber debris. Certainly there had been others logging in the area before the Emersons, including early French Canadians, who had claimed their 160-acre homesteads, but not to farm. They cleared the timber and then moved on.

Around the Emerson mill a small settlement developed. In 1905, the entire settlement, mill and all, was destroyed by a fast-moving forest fire. Only one house was left standing. Houses were hastily and partially rebuilt in time to serve as shelters for the approaching winter.

In 1906, larger and more modern mill equipment was hauled in. For the next few years the mill ran at full steam. The need for power was so great that a second steam boiler and smokestack were added.

Houses were built for one-half mile on both sides of Main Street. The mill was on the road near the swamp. This time the houses were built of lumber milled at the sawmill rather than logs.

Soon the thirty families in the settlement had enough school-aged children to justify a school building. In addition to the mill and school, Emerson also included a store, a post office, and a town hall, which doubled as a church. At various times the settlement had a visiting pastor, a Reverend Ware from Minocqua. (The reverend later lived and farmed on the old town site.) Emerson was unusual in that it also had a resident pastor, and it had no saloons. According to Hugh, the Emersons were pious and ardent prohibitionists, and they allowed no alcohol in their village. The community also had an active Good Temperance Lodge.

The Emersons were instrumental in securing a viable local form of government for the area. Originally part of the town of Vaughn, which included all of Iron County, the town was managed, according to Hugh, in a corrupt manner in Hurley. Hurley at the time was a hotbed of saloons and brothels. Hugh termed it "the wild and most evil community in the U.S." The Emersons even went to the governor of Wisconsin with their complaints. As a result, the town of Emerson was formed and

Views of the site of the town of Emerson today. (Authors' Collection)

A road sign directing the way to Emerson. (Courtesy of Jodie Fobes Livingston)

the Iron County sheriff was removed from office. The town of Emerson would later be named Sherman after early residents.

A direct connection to the railroad was also needed. So the Emersons blazed a road from the railroad depot at Powell through Springstead and on to the Park Falls Road (now Highway 182). A family story tells that some of the land was mucky

and unstable. At one time a locomotive ran off the rails, sinking into the muck. It is said it took a week for it to slowly disappear beneath the surface. The machinery that would have been needed to pull it out could not be brought in due to the mucky terrain.

One-half mile from the Bear River Bridge toward Powell lies a granite outcropping appropriately called the Powell Outcrop. The ledge is on the north side of Highway 182. If one drives by one can see little stacks, or cairns, of rocks piled up on the ledge. Hugh wrote that a small cave lay directly under the outcrop. When the big logging rigs with the heavy iron-clad horses' hooves passed over the spot, one could hear a distinct hollow sound. Modern autos don't produce the same effect. Hugh wrote that he was probably the only living person to have witnessed the phenomenon. That was back in 1966.

Many believed that Emerson would have developed into a full-fledged village had tragedy not struck. John Emerson, his three sons, and a nephew went fishing on Bear Skull Lake in July of 1908. A sudden storm forced them to seek shelter ashore. The group was waiting out the storm in a makeshift tent pitched by a tall tree. The tree was struck by lightning and John, one of his sons, and a nephew were killed. Stricken by grief, the Emersons closed the mill a few years later and left the region. The village also faded into history.

Hugh tells of an old Chippewa legend. The legend states that Bear Skull Lake is so sacred a spot that any white man who had anything to do with the lake or its vicinity would have everlasting ill fortune. The lake is deep, cold, and amber-colored, a true muskie lake.

An historical marker for Emerson is located at the Sherman Town Hall, off of Highway 182 and just a short distance from the old town site. The town site is on private property. The legend of Emerson lives on in memory.

Hinkle's schoolbus. (Courtesy of Iron County Historical Society)

HINKLE

1901 - 1916

CLASS A

APPROXIMATE LOCATION:
Between Kimball and Hurley (5 miles from Hurley)

In 1910, a lumber camp was operating in the Hinkle area and a side track was established to handle the camps transportation needs. The camp supplied forest products for use by the Lake Superior Iron and Chemical Company, which operated out of Ashland. Several trains stopped daily to pick up and drop off passengers, and a boxcar station was provided. Once the lumber camp ceased operations (approximately 1911 to 1914), service was discontinued and the tracks removed. In approximately 1915, a petition was filed to reinstate rail service to Hinkle.

According to rail records, between 125 and 200 people lived in the vicinity of Hinkle and at least eighteen farmers would use the shipping facilities at the reestablished train station. Records indicate that about a dozen people would board the train to go to nearby Ironwood for Saturday night festivities and that number also traveled to Ironwood during the week for varied purposes.

A proposed road was being built, and, though the terrain was difficult, it was deemed that, due to a small population and the newly constructed road, transportation needs would be adequate and the station was not reestablished.

KIMBALL

1889 - 1942

CLASS A

APPROXIMATE LOCATION:
Northwest of Hurley

Once home to a sawmill and a store, Kimball used to be a bustling community. The mill was known for its high-quality hardwood flooring, which was even displayed at the 1893 Chicago World's Fair. For a time, the mill also built boats.

In 1903, fire destroyed homes and the company store. A larger, more disastrous fire struck the community in 1904. After that fire a new mill, dry kilns, a blacksmith shop, a store, and five homes were part of the settlement. The mill was sold and dismantled in the 1920s.

Ruins in Kimball in 1992. (Courtesy of Iron County Historical Society)

MANITOWISH

1890 – 1968

CLASS C/D

APPROXIMATE LOCATION:
Intersection of Highway 47 and U.S. 51

On the way to Mercer from Springstead is the intersection of Highway 47 and U.S. Highway 51. Every time we'd come to the stop, my mom would say, "There is Chuck and Opal's." The tavern building looked so inviting, and I knew they were family friends. But that is about all the thought I gave the place. It wasn't until recently that I even knew the corner crossroads had once been a thriving village. The community was a railroad town built on the timber economy. It was a shipping point until the 1930s. A sawmill also operated in the area. The post office was rather long lived, lasting until 1968.

I never got to meet Chuck and Opal, but recently I talked with their daughter Joyce and their granddaughter Jodie. They very kindly shared stories and tales of Manitowish as well as photos.

Built upon and sustained by the area's vast timber resources and the Chicago Northwestern Railroad Depot, Manitowish was and is still very much a four-season recreational destination. The region's scenic beauty, fish-filled lakes, and northwoods beauty have always attracted visitors, tourists, and residents.

Without a doubt, it is the stories and memories and the people that bring any town—any place—to life, especially so with long-ago places. Joyce Bednar Young lived most of her life in Manitowish, and it is her remembrances I share. Joyce's

Above: An early image of Kimball in winter. (Courtesy of Iron County Historical Society)
Below: A logging operation in Kimball. (Courtesy of Iron County Historical Society)

Early Manitowish's store and hotel, which later became Chuck and Opal's place. (Courtesy of Iron County Historical Society)

parents, Chuck and Opal Jeskewitz, were longtime residents of the area.

As in many northern Wisconsin communities, it was the timber and the logging interests and the subsequent railroad facilities that first established the community. Chuck and Opal owned and operated the former Manitowish Hotel turned tavern. They purchased the business in the late 1930s and it soon became a local landmark, Chuck's Bar.

As Joyce remembers, in the 1930s, it was a bustling place. There was a logging camp near the end of the tavern's road. Logs piled high and long were a common sight at the depot's side track. Rail traffic consisted of two passenger trains heading south and two heading north, each and every day. At least two freight trains, carrying iron ore or timber, went through the station each day.

Even in those early days, folks frequented the northern woods and lakes. According to Joyce, the weekenders who worked south in the cities would leave their cars at Chuck's during the week. On Friday nights, they would bring the train up to Manitowish, pick up their cars, and spend the weekend at the lake or in the woods. Come Sunday, they would come back to Chuck's, park their cars for the week, and head home.

Electricity was not common in those early years, so ice harvesting was a necessity, especially for resorts and businesses. Ice would be cut from area lakes, put in ice houses and covered with sawdust, which, thanks to the logging activity, was plentiful. Every home, cabin, and resort used generators and ice boxes. Chuck and others supplied that ice, filling over forty area ice houses.

Every January, the crew and equipment were readied. Chuck got his ice from Sparkling Lake in Arbor Vitae and

Top: A river scene from Manitowish. (Author's Collection)
Middle: Logs at the Chicago & Northwestern side track circa 1938. (Courtesy of Joyce Bednar Young)
Bottom: A cabin just about buried in snow in Manitowish. (Author's Collection)

Above: The Lazy Ace Saloon today. (formerly Chuck and Opal's) (Courtesy of Jodie Fobes Livingston)
Below: A sign commemmorating Chuck, of Chuck and Opal's. (Courtesy of Jodie Fobes Livingston)

Frog Lake in Manitowish, as well as a few others. Once the ice was nineteen inches thick, the harvest could begin. A large pond and channel were cut to float the ice blocks to the waiting trucks. A conveyor laid against the bed of the truck was used to guide the blocks to the truck's bed. At one time, several school children and a PBS television station came to record the activity. During the summer months, the ice was also used for packing visiting fishermen's catches for shipment by rail to their homes.

During the 1940s, Manitowish had a gas station, Gerlach's on Highway 51, a Homestead Restaurant (now a VFW), the Corner Inn (now the Ding-a-Ling), and Chuck's Bar, now known as the Lazy Aces Bar. At one time, Chuck's included a grocery store and three cabins.

Hunting and fishing camps were annual events. When Highway 51 was restructured in the 1950s, much of original Manitowish was lost. Those years were special and as Joyce recalled, everyone knew each other and helped each other. That is true of most long-ago and lost towns. It is the people and the memories that bring them to life.

POWELL

1908 – 1942

CLASS A/C

APPROXIMATE LOCATION:
Just off Highway 47 and Powell Road

On May 30, 1942, Hattie Holbrook closed the Powell post office for the last time. She had just stamped a handful of last date cancellations that had been requested. Every day Hattie would hitch up the team and drive to Powell, five miles away, and deliver the mail pouch. The mail was in a leather-like sack that had catches on both ends. Alongside the railroad tracks, a metal arm would catch the mail sack when the train passed by. Hattie's daughter Charlotte remembered that, every once in a while, the conductor would throw a bag of candy out. The old box car that had once served as a depot still stood.

Above: Manitowash in 1907. (Courtesy of Joyce Bednar-Young)
Below: Gerlach's gas station on Highway 51, taken in August 1942. (Courtesy of Joyce Bednar-Young)

Above: The first Powell Post Office. (Courtesy of Audrey Holbrook Clark and Charlotte Holbrook Morrill)

Right: Hattie Holbrook, Powell's last postmistress. (Courtesy of Audrey Holbrook Clark and Charlotte Holbrook Morrill

Above: The Powell depot, circa 1920s to 1930s. (Courtesy of Audrey Holbrook Clark and Charlotte Holbrook Morrill)
Below: The Powell Outcrop. (Courtesy of the Wisconsin Geological and Natural History Survey and Tod Roush)

Above: An old photo of the Powell schoolhouse. (Courtesy of Audrey Holbrook Clark and Charlotte Holbrook Morrill)
Below: The Powell school today. (Courtesy of Norbert Vissers)

Hattie, Lester, and their six children moved to Powell in 1934. Powell's first post office was in Frank Sherman's place, as were the store and gas pumps. The town of Sherman was named in Frank's honor. When Hattie became Powell's postmistress, the last one, the family lived in Springstead, a few miles away.

Powell had a school at one time. In the 1920s, tragedy struck the school at the year-end picnic. The five-year-old cousin of the teacher went missing. Her body was found just two hundred feet from the schoolhouse. A woodsman was arrested and taken to Ashland for trial. He was found guilty and sentenced to life in prison.

In 1934, just a few miles from Powell, an infamous FBI encounter with John Dillinger at the Little Bohemia Lodge took place. Dillinger made his escape. Some thought he might come through Powell, so a few area residents set up a stakeout and were armed with shotguns. They quickly disbanded when

Lester Holbrook told them that if Dillinger did indeed come by, he would most likely have a machine gun and he didn't think they'd have a chance.

Sandy Beach was near Powell and was a popular recreational spot with a swimming beach.

Powell's train depot was a busy place. Many passengers came to Powell on their way to the area's many resorts. Powell was also known to be a bit of a gambling town. Slot machines were common in many resorts and the store.

SPRINGSTEAD

1920 - 1933

CLASS A/C/F

APPROXIMATE LOCATION:
16 miles east/northeast of Park Falls on Highway 182

Top: Springstead school, 1934-1935. (Courtesy Charlotte Holbrook Morrill)
Bottom: Springstead school in 2010. (Author's Collection)

Springstead is special to me. It is the place of my mother's and her siblings' youth. It is the place of family memories and stories. It will always hold a place in my heart. By the time I came into being, Springstead was already a lost town, but family stories and research have filled in the blanks of Springstead's early history.

Springstead's beginnings go back to 1901, when Bernhardt and Lulu Pripps came to the area. Built on a logging economy, Springstead and its surrounding area was and is a recreational destination with numerous resorts and lodges.

The earliest loggers were French Canadians. They claimed the 160-acre homesteads available, but not to farm. The stayed long enough to clear the timber and then left the region.

With time, the loggers brought their families and soon there were enough school-aged children to necessitate the building of a school. Springstead's first school was a one-room log cabin on the north end of Springstead Lake. The second school, built in 1917, was known as the Maggie Murphy School. Maggie was a nurse who vacationed in the area.

By the end of the 1930s, the community built a larger school. It was a two-story brick building with a stage and a downstairs kitchen. Young Charlotte Holbrook, along with her sisters and a couple of cousins, attended the school. Charlotte would grow up and become a teacher at her old school in the late 1940s. She fondly remembered the iodine pills. Every so often the teacher would pull out the cylindrical bottles and dispense the pills to the children. Charlotte and the others loved the pills, as they tasted like chocolate. It was a big day when Charlotte became the teacher and had control of the iodine pills.

Valentine's Day was a special day at school. Hattie Striegel baked each child a heart-shaped cookie with icing. Each child's name was written on the cooking in icing. The cookies became a school tradition for over twenty-five years.

The school was used until 1950, when it consolidated with the Park Falls School District. The school building was later used as the town hall for Sherman, until the town built a new one in recent years. A few years back, the old school was for sale. The building is still majestic. Tall pine trees surround the school building and stand nearly eighty feet in the air. Those trees were planted in the 1940s by the schoolchildren, including my mother, Jacqueline and her sister, Jeannie. Today the school is a private home.

Springstead was a deeply wooded area, and deer and other wildlife were plentiful. At one time the Holbrook children had a pet deer, Dickie. Dickie was found along the roadside, her mother having been killed by a car. As Dickie grew, she would leave for a while and then come back. One time she was gone an exceptionally long time. When she returned she was so weak she could barely walk. She had been shot in the jaw. My grandmother cleaned up the wound and splintered it. Dickie, by then a full-grown deer, didn't flinch.

During deer hunting season, Dickie wore a red jacket on her front quarters, with a belled collar. The family left the region for a few years and during their absence Dickie would visit the neighbor. One time Dickie came by and had twin fawns with her. Once the family returned, Dickie greeted them like a dog, jumping on their shoulders and licking their faces. One evening they heard shots. The next day they found Dickie's head and collar. Evidently a poacher had killed the deer.

A schoolbus from early Springstead. (Courtesy of Audrey and Don Clark)

Top: A sign welcoming visitors to Springstead today. (Author's Collection) Bottom: Flambeau River flowage, taken in 2001 from Springstead Landing off of Highway 182 (Courtesy of Joyce Bednar-Young)

When the bulk of logging as an industry ended (the area is still home to much logging activity), tourism became the area's mainstay industry. Springstead was and is home to some fantastic fishing, hunting, lodges, and resorts. It is a vacation destination year round.

Springstead has an historic district. Much of the research on it was done by the late Daniel Stanley. The district was placed on the National Register of Historic Places in 1997. The district is north of Highway 182 and across from the old Springstead tote road, thirteen miles northwest of Manitowish. Springstead was the site of sugar bushes, and in the later years (1900s), maple syrup was processed in and shipped by rail from the town.

The district includes five buildings on just over five acres of land. Four of the five buildings are constructed of logs, and only the barn is of wood siding. Three of the buildings have the same windows. The buildings are the French Canadian cabin, the main house, the garage/post office/general store and the barn. Springstead's post office moved to Park Falls in 1933. The buildings represent traditional and rustic architecture of northwestern Wisconsin.

Below left, below, and next page: Buildings in the Springstead Historic District. (Courtesy of National Register of Historic Places, Springstead, Iron County, Wisconsin, #97000326)

VAN BUSKIRK

1890 – 1933

CLASS A

APPROXIMATE LOCATION:
6 miles south of Hurley

Van Buskirk's one-room schoolhouse. (Courtesy of Iron County Historical Society)

Beginning as a logging town, Van Buskirk was named for the Van Buskirk brothers and their sawmill. At its peak, Van Buskirk had three general stores, a co-op, two gas stations, and a one-room school. One early resident said it had everything it needed. The community also had an active chapter of the Finnish Workers and a Temperance Society.

By the early 1900s, the pine was gone. The mill closed in 1908. The workers moved on and Van Buskirk faded.

Early images of Van Buskirk. (Courtesy of Iron County Historical Society)

Jackson County

GOODYEAR - MCKENNA - ZEDA

1888 - 1895

CLASS A/B

APPROXIMATE LOCATION:
Near the vicinity of Merlin Lambert County Park,
McKenna Road

Most research sources on Wisconsin's logging towns combine the histories of Goodyear, McKenna, and Zeda. Since the three share many commonalities, including time period, general location, parent company, origins, and demise, the three are combined here as well. All three were in Jackson County.

A steam-operated mill began operating in McKenna in 1889. The village was named for C.W. McKenna, the superintendent of the La Crosse and Wisconsin Valley Railroad, a division of the St. Paul Railroad. A sizable village developed around the mill and included a post office (1888 to 1895), a store, a barber shop, forty to fifty homes, a meat market, a planing mill, a dance hall, and several other buildings. Sixty men worked at the mill and 125 in the camps. Output was substantial, with 55,000 feet of lumber, 80,000 shingles, and 20,000 laths being shipped out daily. A telephone line connected the mill to company offices in Tomah.

Meanwhile, another mill was built by the George Warren Company. This one was located along Morrison Creek. Plans were to name the village Wazeda, but its close similarity to Wazeka could be confusing, so the name Zeda was adopted instead. Four carloads of lumber were shipped out daily from this location.

Another settlement developed nearby, around the Goodyear mill. The name had originally been Sperbeck, but was changed to Goodyear. Goodyear included a post office, general store, school, boarding house, and several homes for married men and their families.

In all three mill locations, safety was not a priority and injuries, some fatal, were common.

The year 1891 was pivotal for all three locations. The Goodyear mill burned that year. According to Randall Rohe, historian and author of *Ghosts of the Forest: Vanished Lumber Towns of Wisconsin, Volume I*, the two night watchmen didn't notice the fire until it was too late. No cause was ever determined, but there were rumors of misdeeds and tampering.

That same year, the parent company of the mill in McKenna, McMillian, Salsich and Company moved their headquarters from Tomah to McKenna. McKenna experienced a boom in building, adding a livery, a dance hall, a telegraph office, a meat market, and a barbershop. The hotel was sold to new owners and refurbished. Known as the Hotel Donald, it featured an ice cream and lemonade parlor in the summer. A pool hall and shooting gallery were added later.

Population estimates for 1891 to 1892 were: McKenna, 300; Goodyear, 250; and Zeda, 200. The number of school-aged children necessitated that schools be organized. Goodyear had an enrollment high of forty-seven.

Entertainment and social events were not lacking in the settlements. They occurred often and were varied. Traveling medicine shows, basket socials, cinch parties, turkey shoots, and phonograph parties were just a few of the events hosted. However, the most popular events were dances. Hardly a week or two went by without a dance happening. Dances were held for the holidays, harvest balls, masquerade parties, necktie parties, and ordinary dances just because. Folks, sometimes as many as forty couples, came from as far away as Camp Douglas and Black River Falls.

The Fourth of July was a special celebration. Boxing matches were hosted. Family activities were always well attended and included blueberry picking, cranberry picking, picnics, and boating on the mill pond in McKenna. Theatrical clubs, especially during the winter months, were popular. Skating and sleigh parties made the wintertime pass faster, as well.

Visiting ministers and pastors provided spiritual guidance and conducted services. Held in any building available, the school most often saw services held there. Rohe wrote that people in the area had great interest in national politics. In 1892, the McKenna Democrats erected a seventy-five-foot flagpole. They ordered a flag displaying four large oil paintings of their candidates. When the flag arrived it was too heavy for the flagpole, so they hung the banner across the street and ordered another one for the flagpole.

In the name of equal exposure, the Republicans ordered their own flag. It was five feet shorter than the Democrats' flag, but the Republicans said they would make up the difference in the November election. Alas, Grover Cleveland easily defeated the Republican candidate and the McKenna Democrats celebrated well into the late hours.

Fire was always a danger for logging towns. Logging is not a neat little business, and scraps and slash are left lying about.

All it took was a spark from a passing train and entire villages could be ashes in mere minutes. A forest fire in March of 1891 had Goodyear surrounded on all sides. Every available man was sent to fight the flames. The mill even shut down and sent its employees to battle the blaze.

The vast timber resources didn't last long. By early 1894, the supply was dwindling. The size of the cut timber was also much smaller than in the early days. By the fall of 1894, McKenna and Zeda shut down their mills. A week later, Goodyear followed suit. In October of that year, the train made its last run. With the timber gone and the mills closed, residents moved on to new locations and homes.

The post offices were discontinued and other businesses shut their doors. Some of the buildings were moved, others were abandoned. Local farmers and residents tore down any remaining structures. Nature reclaimed some and fires took the rest.

By the 1930s, only crumbling foundations and mill remnants remained. The McKenna/Zeda school was later used as St. Luke's Evangelical Church and was eventually torn down. The Goodyear school became the Knapp Town Hall. Zeda is now private property. The Merlin Lambert County Park now occupies the former site of Goodyear. The boat landing is where the railroad crossed.

Jefferson County

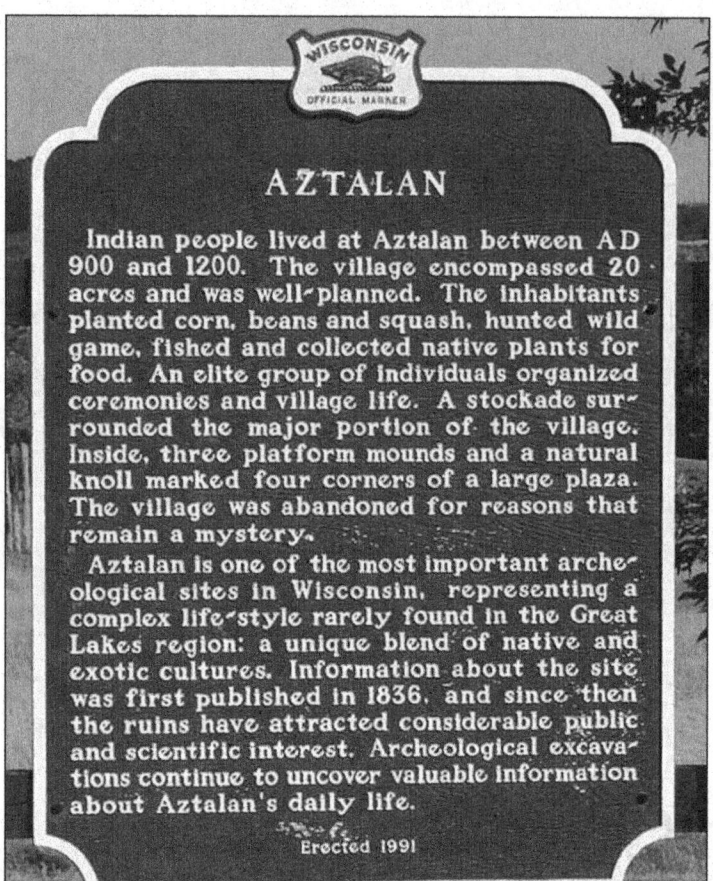

AZTALAN

Indian people lived at Aztalan between AD 900 and 1200. The village encompassed 20 acres and was well-planned. The inhabitants planted corn, beans and squash, hunted wild game, fished and collected native plants for food. An elite group of individuals organized ceremonies and village life. A stockade surrounded the major portion of the village. Inside, three platform mounds and a natural knoll marked four corners of a large plaza. The village was abandoned for reasons that remain a mystery.

Aztalan is one of the most important archeological sites in Wisconsin, representing a complex life-style rarely found in the Great Lakes region: a unique blend of native and exotic cultures. Information about the site was first published in 1836, and since then the ruins have attracted considerable public and scientific interest. Archeological excavations continue to uncover valuable information about Aztalan's daily life.

Erected 1991

Aztalan marker. (Courtesy of Lake Mills Aztalan Histocial Society Inc.)

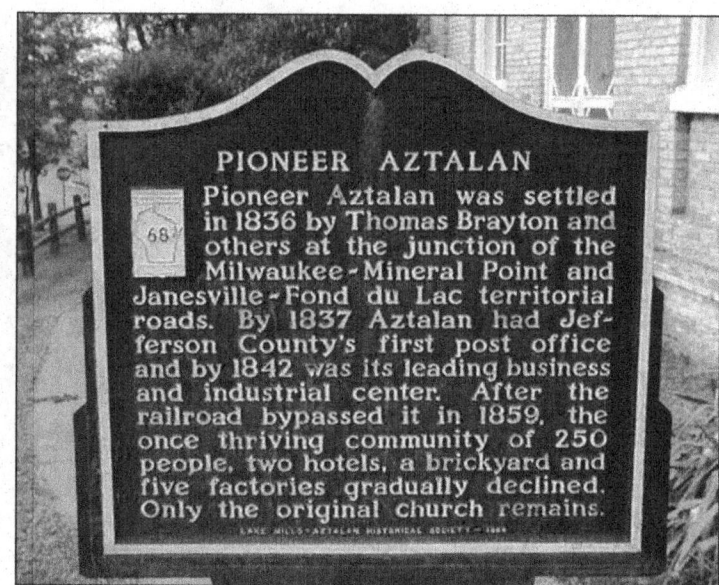

PIONEER AZTALAN

Pioneer Aztalan was settled in 1836 by Thomas Brayton and others at the junction of the Milwaukee-Mineral Point and Janesville-Fond du Lac territorial roads. By 1837 Aztalan had Jefferson County's first post office and by 1842 was its leading business and industrial center. After the railroad bypassed it in 1859, the once thriving community of 250 people, two hotels, a brickyard and five factories gradually declined. Only the original church remains.

Marker for Pioneer Aztalan. (Courtesy of Lake Mills Aztalan Histocial Society Inc.)

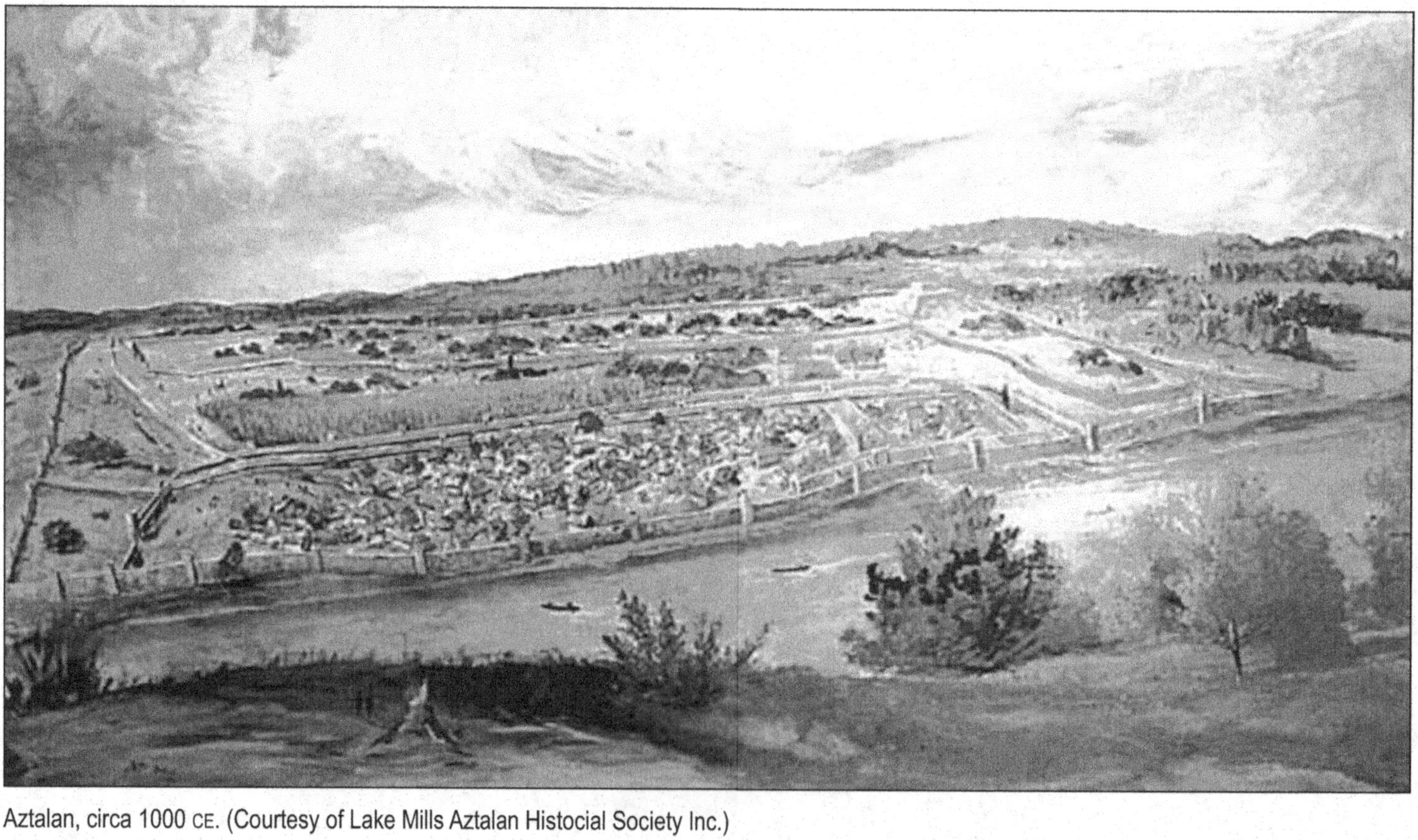

Aztalan, circa 1000 CE. (Courtesy of Lake Mills Aztalan Histocial Society Inc.)

AZTALAN

1839 – 1904 (1250 CE)

CLASS D/F

APPROXIMATE LOCATION:
County Q, Aztalan State Park

Fifty miles west of Milwaukee along the Crawfish River lies what is perhaps Wisconsin's oldest lost village, Aztalan. Forensic evidence dates the village to 1250 CE (Common Era). Centuries later, in the early to mid-1800s, that same location was the site of a pioneer village also known as Aztalan.

In 1836, just prior to the pioneer village being established, a resident of the new village discovered the ancient village. Noticing that many of the region's flat-top rock formation looked man-made, curiosities were piqued. That curiosity would lead to great study of the area. That study would eventually be the largest and most significant archeological survey in Wisconsin.

When reports reached Milwaukee's Judge Nathanial Hyer, who had earlier been in the region conducting surveys, he traveled by horseback to the ruin site. Hyer and later Increase A. Lapham would be credited with drawing the first maps of the site. Early scientists believed that a connection existed between Aztalan and the ancient Aztec culture. Hyer had also heard the well-known legend which said that the Aztec people had come to Mexico from Aztalan, a land by flowing waters way to the north. Maybe this was that land. Hyer called the site Aztalan.

After the erroneous connection to the Aztec, further investigation revealed that the ancient village was a blending of Mississippian and local culture. Studying the mounds and

artifacts, the material makeup of the items proved the site was not Aztec. Remains and artifacts show that the mounds were not used for burial purposes but for rituals and ceremonies. It was also learned that the ancient people of Aztalan cultivated fields of corn, squash, pumpkins, and sunflowers, and could be considered Wisconsin's first farm town. Population estimates were that approximately five hundred people lived in early Aztalan. Other evidence tells that the village was walled, with the crops being grown outside of the walled complex.

Excavation of the village produced remarkable discoveries and led to much knowledge. One mound, located just behind the Baptist church in Pioneer Aztalan, was of note. A body of a female, approximately twenty to twenty-five years of age, with a spinal deformity was found. It was the only burial discovered in a mound. A lack of burial remains leads to a lack of information on the villager's mortuary customs. Buried with the woman's body, who was called "The Princess," were thousands of beads. The Lake Mills Historical Society Inc. writes that the burial was so unique that it was reconstructed as a special exhibit in the Milwaukee Museum. (It is no longer on display.)

Excavation also showed that the ancient city was walled using vertical timbers and plastered with a clay and grass mixture resembling cement. Houses were built the same way, with thatched roofs. There is speculation that cannibalism existed but that has been neither proven nor disproven. Scientists have determined that fire destroyed the ancient village but there is no evidence yet found as to the cause.

Sadly, preservation of historic sites was not strictly adhered to in early American history. When word got out of the ancient ruin discovery, treasure hunters flocked to the region, destroying the mounds in search of relics they might be able

The Princess Mound in 2006. (Courtesy of Lake Mills Aztalan Histocial Society Inc.)

Excavation of a refuse pit in Aztalan. (Courtesy of Lake Mills Aztalan Histocial Society Inc.)

Above: Pioneer Aztalan's post office. (Courtesy of Lake Mills Aztalan Histocial Society Inc.)

Below: Pioneer Aztalan. (Courtesy of Lake Mills Aztalan Histocial Society Inc.)

to sell. Generations of farmers also plowed and cultivated the land, sometimes losing visible features. It wasn't until the twentieth century that preservation efforts were realized.

Located near the site of the ancient city and near two territorial roads, Thomas Brayton's long log house was to become Jefferson County's first incorporated village. The small, bustling settlement, which once was just two votes shy of being designated Wisconsin's state capitol, was the business center of the county. The settlement included hotels, blacksmith shops, a brickyard, a steam-operated sawmill, a stone quarry, and several stores. Since the village was located at the northern end of the ancient village, it too was called Aztalan. For a short time it had been called Jefferson but with the establishment of a post office, officially became Aztalan. Prosperous for several years in part because of its location along the well-traveled roads, the railroad age would prove to be Pioneer Aztalan's demise. The new railroad, which came through in 1859, bypassed Aztalan by just a few miles. Two later rail lines would also bypass the village, one in 1881 and the other in 1882, by just a mile. Only a mile, but it was still enough to cause significant effects to Aztalan. In the early 1900s, little was left of the once thriving settlement.

By 1912, the Baptist church, a creamery, and the general store were all that remained. The church continued for just another year or two. The store burned down in 1925. Nature was slowly eating away at the church by then.

Peaceful Aztalan. (Courtesy of Lake Mills Aztalan Histocial Society Inc.)

Historic preservation of both the ancient and pioneer Aztalan took a positive turn in 1941 with the formation of the Lake Mills Aztalan Historical Society Inc. The society took on the massive task of saving and preserving the site. The Baptist church was restored and is the only original building.

The society continues its efforts today. An annual Aztalan Day takes place on the first Sunday in July. The event features outdoor exhibits, music, food, and more. The society also hosts and maintains an informative website, along with maintaining and operating the site's museum. Check it out at www.orgsites.com/wi/aztalan. Better yet, visit the site in person. Not only will you see and feel the ancient Aztalan and the pioneer Aztalan, but the area is now a great state park.

Plans for the park began in earnest after the Great Depression. Plans were to make it a national park, however, it became a state park. The state of Wisconsin purchased the land in 1948, and the 120-acre park was dedicated in 1952. National landmark designation was awarded in 1964. Over the years, vandals destroyed outdoor exhibits and a lack of funding threatened the park. In 1981, the local township stepped up and offered to maintain the park if the park would remain in state hands. Aztalan State Park's first permanent employee was hired in the late 1980s. Recent interest is sparking preservation, as well. In 1994, the Friends of Aztalan was established.

Above: Aztalan Baptist Church, built in 1852. (Courtesy of Lake Mills Aztalan Histocial Society Inc.)

Below: A map of Aztalan in the 1840s. (Courtesy of Lake Mills Aztalan Histocial Society Inc.)

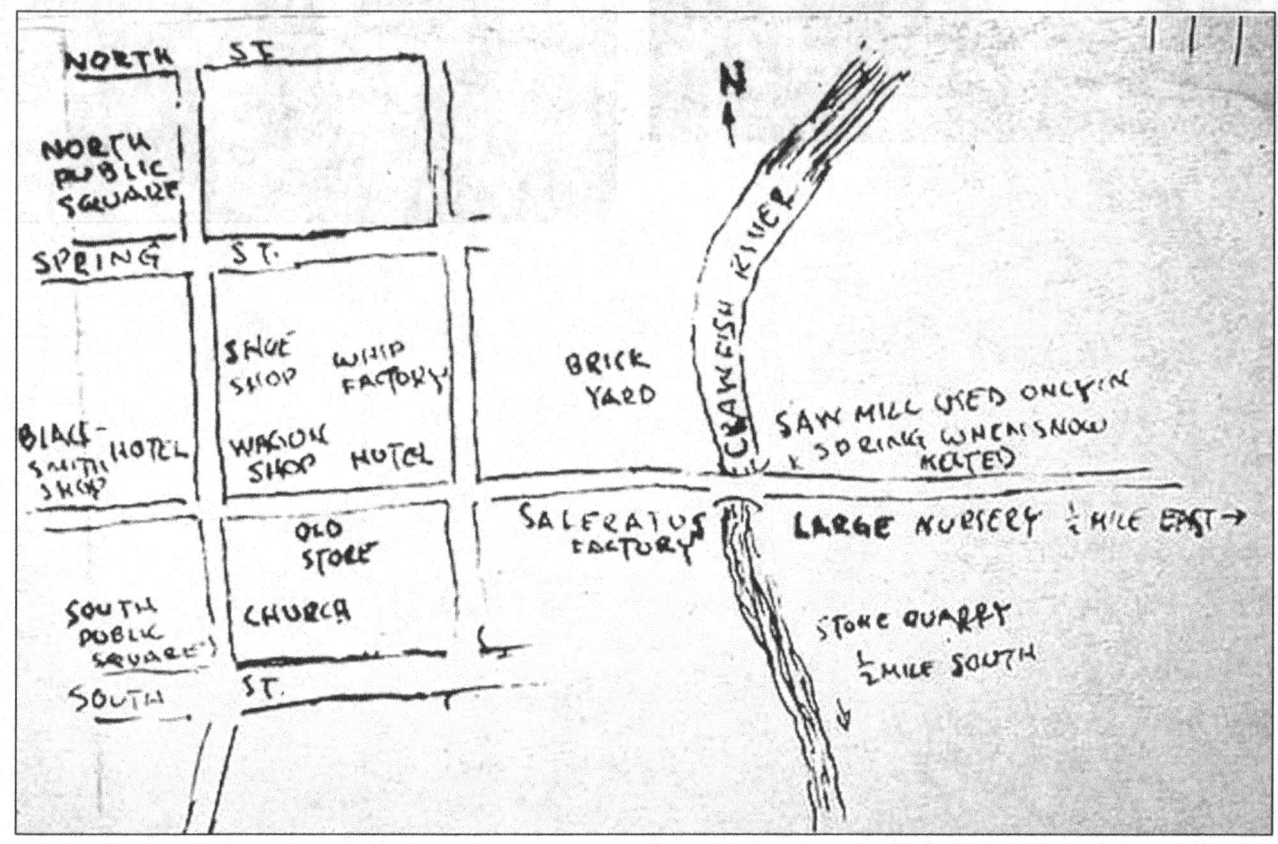

Above: Restoring the Aztalan stockade in 1953. (Courtesy of Lake Mills Aztalan Histocial Society Inc.)

Below: The Aztalan hotel. (Courtesy of Lake Mills Aztalan Histocial Society Inc.)

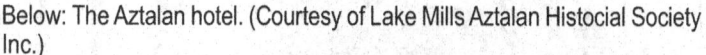

Above: Aztalan's red schoolhouse. (Courtesy of Lake Mills Aztalan Histocial Society Inc.)

Below: The remains of one of Aztalan's stores. (Courtesy of Lake Mills Aztalan Histocial Society Inc.)

Juneau County

Castle Rock County Park, the former site of Germantown. (Author's Collection)

GERMANTOWN (WERNER)

1854 – 1912

CLASS A

APPROXIMATE LOCATION:
Town of Germantown, near Castle Rock County Park

Once a pair of sawmilling settlements, Germantown and Werner were later abandoned, much of the sites lying beneath the waters of Castle Rock Lake today. Located at the juncture of the Yellow and Wisconsin rivers, logging was the basis and the mainstay of the settlements. Laid out with thirty blocks in 1851, the village was incorporated in 1855. Home to Juneau County's first brewery, Germantown also included a Lutheran church, a school, a blacksmith shop, a dance hall, a hotel, a saloon, and of course the sawmill. At one time four sawmills were cutting timber into lumber. After the pine was cut, the logs were made into rafts and floated down the Wisconsin River. For a time a ferry operated from Germantown across the Wisconsin River to Quarry in Adams County.

Plans by the Wisconsin River Power Company were laid in the 1920s to build a dam, and thereby create two lakes. In preparation, buildings in Germantown were disassembled and used for homes in Mauston. The cemetery near Our Lady of the Lakes Catholic Church would remain. However, the Werner Cemetery would be lost to the waters, so the bodies at the Werner Cemetery were relocated to the Our Lady of the Lakes Cemetery.

Today the former settlement of Germantown is in Castle Rock County Park. Werner lies beneath the waters of the lake.

LEMONWEIR (DUSTINVILLE)

1857 – 1899

CLASS A

APPROXIMATE LOCATION:
County N and 19th Avenue, north of I-94

Knowing that settlements often developed around a mill, Newell Dustin built a mill with the plans for a settlement uppermost in his plans. He platted lots and promised to give them to anyone who would start a business in his new village. Dustin also sensed that the region's once-vast timber resources were nearly tapped out, so he built a grist mill, not a sawmill.

For a brief time there was a rivalry with nearby Mauston. All that was settled, over and done with, when the railroad by-passed Lemonweir, also known as Dustinville, in favor of Mauston. Part of the reason for the railroad's snubbing of Dustinville, according to a Juneau County history, was the fact that Dustin had asked way too high of a price for a right-of-way. Cheaper land could, and was, found in Mauston. After the loss of the railroad, Dustin's planned village never amounted to more than a grist mill settlement.

ORANGE MILL

1859 – 1884

CLASS B

APPROXIMATE LOCATION:
2 miles southeast of Camp Douglas

Early settlers were first attracted by the area's location on the well-traveled main road leading to Chippewa, Eau Claire, and Minnesota, as well as its proximity to the Lemonweir River for water power. As with most early settlements, it developed around the activity of the mill.

Soon the community included a school, a post office, a hotel, a general store, and a depot, and it was considered the hub trading center for a wide area. The depot was destroyed by fire in 1869. It was replaced with a small shack, which served as the depot until 1922. A cluster of small motel cabins were also built. The cabins were often used for overflow for nearby Camp Douglas.

At one time a generator was installed in the mill and it provided electricity for lights for Orange Mill, Camp Douglas, and Camp William.

Today, a few buildings and their rubble remains.

STEWART'S SETTLEMENT

1870s

CLASS A/F

APPROXIMATE LOCATION:
County O near Mauston

Though scenic and beautiful, Stewart's Creek was not large enough to power a mill. At that period of time, nearly all settlements were built around a mill.

The one advantage Stewart's Settlement had was its location along a well-traveled and important wagon road. It is said that most settlers who came through Juneau County passed through Stewart's Settlement. The wagon traffic kept Stewart's Settlement going. However, with the advent of and ever-increasing railroad traffic, Stewart's Settlement's importance declined. Travelers who had before come through the settlement now rode trains to Mauston, New Lisbon, and Lyndon Station. Without a railroad and with the institution of Rural Free Delivery, Stewart's Settlement never went past the pioneer town stage.

Orange Mill's school today. (Courtesy of Michael Huebner)

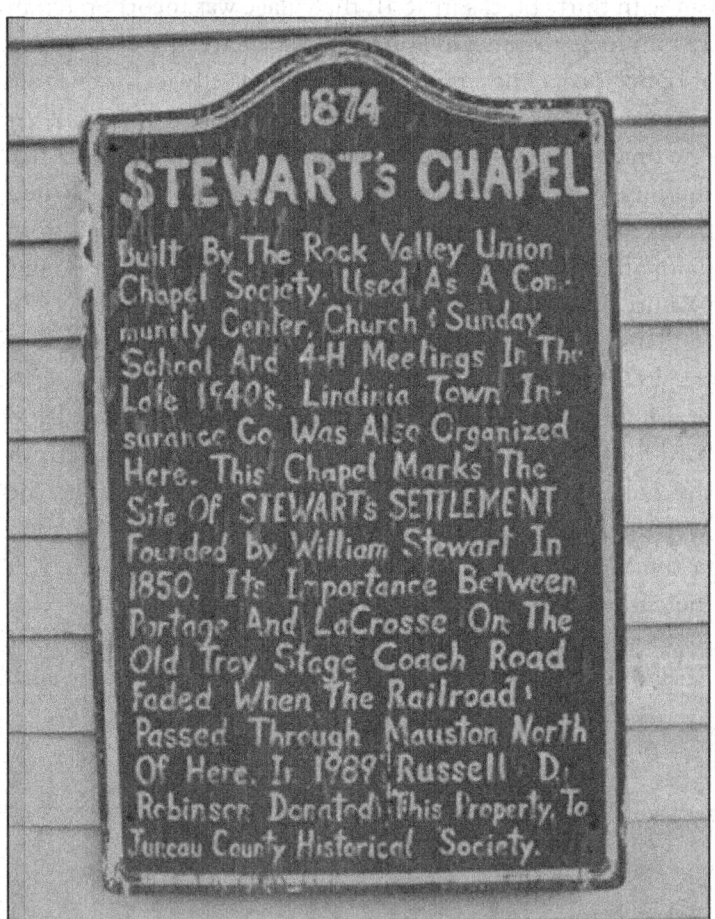

The marker on Stewart's Chapel. (Author's Collection)

Kewaunee County

Early Euren/Bottkol. (Author's Collection)

The New Tippy Canoe Bar and Grill in Euren. (Courtesy of The New Tippy Canoe Bar and Grill)

Downtown Euren today. (Courtesy of "Royalbroil," Wikimedia Commons, http://commons.wikimedia.org/w/index.php?curid=46727536)

EUREN (BOTTKOL)

1879 – 1904

CLASS C/D

APPROXIMATE LOCATION:
County C & S, 8 miles west of Algoma

Michael Bottkol had been forced to serve in the Napoleonic War. As Virginia Feld Johnson, area historian, wrote, Michael's sons had also been forced to serve in the German army. Bottkol grew to hate war and Germany's glorification of it. When he heard that military service in America was not compulsory, and that good land could be had for just one dollar an acre, he was astounded. Furthermore, in America there was freedom of speech and religion and people could eat meat any day they wanted, not just on Christmas or Easter. He made the decision to go to America.

Initially Bottkol was denied the right to emigrate. However, for reasons unknown (bribery or something else?) the Bottkols escaped to France and then on to Wisconsin, where they purchased four forty-acre parcels on the peninsula.

He built a store, a three-story sawmill, a four-story grist mill, a tavern, a cheese factory, and more. When a post office was approved, he was appointed postmaster.

A devastating fire in 1894 destroyed the mill and other buildings.

Today there is a historical marker at the site (on private property).

The ever-popular New Tippy Canoe Bar and Grill is in Bottkol. On game days, the population swells. Open seven days a week, the beer is cold, the food warm, and the atmosphere welcoming.

One note, the German pronunciation is far different from the American.

FROG STATION

Mid-1900s

CLASS A/C

APPROXIMATE LOCATION:
County K and AB

Named for the very loud bullfrogs residing in the nearby headwaters of the Kewaunee River, the community was an early stopping place for farmers picking up supplies in Luxemburg.

Cooya was also popular and Saturday card games days were well attended. Cooya is a card game played with trumps and tricks, similar to Smear. The Belgian residents of the area were particularily fond of the game.

Today smaller species of frogs still are loud, and folks still stop for a respite at the crossroads tavern.

Above: Downtown Frog Station. (Courtesy of Creative Commons)
Below: The road to Frog Station. (Courtesy of Creative Commons)

La Crosse County

NESHONOC

1852 - 1881

CLASS A/C

APPROXIMATE LOCATION:
1 mile from West Salem

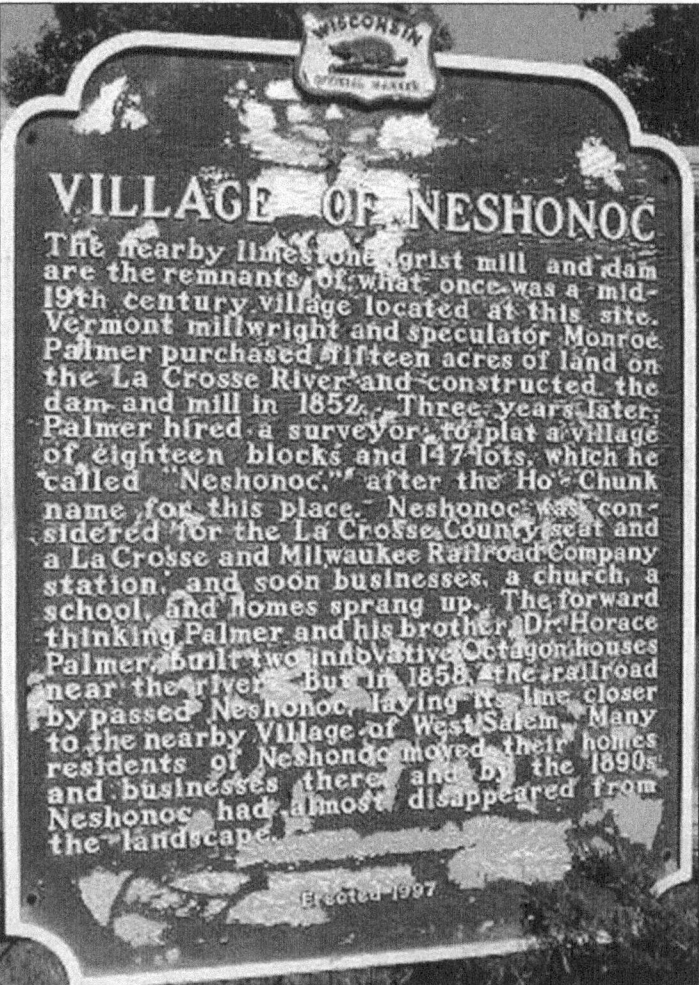

The marker at Neshonoc today. (Courtesy of Creative Commons)

Neshonoc began the same way most early settlements began, with the establishment of a mill. Vermonter Monroe Palmer, in 1851, purchased fifteen acres of land on the La Crosse River. Soon his grist mill was supplying large amounts of feed and flour to the area's many logging camps. Shortly after his business was up and running, he hired a surveyor to lay out a village which he named Neshonoc, after the Native American word for the area.

A post office, the only one between La Crosse and Sparta, was established in 1852. At first the mail was delivered by foot but was later delivered three times a week by stage.

As the settlement grew, Neshonoc's importance grew as well. There was even talk of Neshonoc being designated the La Crosse county seat once the railroad arrived. The expected railroad never happened. Land was donated to the railroad just a mile from Neshonoc at the site of West Salem. Rumor was that Palmer wanted to sell the railroad land and a resident of West Salem donated land. That one-mile distance would prove disastrous for Neshonoc. Without shipping and transportation outlets, Neshonoc businesses could not compete. Residents, businesses, and their buildings made the move to West Salem.

Palmer's original mill burned but was rebuilt with limestone. By 1890, all of Neshonoc was gone except for the rebuilt mill. Today a historical marker notes the former village site.

Neshonoc's octaganal house. (Courtesy of Creative Commons)

Lafayette County

The Buncombe tunnel today. (Courtesy of "Jeff_Tendick," Wikimedia Commons, http://en.wikipedia.org/w/index.php?curid=13108731)

The railroad bed near Buncombe today. (Courtesy of "Jeff_Tendick," Wikimedia Commons, http://en.wikipedia.org/wiki/File:Old_roadbed_near_the_Buncombe_Tunnel,_Galena_and_Southern_Wisconsin_Railroad_(2007).jpg)

BUNCOMBE

1875 – 1903

CLASS B

APPROXIMATE LOCATION:
Buncombe Road east of Highway 80

Prone to persistent flooding, a 350-foot tunnel to protect the rails was constructed. It followed the rail line, which ran north and south along the Coon Branch and the Fever River Valley. In recent years some vestiges of the tunnel were visible.

At its peak, four passenger trains a day visited Buncombe. As reliance on railroads declined, the Buncombe line was abandoned, making Benton the end of the line. A post office operated from 1875 to 1903. A store, a school, and several houses existed until the 1950s. The tracks to Cuba City were removed in the 1980s.

ETNA

1857 – 1915

CLASS B

APPROXIMATE LOCATION:
3 miles north of New Diggings

Primarily a mill town in a mining region, Etna was also considered the cultural center of the area. The four-story stone grist mill overlooked a dam on the Shullsberg Branch. Since it was close to the mines, Etna was a convenient location for the miners to live. The post office was located in the stone store building and provided miners with a mail connection to family and loved ones back home. Able to seat 300 people, Etna Hall, at thirty by sixty feet, hosted many cultural events, traveling shows, and school graduations.

The stone store building was still standing in the early twenty-first century and was the only remnant of Etna remaining.

FORT DEFIANCE

1832

CLASS A/F

APPROXIMATE LOCATION:
5 miles southeast of Mineral Point

When the Black Hawk War broke out, area settlers were concerned about their safety. Tensions were high, as were emotions, and the situation volatile. To reassure settlers, Fort Defiance was built.

Fort Defiance was the last garrisoned stockade fort in Wisconsin Territory. Forty specially trained militiamen were stationed at the fort. It was never attacked. Today there are no visible remains of the fort. While not a village, per se, the fort was a settlement of necessity.

The site of Fort Defiance today. (Courtesy of "Rattis irrittis, "Wikimedia Commons, http://en.wikipedia.org/w/index.php?curid=12799533)

GRATIOT'S GROVE

1828 - 1846

CLASS A/C

APPROXIMATE LOCATION:

County W near Sedgwick Road and County U and Rennick

Years before Wisconsin became a territory in 1836, lead was discovered in what would become southwestern Wisconsin. For the next two decades or more, mining and the arrival of settlers progressed at a fever pitch. One of the main arteries to the area was called the Old Lead Road. It ran from Galena to Mineral Point and on to Milwaukee, a distance of 150 miles. It is interesting to note that at the time Milwaukee had a population of two hundred while Mineral Point was home to over two thousand.

At about the time lead was discovered, prominent St. Louis brothers Henry and Bion Gratiot made the journey to the region. They wanted to check out the mining prospects. Finding it all they had heard about and hoped it would be, the brothers began building log cabins and log smelting furnaces. The next spring, they sent for their families.

The Gratiots had long been instrumental in the fur trade and were respected and trusted by the Native Americans in the region. This amicable relationship helped secure mining rights and land in the area. That bond would later prove valuable when the Black Hawk War was imminent.

After the war, Gratiot's Grove grew and prospered and in 1836 was considered the most important place between Galena and Chicago. Some estimates record the area's population from several hundred to near 1,500. The village itself included the first school in the county, several stores, two hotels, furnaces, shops, and homes. The Gratiot House was built on high land in the area in 1835. It was of Georgian style, and one account states that it is supposedly the oldest continuously occupied residence in Wisconsin and is one of the earliest buildings surviving from the lead mining period.

In recent years, the house has undergone extensive renovations, stripped to its studs and remodeled, the Gratiot House Farm is operating as a bed and breakfast and is now open for reservations. What a great way to explore the area's history,

Right: The Gratiot farmstead. (Courtesy of www.gratiothousefarm.com)
Below: The Gratiot House today. (Courtesy of National Register of Historic Places, Shullsberg, Lafayette, Wisconsin, #80000153)

Berry's Tavern and its historical marker. (Courtesy of Cory Ritterbusch)

Gravity Hill near Gratiot's Grove. (Courtesy of www.wisconsinosity.com)

all from the comfort and splendor of the historic building and scenic countryside. Visit www.gratiothousefarm.com to book your trip back to history.

One of Gratiot's Grove's hotels was built by another important settler. Frontenac Berry came to the region at about the same time as the Gratiot brothers. He built a crude hotel, which included a post office. With the advent of the stage route, he built a larger hotel. Also included was the Berry Tavern, which still stands today. The tavern has also been undergoing restoration and a historical marker placed in the 1930s marks the site as well. The Friends of the Berry Tavern have undertaken its upkeep and one can learn more at the tavern's Facebook page.

A recent Lafayette County book, *A Tour Guide to the Mines of Lafayette County*, by area historian Loren Farrey, tells of a mysterious nearby phenomenon. Called Gravity Hill, it is located just north of the intersection of County U (south Judgement Street) and Rennick Road. At the spot, it is said a vehicle will, after being stopped and shifted into neutral gear, roll uphill! When traveling the route, stop at the bottom of the road just before it starts up the wooded hillside and near the farm gate on the right. Please watch for traffic. No explanations have proven or disproven the phenomena. Is it an optical illusion, the lead mine factor, or something else? (www.roadsideamerica.com/tip/10634 has reader comments that seem to support the claims.)

A recent article in *The Voice of the River Valley* by Cory Ritterbusch tells of Gratiot's Grove history. One historical tidbit he shared was that of a murder committed at Berry Tavern by William Caffee in 1942. Caffee was hung in Mineral Point with an audience of 5,000 watching. Caffee's last meal request was a "slice of the heart of Judge Jackson." It is said his ghost still haunts Mineral Point's Walker House today.

Business in Gratiot's Grove was brisk until the lead ore was mined out. After that, village residents left in droves and Gratiot's Grove faded into history. However, with the efforts being taken by the Friends of the Berry Tavern and the owners of the Gratiot House Farm, history lives on. The Gratiot House is also listed on the National Register of Historic Places.

JENKYNSVILLE

1830s – 1880s

CLASS A/C

APPROXIMATE LOCATION:
County H south of Highway 81

Jacob, John, and Abraham arrived in the area in the mid-1830s. Jacob built a mill and the other brothers farmed. The City of Benton tells that Jacob's house still stands. The 1861 Primitive Methodist Church still stands and is a Lafayette County Historic Site.

The church in Jenkynsville still stands today. (Courtesy of www.wisconsinosity.com)

The Leadmine Tavern. (Courtesy of Clayton McSheridan)

LEADMINE

1883 – 1953

CLASS C/D

APPROXIMATE LOCATION:
County Road 1 near Wisconsin Highway 11

With the name "Leadmine," it's easy to determine what spurred the settlement's establishment. Several lead mines were located in the region and the miners, wanting to be close to them, built their cabins nearby. The cluster of homes became Leadmine. The village was first known as Leadville but was also known as Democrat, not for political reasons but for the nearby mines. When a post office was established, the postal service notified the postmaster that the name Leadville was already taken, so Leadmine it became. The post office operated for nearly seventy years.

In addition to the post office, Leadmine included two stores, a blacksmith, a three-room school, a town hall, two churches, an Odd Fellows Hall, and a tavern. According to a Lafayette County history written by Loren Farrey, the Longhenry Saloon was a long, narrow, two-story building with a porch extending across its entire front. The saloon was on the first floor. A dance hall was in the back of the second floor while the front part of the second floor had four bedrooms for the owner and his family.

A town pump was located on the main street. A wooden bucket for watering horses and a tin cup for travelers was provided. The pump was removed in 1972, when curbs and gutters were added to the street.

Today there is a Leadmine Tavern.

OLD BELMONT

1836

CLASS D/F

APPROXIMATE LOCATION:
North of Belmont off of U.S. 51

Not to be confused with today's "new" Belmont, Old Belmont had a brief, contentious, yet historic past. When the United States Congress created the Territory of Wisconsin in 1836, then–President Jackson appointed Henry Dodge of Mineral Point as governor of the territory. At that time in history, Mineral Point was the most populous region of the territory, so it made sense to locate the new territorial capital where the people were. From its inception, the choice was unpopular. Beautiful and scenic, a prettier spot couldn't have been found.

John Atchison, a Galena promoter, assured Governor Dodge that he could build a capitol city and have it done by fall. Four buildings—one to house the legislature, one for the supreme court, a governor's residence, and a boarding house for the legislators—were to be completed by the upcoming legislative session. Territorial newspapers scorned the Belmont location and opposition steamrolled, but plans went forward.

Atchison promised more than he could deliver. When the legislature convened in 1836, only one building was completed. The boarding house was far from being finished. It had few, if any beds, but since it was the only place to board the legislators, they were left to sleep on the floor wrapped in their own coats. October and November can be downright chilly in Wisconsin and the one small stove threw off little heat to warm the two-story building. The legislators were not happy. The first session lasted just forty-six days.

Area land speculator James Doty realized Belmont's days as the territorial capitol were numbered. He purchased land near Four Lakes (later Madison), where he proposed the next capitol be located. The legislature was hesitant at first, but when Doty offered "incentives," the proposal gained favor. Thus the thirty-six legislators approved the proposal and each went home with a "parcel" of land, the incentives offered by Doty.

After the first legislative session in Belmont adjourned, furniture and supplies were auctioned off. The store and its stock moved to Galena. Within a year, Old Belmont was in significant decline. Charles Dunn, the newly appointed chief justice, purchased the supreme court building, and he and his family lived there until his death, thirty-six years later.

On the left, Wisconsin's first state capitol building, and on the right, the Council House. (Courtesy of www.wisconsinosity.com)

Belmont continued on as a sleepy little village until after the Civil War. When the new railroad line bypassed Old Belmont, locating just three miles to the south, Old Belmont's fate was sealed. The legislative building and the court building were moved a short distance and were converted to barns.

In 1910, the Wisconsin Federation of Women's Clubs became active in preserving Wisconsin's historical sites. After looking at the buildings, they were deemed "restorable" and preservation efforts on Old Belmont began. The buildings (barns) were purchased and moved back to their original foundations. Seven years later, the Wisconsin Legislature allocated funds to help with the restoration.

Today Old Belmont is a true historic site and is part of Belmont Mound State Park. The original buildings serve as museums and a glimpse to Wisconsin's past. One note: that old stove still stands in one of the buildings.

Langlade County

HEINEMAN

1901 - 1919

CLASS A

APPROXIMATE LOCATION:
Heineman Road

Once plans were laid, it didn't take long for Heineman to be built. Plans were announced in 1900 and soon a village store (two stories with a large basement), twenty-two homes, a boarding house, a blacksmith shop, and other buildings were up and functioning. The construction boom didn't stop there. In 1901, a mill pond was completed, as was a two-story hotel with a capacity of seventy-five. The hotel took less than an month to erect. A grand opening dance was held in the hotel with the general public invited. It is said the hotel was the best around, and it was well known for its trout dinners.

By 1901, the village, originally called Trout Lake, included a general store, a drug store, the hotel, and a saloon. As Randall Rohe, a Wisconsin historian, writes, a company town with a saloon, let alone one operated by the company, was a rarity. Most company towns made an effort to keep alcohol off-site.

Extensive logging operations began in 1903, and a second large hotel was needed. A school joined the community, which then had a population of 150. In 1904, a larger school was constructed. It had two rooms, one for the first four grades, the other for the upper grades. The year 1904 also saw the establishment of the Maccabee Lodge, which quickly became the social center. By 1905, the population of Heineman was at 300.

The building and construction continued in 1906. The company built a large building that held a department store, a bank, a meat market, and company offices on the first floor. On the second floor, a hall and club rooms were located. In 1909, an opera house was built with a dance floor on coiled springs, electric lights, and steam heat.

Baseball was popular, and the village had its own team and ballfield.

In 1910, the town boasted seventy-five homes. That was its peak, and it would soon end. In April of 1910, the mill burned. Hard work by the fire department prevented further damage to the village. However, on July 20, the village was totally destroyed by an unlikely and unexpected fire.

The fire was eleven miles away, just north of Merrill. Heineman residents could see the smoke, but it was so far away no one was overly concerned. The winds suddenly changed and soon the village was in danger. The decision to evacuate the village was made. Valuables were put in boxcars and shipped out. Automobiles and trains carried most of the residents to safety. A small group of men stayed behind to do what they could, which was little, and they soon had to flee as well. Shortly after the last of the residents and men got out, the village was engulfed in flames.

Randall Rohe writes that three fires met up that day in Heineman and once the lumber piles caught fire, there was no hope of saving the village. Eyewitnesses said that the winds were fifty to sixty miles an hour and that the flames shot more than 200 feet in the air. Heineman burned in less than an hour. The population at the time of the fire was 350 to 400 residents.

The destruction was devastating, and rebuilding was impossible. The company, which had a twenty-year timber right, built a new plant in Merrill.

A few foundations are all that remain at the site, which is now known as Heineman Road.

Lincoln County

DUDLEY

1880 – 1881

Class A

The post office and store in Dudley, Wisconsin. (Author's Collection)

Manitowoc County

The bridge over Cato. (Courtesy of Tobe Resch)

Cato today (Courtesy of "Royalbroil," Wikimedia Commons, http://commons.wikimedia.org/wiki/File:CatoWisconsin.jpg)

CATO

1870 - 1998

CLASS A/C

APPROXIMATE LOCATION:
Highway 10 and County J

When Highway 10 was improved and expanded in the 1990s, much of historic Cato was lost. The once-bustling community was originally called "Nettle Hills" because the itchy weed was abundant. An early settler renamed it Cato, after his hometown of Cato, New York.

At one time, eight trains a day stopped in Cato along a line the ran from Manitowoc to Forest Junction. Local folklore has it that Al Capone also visited Cato, or at least some of his mob did. Supposedly returning from their "still" on an area vacant farm, they had an accident with another vehicle. The vehicle they hit slammed into Reitmeyer's Tavern, and the driver was killed.

Reitmeyer's Tavern was one of only two drinking establishments in the village. Reitmeyer's was at the top of the hill at the community's main intersection. The top floor was later converted to a hotel. The other tavern was below the hill (north side of Highway 10). Originally it was built as a community center by the Order of Foresters. It was converted to a tavern in the 1920s.

A school operated from the early 1900s until the 1930s. A Presbyterian church was built in the 1930s and was razed in the 1960s. Extremely long-lived, the post office lasted over 100 years—128, to be exact.

In 1992, the Highway 10 project required the purchase of much of the former town site and many of Cato's historic buildings were later demolished.

Cato's grain elevator. (Courtesy of Dave Weller)

Reitmeyer Tavern. (Courtesy of Library of Congress, Historic American Buildings Survey, call number: HABS WIS,36-CATO,2--2)

A barn-raising in Cato. (Author's Collection)

Cato store and post office. (Courtesy of Library of Congress, Historic American Buildings Survey, call number: HABS WIS,36-CATO,1--1)

COOPERSTOWN

1848 – 1912

CLASS C/D

APPROXIMATE LOCATION:
County R and Zander Road

Not far from the former town site of Cooperstown lies Manitowoc County's first county park, Cherney Maribel Park. The park's seventy-five acres lies along the West Twin River. Geographically significant, the park is home to seven caves: Cooper, Pancake, Tunnel Passage, Spring Lake, New Hope, and Staircase. Some of the caves are open for exploration, others are not. The scenery, however, is always open for visitors. The park offers a full slate of park amenities. The park was heavily damaged by a 2013 tornado, but is now completely restored. If you are in the area, it is a must-see. While in the area, take a short detour and head to the Maribel Hotel historic site. The hotel was built in the 1900s and abounds in haunting, sinister tales. The shell of the hotel still stands, a historical marker details the history, and visitors can see for themselves just how eerie and haunted the site may or may not be. A quick Internet search will give all the details and then some. Haunted or not, the site is also a must-see.

Cooperstown, located at a central point along the stage-coach line running from Green Bay to Two Rivers, is one of Manitowoc County's earliest villages. The first settler arrived in 1841 and subsequent settlers were New England Yankees and French Canadians. By 1856, the population was eighty-five. Due to its location along an important travel route, Cooperstown had several hotels. Other businesses included a general store/post office, a dance hall, an undertaker, a meat market, a hardware store, a dressmaker, a grist mill, and several doctors. The store served as the social center and many a dance was hosted. Most dances were followed by a large, home-cooked meal.

Memorial Day and the Fourth of July were huge celebrations, attended by all villagers. The day-long celebrations included veterans, speakers, a dance, and supper. St. James was also an important part of the community.

Maribel Caves Park. (Courtesy of Joshua Mayer, www.flickr.com/photos/wackybadger/7351146890)

GREENSTREET

1875 – 1904

CLASS A

APPROXIMATE LOCATION:

The small, mid-1800s Bohemian settlement was named after the first settler, Zeleny (Bohemian for "green"). Zeleny operated a store, a tavern/dance hall, and a post office. A Catholic church, a school, and several homes were also part of the community.

GRIMMS

1874 – 1955

CLASS A/C

APPROXIMATE LOCATION:
14 miles east of Manitowoc

Manitowoc County had two limestone quarries within its borders, one in Quarry and the other in Grimms. Grimms's quarry was considered one of the largest in the state of Wisconsin. It also produced the largest high calcitrate limestone in the world.

A small settlement grew around the quarry. Manned primarily by Italian immigrants, records tell that sixty-five families

Grimms lime kilns, which would have been along the ridge. (Courtesy of Tobe Resch)

Top: East Grimms Road. (Courtesy of Tobe Resch)
Bottom: Grimms School, shortly before it was demolished. (Courtesy of Tobe Resch)

were brought over from Italy. The kilns ran twenty-four hours a day, with two twelve-hour shifts. Wages were $180.00 per month, with six dollars going to rent.

In the 1930s, the quality of the limestone declined significantly. Coupled with the Great Depression, the kilns shut down. The post office continued until 1955. The Grimms School stood until recent years.

For those who love old-time and polka music, bandleader Romy Gosz was born in Grimms.

KING'S BRIDGE

1876 – 1903

CLASS A

APPROXIMATE LOCATION:
County Highway Q

Naming the settlement couldn't have been simpler. Since the village mill was founded by King and it was by a bridge, King's Bridge it was.

In addition to the sawmill, King's Bridge had a tavern/dance hall and a store/post office, all located in the same building.

King's Bridge was a stopping place for travelers. Both humans and horses could rest and refresh. Gypsies were also said to stop by on occasion.

King's Bridge was also visited by a "ghost." For a time, a gray, wolf-like creature stalked small children, but never attacked. Lonely howls and wailing were heard at night. One morning a flock of geese was found butchered. Fearing for the safety of their children, residents hired a hunter. Finding his prey, the hunter killed the creature in one shot. Upon closer inspection it was discovered that the "ghost" was, in reality, an unkempt collie, covered in burrs and dirt. Apparently the collie had been abandoned and had resorted to fending for himself. It is assumed he had been around children in his earlier life, thus he followed them around. It was said that some of the children buried the dog near the school, so he could always be near the children. I'd like to think they did.

NILES (SLAB CITY)

1856 - 1904

CLASS A/C

APPROXIMATE LOCATION:
Highway W north of Highway 51

Slabs of wood used to be piled alongside the road, thus the name "Slab City" came about. The small village was established along a mill and included a post office, a school, a saloon, a cheese factory, and a Presbyterian church. The church was later moved to Manitowoc County's Pinecrest Village and was restored. The school building still stood in 2000.

OSMAN

1878 - 1904

CLASS D

APPROXIMATE LOCATION:
Highway 42

Osman's first school was built in 1853. The second (a frame building) came in 1868, and in 1920, a brick building was constructed. The last school term was 1963–1964. After that, the building was sold and demolished.

Over the years, a general store, an ice cream parlor, a tavern, and a small hall comprised the community. The store building was later used as a blacksmith shop, which later became a garage.

QUARRY

1900 - 1945

CLASS A

APPROXIMATE LOCATION:

Booming in 1900, by the 1950s, Quarry had disappeared from the landscape.

Original plans in 1880 were to quarry granite, but the stone was not hard enough. After a succession of owners, the quarry began to excavate limestone. The advent of the railroad lines running adjacent to the quarry helped spur the industry.

Another boom was the enactment of the 1911 State Aid Road legislation, which increased the demand for limestone. Soon the quarry employed fifty men, primarily Italian immigrants as well as a few from Mexico and Puerto Rico. The village of Quarry grew up around the quarry and soon included a hotel/saloon (which housed and fed twenty-five to thirty single men), two other saloons (one with a dance hall), a post office (until 1945), an ice house, a blacksmith, a grocery, a shoemaker, and a school, which had to be later expanded to two rooms.

As it is with one-resource, one-industry towns, there is no backup plan. When the Great Depression hit and the demand for limestone bottomed out, no other industry took up the slack. Coupled with the fact that no roads connected it to other communities, Quarry had run its course.

With no quarry work and no alternative, workers left. Piece by piece, the equipment was also moved out. A Manitowoc County history tells that even the timber and wood that had been cut and stacked for the kilns was sold and carted out.

In the 1970s, only six families lived in the area. For a time, the quarry became a dumping ground and is now private property.

SHOTO

1894 - 1904

CLASS A

APPROXIMATE LOCATION:

Shoto's post office lasted just ten years (1894-1904). A sawmill and grist mail were operating in 1899. The two mills were destroyed by fire in 1948.

STEINTHAL (STRONG VALLEY)

1875 - 1902

CLASS A/B

APPROXIMATE LOCATION:
Town Line Road and Steinthal Road

An early historian, name unknown, wrote that Steinthal (Strong Valley) was a "quaint village built in a setting that could do justice to the tales of Bram Stoker (author of *Dracula*)." The area was full of springs, bubbly quagmires, loose quicksand, winding roads, and nighttime wisps of fog.

Settled by immigrants from Holstein, Germany, Steinthal had a sawmill, a store/tavern (later a senior center), a blacksmith, and a "monster." Appearing in recent years, the monster seemed to roam at will in a rural vacant house. Upon closer investigation, the "monster" was found to be a practical joke. Built by a prankster, the "monster" was a dressmaker's dummy, draped in white fabric with green reflectors.

TAUS

1886 - 1904

CLASS C/D

APPROXIMATE LOCATION:
3 miles north of Cato, 15 miles west of Manitowoc

Built around an early sawmill, Taus would include a blacksmith shop, two groceries, two taverns, a cheese factory, a slaughterhouse, and a machine shop that doubled as a dance hall. The school was half a mile to the west of the village. The community was named for a town in Bohemia. It also had a post office for just eight years.

As automobile travel became the norm, people could more easily travel to larger cities. With time, the Taus businesses closed and residents left.

TWO CREEKS

1862 - 1864

CLASS D

APPROXIMATE LOCATION:
Highway 42 and Two Creeks Road

Looking at the small crossroads community amidst the rolling farmland, it is hard to imagine Two Creeks as a busy port community near Lake Michigan.

A tannery was established in 1861, and by 1863, the settlement included a sawmill, a planing mill, a school, a general store, boarding houses, a blacksmith shop, a wagon maker shop, a tailor shop, a meat market, a telegraph office, and a tavern.

Schooners visited the port often and were used extensively to haul freight. At one time, Two Creeks was one of the leading shippers of baled hay and seed peas.

Much of the area's rich, dense timber had been destroyed by an 1870 fire. In 1882, the tannery moved to Milwaukee.

Looking north toward downtown Taus, Wisconsin. (Courtesy of "Royalbroil," Wikimedia Commons, https://commons.wikimedia.org/wiki/File:Taus_Wisconsin_Downtown_Looking_North.jpg

October of 1918 was especially dry and arid. In fact, the previous several years had been abnormally hot and dry throughout the Midwest. Minnesota lay victim to several large fires that same month. The Two Creeks's area soil was tinder dry, and water for livestock was a precious commodity, despite the rather close proximity to the lake.

It was so hot, tires slipped off the rims of wagon wheels. Ernie Kochler, the area blacksmith, was beyond busy. The day of October 5, 1918, he spent re-tiring rims onto wagon wheels. Re-tiring required a bonfire, so Ernie set three of them. When he left to visit an area farm that evening, he made sure the fires were put out. One flared up and burned the blacksmith shop down. Sparks traveled to the general store porch. By morning, nine buildings were destroyed, including the general store and the dance hall.

originally the general store. The one-room schoolhouse had a library upstairs and restrooms on the lower level. For years after the school was torn down, the sidewalk in front of it remained.

WELLS

1894 – 1898

CLASS A

APPROXIMATE LOCATION:
County Road JJ between Potter and Collins

Lasting just ten years, Wells was home, at various times, to a tavern/dance hall, a cheese factory, and a handful of homes. Little remains of Wells today. The tavern was

Wells today. (Courtesy of "Royalbroil," Wikimedia Commons, http://commons.wikimedia.org/wiki/File:Wells_Manitowoc_County_Wisconsin _Looking_Southeast_County_JJ.jpg

Marathon County

In Dancy, looking east on County C. (Courtesy of "Royalbroil," Wikimedia Commons, http://commons.wikimedia.org/w/index.php?curid=47587279)

BRUCKERVILLE (BRUCKER)

1882 - 1884

CLASS A

APPROXIMATE LOCATION:
Intersection of Brucker Avenue and County A

Since Joseph Brucker owned the land, the store, the postal station, and a nearby sawmill, the settlement was named for him. When the two-room schoolhouse was built, it was, at the time, the only two-room school in Holton Township. A long-lasting cheese factory operated until it merged with the Dorchester Cheese Factory in 1953.

DANCY

1887 - 1959

CLASS C/D

APPROXIMATE LOCATION:
Highway 34 and County C

During the 1990s, the University of Wisconsin–Stevens Point did archeological digs in the Dancy area. What they discovered over the course of several digs was quite a history of the region. According to the Marathon County Historical Society, Tom Willems, the director, said that people have been gathering in the area since the Ice Age glaciers began to retreat, about 11,500 years ago. Evidence uncovered also supports people in the area in the Copper Age 4,000 years ago, to Woodland Indians who operated a trading post there, to early European settlers in the 1800s.

In more recent times, 1874, the Wisconsin Valley Railroad had a station at the site, which was first called Huntington. The town's name was later changed to Dancy in 1887.

A post office operated until even more recently, 1959. A community post office then operated from 1959 until 1964. Records tell that postmasters changed depending on what party was in office at the time, Democrats or Republicans.

The community had a general store, a boarding house, a dance hall, a sawmill, and a school. St. John's Evangelical Lutheran Church was founded in 1893. Farming activity followed the logging days. Today there are some buildings in the area, as well as a saloon.

GRANITE HEIGHTS

1889 - 1953

CLASS A/C

APPROXIMATE LOCATION:
East bank of the Wisconsin River, 7 miles north of Wausau

Styles come and go and change with the times. Even granite has its trends and fads. Back in the 1880s, the "in" thing with granite was granite paving stones. When the trend changed, it changed a company and a community.

At about the time the railroad arrived in Marathon County in the 1880s, granite was also discovered. Primarily Swedes and Norwegians settled near the river where the granite was found. As the demand for granite grew, so did the settlement that took its name from the stone, Granite Heights.

There were actually two phases to Granite Heights, an Upper and a Lower Heights. The Lower Heights had most of the homes, the depot, the store/post office, and the hotel. The Upper Heights was further north and had the granite finishing plant and a few homes. The granite itself was south of Lower Heights and east of the railroad tracks.

The first quarry and its activity was done and gone by 1886, due to the downturn in the popularity of granite pavers. Some granite was still sold for decorative purposes, such as statues and grave markers. The operation was sold to a group of businessmen from Wausau, and it became the Marathon County Granite Company. In 1901, the business was moved to Wausau, abandoning the Granite Heights quarry. The rail station was torn down and the village faded away.

Today a row of houses along the river are all that remains.

HALDER

1887 - 19??

CLASS A/C

APPROXIMATE LOCATION:
Halder Drive south of Highway 153

Fleeing to escape the potato famine in Ireland, the first settlers came to the Halder area in 1856. First called Irish Hill and Irish Settlement, the name Halder came from an early resident. A post office operated from 1889 to 1908 or 1909. St. Patrick's parish operated a school, St. Robert's, until 1970. A one-time resident, in his younger days, remembers the Halder feed mill and elevator. On Saturday nights, movies would be shown on the buildings' outer walls. The area converted to dairy farming in the early 1900s. Both the saloon and the Catholic church played large roles in the community.

LAMERDIN

1895 - 1896

CLASS A

Built near a spot along the Big Rib River and settled by former coal miners, the settlement was short-lived. The settlers found rural life difficult so after only two years they left.

The land was logged until 1931. Even today the area is forested and much of it is owned by the Wisconsin Department of Natural Resources and other large land owners as forest crop land.

MARCH RAPIDS

1892 - 1922

CLASS A

APPROXIMATE LOCATION:
On Big Eau Plaine River

Early mill towns depended on rivers and waterways to power their mills and their livelihoods. On the flip side, those creeks and rivers also wreaked havoc on the towns, sometimes totally destroying them.

For March Rapids, the Big Eau Plaine River was its nemesis but also the reason for its creation. In 1877, a waterwheel mill was established on the river. First called Hope, the town was later called March and March Rapids after Thomas March purchased the property in the late 1870s. March had the settlement platted and lots laid out. Just as he was preparing to sell the lots, the Big Eau Plaine River went on one of its many rampages, damaging vital mill machinery.

The next spring the dam gave way, causing March to lose over 100,000 feet of lumber. March had had enough and sold the mill property, lock, stock, and barrel (forty buildings) to Doud and Sons of Winona, Minnesota. March Rapids then suffered a number of fires, with the one in March of 1902 being the most destructive. The company store and everything in it was consumed. That same year, the settlement was hit with a smallpox outbreak.

In 1904–1905, the school had an enrollment of fifty students. The school had been built in 1880 on an acre of donated land. A parochial school reported a roster of thirty students. Attendance was said to be irregular. Influenza outbreaks, bad roads, and snowstorms often kept students from attending daily.

Tragedy was a repeat visitor to the area, as well. In June of 1904, it rained eleven inches in just two hours. The Big Eau Plaine River swelled to eighteen feet over flood stage, and its rampage damaged the village.

In 1911, the old steam engine *Old Rose*, overloaded with logs, caused the bridge to collapse, sending the engine into the stream below. The engine then exploded, killing the fireman.

January of 1913 was March Rapids's most serious disaster. Fire totally destroyed the mill. No watchman had been on duty, so by the time the alarm was sounded, the mill was engulfed in flames and the roof near collapse. A mill in Fenwood was purchased, dismantled, and moved to March Rapids.

World War I saw a boom in demand for wood products. The mill operated overtime. Everyone was growing Victory Gardens. Clocks and watches were set one hour ahead so that mill workers could have an extra hour of daylight to tend their gardens.

Doud and Sons donated an acre of land for the building of the German Evangelical Lutheran Church. In 1917, the church was moved across the street to its present site. It was completely remodeled with a full basement added.

A Modern Woodmen of America Hall hosted many social events, including wrestling matches, plays, dances, roller skating, and movies. The community even had a Bachelor's Club where the men got together to play pool and cards. A baseball and basketball team were popular attractions.

The population in 1917 was 160, but already the settlement was showing signs of decline. The company began to dispose of its buildings. By 1921, the population had dwindled to 100. The mill was closed in 1922. The boarding houses were torn down. The dance hall (the Forests Hall Saloon) stood until a few years ago.

At its peak, March Rapids included several stores, a coffin shop, a few saloons, a hotel, a boarding house, a dance hall, and a popcorn stand.

NUTTERVILLE

1889 - 1901

CLASS A

APPROXIMATE LOCATION:
North 85th Street and Highway 52

The once-thriving crossroads community had a blacksmith shop, a post office, a grist mill, a cheese factory, a sawmill, a saloon, and dance hall by 1878. By 1991, according to the Marathon County Historical Society, only the Homestead Inn and one house remained.

Nutterville was said to be known by everyone as the place where the dances were. Dances were held on the second floor of the ice house—the shaky second floor. Early residents said that underneath was the ice house with "rats as big as cats."

PEPLIN

1838 -- 1841

CLASS A/C

APPROXIMATE LOCATION:
Highway 153 and County X

The Worzella Brothers purchased 26,000 acres and decided they wanted to build a Polish community. They printed and mailed brochures, written in the Polish language, to all major U.S. cities touting the virtues of their region. The brochures included photos of beautiful farms to entice the Polish to come. And come they did. The brothers built homes for settlers. The price for a three-room house was $350, while a five room house was $450.

Peplin had a sawmill on the corner, a store, an office, a blacksmith shop, and living quarters for workers. Peplin Hall was built in 1928. The brothers also owned a long barn for horses with a dance floor on the upper level. In 1928, a tavern was opened at the corners and operated until the owner's death in 1936. A cheese factory also operated at the corners.

TRAPP

1872 - 1898

CLASS A

APPROXIMATE LOCATION:
Town of Texas

Early mail delivery was by train; the mail was dropped off at the depot, picked up and taken to Callon's Halfway House, which was the post office.

In 1873, land was donated for a school. A new school was built in 1886 and remodeled in 1933.

The Marathon County Historical Society tells of an early resident, John Muschel. John was a cigar maker and worked at a cigar shop in Wausau. He walked back and forth every day (he lived on what is now Shady Lane Road). For unknown reasons, he became separated from his family and became a recluse. He built himself a shanty in the woods alongside the railroad tracks. He picked willows and made baskets until he was elderly and moved to the County Home.

Marinette County

PESHTIGO HARBOR

1838 - 1897

CLASS A

APPROXIMATE LOCATION:
8 miles southeast of Peshtigo

The land around the mouth of the Peshtigo River was and is marshland. For sixty years, it was also home to over five hundred people, fifty dwellings, and all the necessary businesses of a busy village.

Peshtigo's first mill was built in 1838. To get the lumber to market, the logs were made into rafts and floated to the mouth of the Peshtigo River. Only eight miles by land, the water route was sixteen miles because of the winding waterway. At the mouth, the lumber was pulled out for shipping, usually to Chicago. The waters were too shallow for larger ships, so they anchored in the Lake Michigan bay and smaller scows brought the lumber out to them. The men doing the work needed housing, so a boarding house was built. According to a short history by F.E. Bruce, the boarding house, built in 1839, marked the beginning and establishment of Peshtigo Harbor.

In conjunction with the lumber milling, William Ogden wanted and needed rail transportation. The land was just too marshy to support a rail line, so building up the land was begun. Using sawmill refuse (sawdust, slabs, etc.), the marshland was raised. The project took two years, but also included the construction of docks, a store, a school, a blacksmith shop, and two homes for mill officials. Two docks, each 1,500 feet long and 100 feet wide, started at the mouth of the river and extended into deep water. Building a railroad required canals, and they had to be dredged. With the completion of the railroad, lumber could be shipped anywhere.

According to Bruce, an early resident who wrote down his memoirs, the village was built on three steps of land. The working men built their own homes using lumber, hardware, doors, and windows supplied at no charge by the company. Built after work and on weekends, beer was offered to encourage help. The company never allowed a tavern. The employees didn't mind that, as the temptation to spend their hard-earned money was removed.

Peshtigo Harbor's boarding house accommodated 150 men. The building included a dining room large enough to seat the 150 boarders. In addition, it included a butcher shop and a large bakery with a brick oven. All foods were ordered from the company store in Peshtigo. There was also a smaller boarding house a half-mile upriver.

Company stores, at first, only carried groceries and a few staples. In later years, they stocked yard goods, overalls, and notions. The post office and the only telephone were in the store. Mail came daily in winter but in the summer, whenever. Water came from the river. Occasional outbreaks of typhoid fever occurred, but of course no one knew it was caused by the water.

Meat was purchased in Peshtigo. An on-site meat market was tried in the village but was not successful. After closing, the building was used as an additional school.

Perhaps the first insurance plan in the area was offered to the employees. In 1885, Marinette doctors negotiated a deal with the company to care for the workers' medical needs at a fee of $1.25 for families and seventy-five cents for single men per month. The cost was deducted from the workers' pay checks. Employees could call on any doctor in the group.

From all accounts, the company seemed to truly care about their employees and offered them many benefits. Pine shingles for heating were offered free of charge. Employees only had to put their order in for the year, and the wood was delivered to their front door.

Social activities were varied and plentiful. A village band was formed and practices took place in a large room over the store. Dances were held in private homes. They would start at 10:00 P.M. and go on to Sunday morning's dawn. An added feature, beer on tap, helped boost attendance.

Most early settlements celebrated the Fourth of July with great gusto. Peshtigo Harbor was no different. The company furnished lumber for the building of a dance pavilion. A carload of fresh evergreens were placed around the grounds and tables and provided much-appreciated shade.

October of 1871 saw one of the most destructive forest fires in recorded history. The village of Peshtigo was at the heart of the inferno. Over 1,500 lives were lost, and many villages were completely destroyed. Peshtigo Harbor escaped with no damage. Following the fire, the mills ran day and night to supply the lumber needed for rebuilding. Chicago's famed fire was also that day.

In 1884–1885, sixty-seven families and 165 single men lived in Peshtigo Harbor. School enrollment was sixty-five and the school building was bursting at the seams. Also feeling the fray was the one and only teacher. The former meat market was set up as a school and another teacher was hired. By 1890, the population was 600, In 1894, that number had dwindled to 400, and in 1897, only four families remained.

Financial difficulties beset the company. Agents eventually seized all of the company's assets, including the rail terminus. After the mill's closure, residents moved on. The buildings were sold to house wreckers.

Today the area is once again marshland and part of the Peshtigo Harbor Unit. Encompassing nearly 5,000 acres, the land has reverted back to its original state and the area is now a protected wetland and woodland. But if you look close, in times of low water, the pilings for the wharf can be seen.

Milwaukee County

Postcards of Bay View Park (top) and Bay View roller mills (bottom). (Author's Collection)

Three views from historic Bay View. (Courtesy of National Register of Historic Places, Bay View Historic District, Bay View, Milwaukee County, Wisconsin, #82000686)

A marker for Bay View's earliest settlers. (Author's Collection)

BAY VIEW

1879 – 1886

CLASS F/G

APPROXIMATE LOCATION:
Shores of Lake Michigan south of downtown Milwaukee,
now part of the city of Milwaukee

Historically significant in the fight for worker's rights, Bay View was the site of a massive strike and subsequent tragedy.

March 1, 1886, was a Saturday. Hoping to institute an eight-hour work day, nearly seven thousand workers joined forces with five thousand Polish workers. The strikers numbered nearly 14,000. The strike shut down every business, except one, in the village. Two-hundred-fifty National Guardsmen were deployed. Orders were issued that if any workers entered the building, they were to be shot. As often occurs in times of stress and turmoil, the orders were misunderstood, with tragic results. Ordering the soldiers to pick out a man and shoot to kill, pandemonium ensued. When it was all said and done, seven people, including a thirteen-year-old, were killed. The incident is known as the Bay View Tragedy or the Bay View Massacre. Each year the Wisconsin Labor History Society honors the event with an anniversary gathering. Learn more at www.wisconsinlaborhistory.org/resources/bay-view.

The Milwaukee Iron Company began operating in 1866. Specializing in rail, over 135 employees worked that the company. Just four years later, the Iron Company was the second-largest manufacturer of iron rail in the country, employing more than one thousand workers. All those workers needed housing and support services, so a large company town developed. Cottages and boarding houses were built. Lots were sold to the workers with easy payment terms. Land was donated for churches. With the population burgeoning, municipal services were required. Overwhelmingly, in 1879, residents voted to incorporate into a village, becoming Milwaukee's first suburb.

Seven years later, residents wanted city services and amenities. An election was called to allow annexation to the city of Milwaukee. The measure passed easily. Though now a part of Milwaukee, Bay View has managed to maintain its identity. In fact, it is said to be one of Milwaukee's strongest neighborhoods.

History preservation is an important aspect of Bay View. The *Bay View Compass*, a neighborhood journal, features a monthly history column. The original village is now listed on the National Register of Historic Places and is known as the Bay View Historic District. The district includes 1,040 acres and 329 buildings.

One note: legendary actor Spencer Tracy was from Bay View.

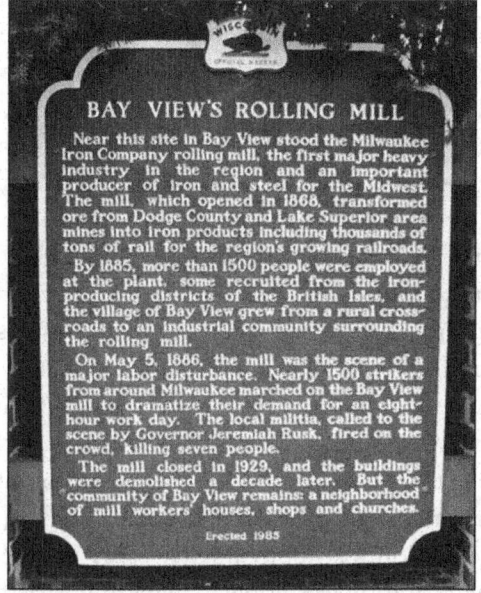

A marker for Bay View's rolling mill. (Courtesy of Wisconsin Labor History Society)

An early rendition of the rolling mills in Bay View. (Courtesy of the *Bay View Compass*)

GRANVILLE
(STATION, CENTER, WEST)

1847 - 1962

CLASS G

APPROXIMATE LOCATION:
Now part of Brown Deer and Milwaukee

Granville Depot. (Author's Collection)

Three hamlets, all of them with Granville in their name, were early Milwaukee County communities. Today, any remains of the original settlements have been long gone. Over the twentieth century the sites have been built upon, expanded, industrialized, commercialized, and annexed. Today they are population centers, retail and trade centers, and industrial areas. Traveling the area's busy thoroughfares, one would never guess small hamlets once occupied the sites.

Granville Center was in the area of Dean Road and Seventy-sixth Street. Early structures included a school, St. Catherine's Catholic Church, a general store, a blacksmith shop, and a shoemaker shop. In the late 1800s, the Servite Fathers built a five-story limestone monastery and named it Mount St. Philip. It served as a two-year novitiate until 1973. After that time, Servite Woods was built on the land. Over the ensuing years, buildings were razed, new ones built, businesses discontinued, and other establishments here and gone.

Granville Station's history parallels that of Granville Center, as it was built on excellent rail connections with the usual business entities (store, hotel, etc.). The two communities are nearly identical in history and makeup. The population of Granville Station was approximately 1,000 in 1879.

Granville Station was home to many and varied businesses over the years. One unique one was the Orinda Springs. The Springs was, as the name suggests, a spring located on a nearby farm. An investment group was formed and mineral water was sold. Sales were brisk, so much so that the investors decided to go for broke. Their plans were to create an exclusive residential community. Crews excavated a large lake in the Little Menomonee River. Scenic roads were graded and lots were platted. Advertising was targeted to wealthy Milwaukee residents. An auction sold thirty lots in less than an hour. Alas, the investors quite literally did go for broke. The project never developed and all traces of the improvements, including the lake, have long since vanished.

As the area grew, farming declined. By 1960, only one farm existed south of Brown Deer Road. According to a Milwaukee County history, previously, more wheat had been grown in Granville Station than any of Milwaukee County's six other townships.

In 1954, the newly created village of Brown Deer began to annex portions of Granville. The city of Milwaukee also began annexing Granville acreage.

With time and growth, Granville Station was built upon and occupied by an industrial park, retail shops, and other businesses. The old village site is now a major thoroughfare with homes, apartments, and other residences.

JONES ISLAND

1870 - 1920s

CLASS G

APPROXIMATE LOCATION:
Milwaukee Peninsula

Looking at Jones Island today, it is hard to imagine how very different it was in the early days. Today, the mile-long, three-block-wide peninsula along the shores of

Granville's school. (Author's Collection)

Lake Michigan is the site of Milwaukee's sewage treatment plant, its port facilities, and other industrialization.

In its very earliest days, long before European immigrants came to the area, the island was the summer home of Native Americans. The area teemed with wildlife, wild rice, blueberries, and other natural resources. In 1818, the island was the winter trading post of the American Fur Company's Solomon Juneau. Records indicate that the island was all marshland, nearly impossible to walk across. According to author Ruth Kriehn, who wrote a book on the fisherfolk of the island, the island was indeed marshland. Some say it was only good for two things: fishing and hunting. Fishing was what defined life on Jones Island.

In 1854, shipbuilder James Monroe Jones established a shipyard on the island. His fleet of sleek schooners helped launch Milwaukee as a Great Lakes port. It was the arrival of the Kashubian fishermen in the 1870s that produced the picturesque fishing village. The settlement was a hodgepodge of homes, fishing shacks, and saloons. The result was a semi-rural, village-oriented way of life, unique to the region and perhaps to America.

The Kashubian were Polish immigrants from the Baltic Peninsula, descendants of Slavic peoples. They began to settle on the island in the 1870s. They were considered "squatters," settling on land they did not own. They, along with some Germans and people of other ethnicities, would define life on Jones Island well into the twentieth century.

The first fishermen were too poor to own large fishing boats, so rowboats and netting were used. Winter fishing was too difficult, so many islanders took jobs on the mainland. During the summer doldrums, the boats were used to haul freight. The Kaszubes, as they were known, were considered second-class citizens by the mainland people, and were looked down upon. The Kaszubes were well aware of their image.

Jones Island became a culture and community of its own with a population of nearly 2,000. Fishing shacks, cottages,

A cottage on Jones Island. (Courtesy of Carl Mydans, Library of Congress Prints and Photographs Division, http://hdl.loc.gov/loc.pnp/pp.print)

Fishing shacks on Jones Island. (Courtesy of Carl Mydans, Library of Congress Prints and Photographs Division, http://hdl.loc.gov/loc.pnp/pp.print)

The tiny Kazube's Park on Jones Island. (Courtesy of Creative Commons)

Above: Fishing nets on Jones Island, circa 1912. (Courtesy of Creative Commons)
Below: Jones Island's dock. (Courtesy of Creative Commons)

homes, and saloons—especially saloons—abounded. Every block had at least one saloon, and oftentimes many. Grocery stores, butcher shops, bakeries, and other establishments were also on the island. Music was an important aspect of life on the island. Jones Island was considered one of the toughest neighborhoods in all of Milwaukee.

Since there was no church on the island and many islanders were stout Catholics, they would row to the mainland on Sunday mornings for Mass. In its earliest days, Jones Island did not have a school building, either. Children were ferried across the water to attend school, where the Jones Island students were looked down upon. In 1896, a small school finally opened on the island. For nearly one-third of the island's children, it would be the first time they attended school. Their parents had been leery of sending their children on the ferry.

Three hundred feet offshore sat a 100-foot diameter octagonal structure. Its purpose was to provide Milwaukee with better drinking water. It was dubbed the "Cribs." A wooden shack sat on top of the Cribs' platform. The shack provided living quarters for the fifteen men—engineers and a cook—who worked the Cribs.

On August 19, 1893, gale-force winds hit Milwaukee. Anxious wives feared for their husbands at work on the Cribs. They were reassured that the Cribs was safe and there was no need to fear for the workers' safety. Experts told the wives that the Cribs was anchored to the bottom of the lake and twelve-foot timbers reinforced the structure. Sadly, the structure did not hold. The next day, a Coast Guard cutter rescued the one survivor. The remnants of the Cribs, later dubbed the Love Rock, became a navigational hazard and a hotspot for vandals. It was demolished and removed in September of 1986.

In 1896, a multi-million dollar entity, the Illinois Steel Company, claimed ownership of the island, putting life for the 150 families living on Jones Island in jeopardy. With top-notch lawyers and unlimited funds, the steel company was no match for the poor squatters. A long, drawn-out legal battle ensued and lasted for years.

In 1910, a bond issue was introduced that would provide funds to purchase Jones Island and improve the harbor. By 1915, the northern half of the island was condemned. Life for the islanders was nearing its end. Worry set in as compensation did not provide enough funds for islanders to purchase homes on the mainland. Fishing would no longer provide an income. A way of life was fading. The next years saw low prices for fish. Over the years, fishing became more and more unprofitable. Commercial fishing would disappear in Milwaukee in the 1980s. The younger generation didn't want to work as

A marker in Kazube's Park. (Courtesy of Creative Commons)

hard as their fisherman fathers had, and the waters were overfished.

In 1920, only twenty-five islanders remained on the peninsula. One stronghold held out until 1943. Jones Island as a community was no more. Yet the history and legacy continue on. In 1974, Kaszube's Park was designated. Set among the industrial activity, the small lot became a park sporting one picnic table, two trees, and a historical marker. On the first Sunday in August, an annual Kaszube Picnic is held at the park.

SCHWARTZBURG (NORTH MILWAUKEE)

1893 – 1929

CLASS G

APPROXIMATE LOCATION:
North Milwaukee

From the beginning, Schwartzburg was a railroad community. In 1856, the Milwaukee and Superior Railroad crossed the area. That line was abandoned in 1858 but was later acquired by the Milwaukee and Northern Railroad. The tracks were extended from Schwartzburg to Cedarburg. Later the Chicago, Milwaukee and St. Paul, the Milwaukee Road, and Amtrak would operate the line.

Due to the excellent rail connections, businesses were established and the population grew. Over six hundred residents called the area home in 1897. The village was incorporated at

that time. When the city of Milwaukee annexed the village in 1929, Schwartzburg became North Milwaukee's Ninth Ward. During the Cold War years, the area was home to a Nike-Hercules Missile site.

ST. MARTIN'S

1862 – 1903

CLASS G

APPROXIMATE LOCATION:
West St. Martin's Road near intersection with Church Road

Local legend has it that Al Capone frequented St. Martin's while on his way from Chicago to his family cabin in Mercer, Wisconsin. Once billed Milwaukee County's smallest town, St. Martin's was first settled by the Irish and later the German Catholics. Both groups started churches of their own (Holy Assumption in 1847 and Sacred Heart at an unknown date), and church life was a major influence on the community. In fact, the community was said to be named for an early parish priest, Father Martin Kundig. Each church had its own cemeteries. Today they are side by side and appear as one, but each has its own records. According to a church history, the shortage of priests in the late twentieth century necessitated the two churches combine. The merged parish is known as St. Martin's of Tours.

Platted in the mid-1800s, at one time St. Martin's included a post office (1862 to 1903), a telephone exchange, a dance hall, a tavern, stables, and more. Those original businesses are all gone. Even though the post office was discontinued in the early 1900s, the community lived on. In 1987, a newspaper account reported that St. Martin's had an area population of 200 and included the two churches, three taverns, a convenience store, and a farm implement dealer.

To this day the community hosts Sale Days. Usually held on a Monday with extended length over Labor Day, it is said you can buy anything and everything at the sale. The historic St. Martin's Inn is a great spot for lunch, dinner, and ethnic meals. The community is also home to several businesses.

St. Martin's Inn today, still a great place to stop for a meal. (Courtesy of Dennis Wegner, www.stmartinsinn.com)

Monroe County

The former Glendale school, as it looks today. (Courtesy of Andy Zuhlke)

GLENDALE

1856 - 1926

CLASS A/C

APPROXIMATE LOCATION:
Wisconsin Highway 71, 1½ miles east of Kendall

Both the township and the settlement were named Glendale. The village had a post office from 1856 until 1926.

OIL CITY

1873 - 1902

CLASS A

APPROXIMATE LOCATION:
Wisconsin Highway 131, halfway between Wilton and Ontario

The smooth-talking newcomer sure sounded like he knew what he was talking about. He claimed to be an expert in the oil business and folks took him at his word. Tichnor was his name, and when he told residents that their area looked exceedingly promising for the discovery of oil, they were more than excited. After briefly exploring the area, Tichnor told the folks that he had indeed found oil. Excitement burgeoned and everyone had to see for themselves. Sure enough, a small pool in the ground was oil. That's all it took.

Tichnor formed the Gem Petroleum Company, of which he was the chief officer and major stockholder. He leased land from area landowners. Everyone wanted in on the action so Tichnor "reluctantly" sold much of his stock. More wells were dug. but only water was found. One well, seven hundred feet deep, hit a geyser—not of oil but of pure, clean water.

Folks began to get discouraged and suspicious, Upon investigating, locals found that a barrel of oil had been buried and well hidden in the ground. That was the oil Tichnor had "discovered." They had been duped, and by the time they learned it, Tichnor was gone. There was no oil, but on a side note, the water found was some of the cleanest and healthiest in the region.

The first settlers arrived in the Oil City area in the early 1840s. There was no real community activity until 1866. By 1871, the school's enrollment was 121 students! A post office was established and operated from 1873 until 1902. A grist mill, a sawmill (powered by the Kickapoo River), a cooper shop, several blacksmith shops, and at least two stores made up the settlement. By the late 1800s, several hundred people called Oil City home. Then things changed.

The Oil City train depot. (Author's Collection)

Oil City today. (Courtesy of "Osirisx11," Wikimedia Commons, http://en.wikipedia.org/w/index.php?curid=6024966)

The lack of a railroad greatly hampered the community's growth. A rail line planned by the Kickapoo Valley and Northern Railway from Wauzeka to Wilton (four miles from Oil City). The line never reached Oil City. Wilton and Ontario grew and Oil City declined.

A community cemetery was used from the 1860s until the early 1900s. A local farmer plowed over the cemetery in the 1940s. The cemetery has since been restored but many of the original headstones are gone. The settlement's last remnant, the school, closed in 1959. Today there is handpainted wood sign stating "OIL CITY, POP. 16."

SHENNINGTON

1893 - 1928

CLASS C/D

APPROXIMATE LOCATION:
Wisconsin Highway 21

Side by side is a great way to travel through life. There was even a popular song titled "Side by Side" during the Depression years. For the two Lutheran churches in Shennington, it's a way of life.

Early settlers from Germany and Denmark were of the Lutheran faith but each constructed churches of their own. St. John's was the German and St. Peter's the Danish. St. Peter's had originally been located at a site one and a half miles away and was relocated next to St. John's. The two shared a parking lot and members of the same families. When St.

Above: The Shennington depot in its early days. (Courtesy of St. Peter's Church)

Below: Side by side churches in Shennington: St. Peter's and St. John's Lutheran churches. (Courtesy of St. Peter's Church)

John's closed in the early 1980s, it donated its property to the congregation of St. Peter's.

The community of Shennington was established in the early 1900s. Fred Shenning donated the highest parcel of his land for the building of a school. The settlement had a post office that operated from 1893 until 1933.

The church was and is the center of the community.

Oconto County

Above: Early Klondike. (Author's Collection)
Below: Klondike today. (Courtesy of "Royalbroil," Wikimedia Commons, http://commons.wikimedia.org/w/index.php?curid=11655856)

KLONDIKE

1898 - 1906

CLASS A

APPROXIMATE LOCATION:
Intersection of County Z & B

Klondike's school dates back to 1845. The community had a post office from 1898 until 1906.
Today the school serves as the Brazeau Town Hall. The crossroads community has a bar and grill.

The badly damaged Gardner Hotel after the 1876 cyclone. (Courtesy of Oconto County WIGenWeb)

Klondike's school, now the Brazeau Town Hall. (Courtesy of Jill Gondek)

Pensaukee's school today. (Courtesy of Jill Gondek)

PENSAUKEE

1855 - 1957

CLASS A/C

APPROXIMATE LOCATION:
County S and SS

Pensaukee, in 1875, had a lot going for it. As anthe *Oconto County Reporter* journalist wrote, Pensaukee had two mills, the railroad, water power, one of the best harbors on Green Bay, a population of three hundred, and one of the finest hotels in the state. That hotel, built by F.B. Gardner, was indeed grand. Not built of wood as most buildings were at the time, the hotel was brick. It also offered modern plumbing, hot and cold running water, and the finest furnishings.

Two years later, the once-thriving village was devastated by a cyclone. The mills were badly damaged, homes resembled kindling wood, ships and lumber in the harbor were tossed about, and the violent winds tore large sections of the Gardner Hotel away.

The residents made a great effort to recover. F.B. Gardner did all he could to assist in the efforts, even opening a store in a part of the hotel not damaged. The depot became home to the post office. The mills were repaired and up and running. A carload of baled sawdust was shipped to Illinois (for ice packing) daily.

The mill had been the first in Oconto County. At one time there were seven dams on the Pensaukee River. As logging dwindled, many residents began farming small plots of land. Fishing was also a major industry at the time.

Efforts to revive Pensaukee were short-lived. The anticipated railroad line, which would have saved the village, never came. F.B. Gardner gave up and returned to Chicago.

STILES (JUNCTION)

1855 - 1976

CLASS A/C/D

APPROXIMATE LOCATION:
Duarme Road West of Highway 141

I can just imagine the scene would look like a movie set, women and men dressed in formal attire arriving at the grand ballroom in a horse-drawn sleigh. Such was the scene in early Stiles, said to be the region's social center. It was even listed on the social register of the time. However, things weren't always so fine and grand. In fact, Stiles (Junction) would live and die at least twice in its history.

First attracted by the area's pine forests, Stiles was surveyed in 1839. In 1850, Merrick Murphy built a dam across the Oconto River and began full-scale logging operations. Things were slow until 1851, when Anson Eldred partnered with Murphy. By 1855, Eldred took over the entire operation and began building "his" town, which he named after his son Howard Stiles Eldred. The settlement and Eldred's mill grew substantially. An Octonto County history tells that in 1855–1856, Eldred's mills had an inventory of over twenty-one million board feet of lumber and logs. He also owned a fleet of ships, a schooner, six brigs, and a bark barge. Lumber was shipped to points as far away as England and Scotland.

Most of the mill workers were Menomonee Natives, including Chief Machickanee. An Oconto County history tells that the chief would on occasion dress in a Prince Albert coat, with a high hat and no trousers!

After twenty-five years of prosperity, Eldred began to look elsewhere for mill sites. It was evident that Stiles was no longer his main interest and his lack of concern showed. By 1881, a fire destroyed one of the boarding houses and Stiles was, for all intents, a ghost town.

Rumor was that the Wisconsin and Milwaukee Railroad was planning to run a line through Stiles to northern Wisconsin's iron mines. Just the rumor was enough to get the town buzzing. A new town site was laid out and a post office (Eldred) was established in 1882 with Howard as the postmaster. Soon the Stiles Hotel, a creamery, and a saloon were thriving. The Stiles Hotel had been built before the Civil War and was a three-story structure, with forty rooms and a reserved suite for mill owners. It was later converted to a tea room and summer-resort type of hotel in 1928. In 1938, it too was destroyed by fire. Things were again prosperous, at least until the turn of the nineteenth century.

In 1900, fire destroyed a large part of the settlement. The mill continued on until 1910, but was converted to a pulp operation. Yet again, in 1918, fire struck the village. Sparks from a passing train ignited a blaze that destroyed the railroad station and coal dock.

The death knell came in 1924, when the pulp mill was destroyed by fire. An attempted robbery of the post office in 1927 was ruled arson. Now considered at the end of its lifespan, nearly everyone left Stiles, except for a few families.

Today Stiles still has a Catholic church, church hall, and some homes. Stiles Junction is actually a few miles north of Stiles, and it has a gas station, a restaurant, and other highway businesses.

Above: The Stiles Depot in 1909. (Author's Collection)
Below: Stiles Junction Depot in 2011. (Courtesy of *Model Railroad Hobbyist*)

Stiles Junction's second school. (Courtesy of Jill Gondek)

St. Patrick's Catholic Church, Stiles. (Courtesy of Jill Gondek)

Old Main Street, Stiles, Wisconsin. (Author's Collection)

Oneida County

Above: The Mecikalski general store before restoration. (Courtesy of National Register of Historic Places, Mecikalski General Store, Saloon and Boardinghouse, Oneida, Jennings, Wisconsin, #84003751)

Above: The Mecikalski general store before restoration. Notice the cordwood walls. (Courtesy of National Register of Historic Places, Mecikalski General Store, Saloon and Boardinghouse, Oneida, Jennings, Wisconsin, #84003751)

The general store, circa 1899. (Courtesy of National Register of Historic Places, Mecikalski General Store, Saloon and Boardinghouse, Oneida, Jennings, Wisconsin, #84003751)

JENNINGS

1899 – 1920

CLASS C/D
APPROXIMATE LOCATION:
Intersection of County Z & B,
19 miles east-southeast of Rhinelander

It's not often you find a building constructed in the stovewood method still standing, but in Jennings, Wisconsin, you can see and tour the only known commercial stovewood structure in existence. Built in 1899 by Prussian immigrant John Mecikalski, the building was a general store, saloon, and boarding house. Throughout its history it was also an implement dealer, post office, grocery store, candy store, cheese factory, pool hall, and private home.

The stovewood construction method used short, irregular cedar logs laid like firewood. It was joined with a wet lime mortar, which created amazingly strong and solid exterior walls. It allowed for the use of leftover logs.

In Jenning's earliest days, lumber was king. Sources tell that from 1890 until the 1920s, the town was a rough-and-tumble logging center. Fisticuffs and brawls were common, especially when the lumberjacks came to town.

In the 1920s, John sold the building to his brother Henry and it was used as a pool hall and saloon. By 1940, the timber was gone and the building was converted to a co-op cheese factory. Later, a bachelor used the rear of the building as living quarters. The building then fell into disrepair and was abandoned in the 1960s.

Hoping to preserve the building and its history, many local residents worked to save the historic structure. In 1984, the Kohler Foundation began its efforts to restore the building. Three years later, the Kohler Foundation donated the building to the Town of Schoepke. Today, the Stovewood Museum offers tours of the building. Learn more at www.stovewoodmuseum.com.

The restored Mecikalski store today. (Courtesy of the Library of Congress, http://hdl.loc.gov/loc.pnp/highsm.12447)

A closer view of the stovewood walls. (Courtesy of National Register of Historic Places, Mecikalski General Store, Saloon and Boardinghouse, Oneida, Jennings, Wisconsin, #84003751)

Ozaukee County

An early photo of Holy Cross Catholic Church. (Author's Collection)

Ulao's Ghost Town Tavern and Restauarnt. (Courtesy of Tony Graber, www.fridayfishfryguide.com)

HOLY CROSS

1866 – 1904

CLASS A/C

APPROXIMATE LOCATION:

County A

Settled by immigrants from Luxembourg in the 1840s and 1850s, the community name honors their Catholic faith.

ULAO

1850 – 1864

CLASS D/G

APPROXIMATE LOCATION:

County Q

Do a dastardly deed and your notoriety lives on in history. Every person and every place in your life becomes infamous. Ulao was no exception.

Charles's parents, Jane and Luther Guiteau, moved to the Ulao area in the mid-1800s. Charles, said to be "high strung" or even a bit unstable, was a young child at the time. The family stayed just a few years before returning to Illinois. Even that short time was enough to label the community with his presence and with the connection. Over the years, Charles became seemingly more and more unstable with each passing year. He hounded government officials in search of an appointment. He became so bothersome that he was eventually banned from the White House. In July of 1880, Charles shot and killed President Garfield (although some say it was incompetent doctors that actually caused the president's death). Charles was tried, convicted, and hung. To this day, his childhood days in Ulao are noted. His former home still stands. Ulao, aside from the Guiteau connection, has quite a history of its own.

Ulao has a very distinctive landscape. It has sandy shores along Lake Michigan and a 200-foot-high bluff with a remarkably level plateau at the top. Dense forests graced the shoreline. It was perfect for James Gifford's plans. When he arrived in the area in 1847, he purchased large quantities of land, both by the lake as well as the bluff. Under his direction, a 1,000-foot pier onto Lake Michigan was constructed. A 200-foot chute was built from the top of the bluff to the pier. It was perfect for loading off the pier.

In those days, lake ships burned wood as fuel, and a lot of it. It took six hundred cords of wood (equivalent to ten acres of heavily forested land) for the trip from Chicago to Buffalo. Gifford supplied that wood. Cutting the timber on his property and using the chute, he had quite a loading facility. Gifford was also instrumental in building a three-mile roadway. That roadway was Wisconsin's first turnpike and is today's County Q.

During the Prohibition years, Ulao was a wild and crazy place, with all the moonshine one could ask for.

Today there are five original buildings still standing: the Guiteau House, the grain mill and elevator (now part of the Grafton Antique Mall's main building), the dance hall, and the Ghost Town Tavern and Restaurant (originally built in 1902). The tavern is known for its Friday night fish fries.

Ulao today. (Courtesy of "Royalbroil," Wikimedia Commons, http://commons.wikimedia.org/wiki/File:WIS_60_East_Terminus_Ulao_Wisconsin.jpg

191

Pepin County

LITTLE HOUSE WAYSIDE

"Once upon a time......a little girl lived in the Big Woods of Wisconsin in a little gray house made of logs."

Writing about herself and her life here, Laura Ingalls Wilder thus began "Little House in the Big Woods," the first of her famous "Little House" books.

Laura was born here on February 7, 1867. Late in 1868 or in the spring of 1869, the Ingalls family left Wisconsin and traveled by covered wagon to Kansas. They found Kansas to be Indian country, so shortly after Carrie was born in August of 1870, Charles Ingalls brought his family back to the little house near Pepin. In 1871 Mary and Laura enrolled in the Barry Corner School near here. They sold this farm in 1873 and moved to Minnesota.

Laura Ingalls Wilder is loved, both for her delightful writing style and for her good homespun philosophy. Reflecting on her rugged frontier youth, she said "It has been many years since I beat eggs with a fork or cleaned a kerosene lamp. Many things have changed since then, but the truths we learned from our parents and the principles they taught us are always true. They can never change."

The Laura Ingalls Wilder Memorial Society, Inc. of Pepin, Wisconsin, organized in 1974, is proud to provide "Little House Wayside" as a memorial to this great lady and beloved author.

Erected 1978

A marker for Laura Ingalls Wilder at the Little House Wayside. (Courtesy of "Aarongunnar," Wikimedia Commons, https://commons.wikimedia.org/wiki/File:Littlehousewayside.jpg)

The Laura Ingalls Wilder replica cabin near Barry Corner, Wisconsin. (Courtesy of "Jodamiller," Wikimedia Commons, https://en.wikipedia.org/wiki/File:Little_House_Wayside_replica.jpg)

BARRY CORNER

1860s

CLASS A

APPROXIMATE LOCATION:
Near intersection of County CC and Bogus Road

On a farm not far from Barry Corner, Laura Ingalls Wilder was born in 1867. As we all know, Laura would grow up to become one of America's most beloved authors. Young or old, readers cherish the tales of Laura's childhood in the big woods of Wisconsin, on Plum Creek in Minnesota, and her other travels. While most readers and television viewers recall Laura's school days in Walnut Grove, it was in Barry Corner where Laura and her older sister Mary first attended school.

Barry Corner was just a short distance from the Ingalls homestead. Though the Ingalls's original cabin is no longer standing, a replica cabin has been built at the Laura Ingalls Wilder Wayside, just down the road from Barry Corner. The wayside is a respite, a perfect place to have a picnic, read the marker, and see the spot where Laura Ingalls Wilder was born.

Barry Corner's teacher was in fact, a Barry—Mary Barry. She is said to be the Ingalls's girls' first teacher. Be sure to visit Pepin, just nine miles away. The Laura Ingalls Wilder Museum is in Pepin, as are many other places to visit and things to do.

WAUBEEK

1880 - 1888

CLASS A

APPROXIMATE LOCATION:
Near Nine Mile Island

Wisconsin's smallest county, Pepin, was at one time home to the largest pre–Civil War lumber mill in Wisconsin. The mill was located in Waubeek, Pepin County's first town.

According to a history project compiled by the students of Durand schools, Waubeek was located near Nine Mile Island on the Chippewa River bottomland.

As was the case in so many early settlements, a community developed around the sawmill. Platted with thirteen streets and a public square, Waubeek also included a hotel, saloon, general store, post office, a blacksmith shop, a Baptist church, a photography shop, a dance hall, and a boarding house.

The mill was established and owned by Cadwallader Washburn. According to the student report, C.C. Washburn, as Cadwallader was known, was one of seven overachieving sons. Two became governors of Wisconsin, four were elected to Congress, two were ministers to foreign countries, one was secretary of state, and three were authors.

In 1855, C.C. purchased twelve thousand acres of land on the Chippewa River and built a sawmill. The students wrote that during the Civil War, C.C. served his country. Upon his return the mill was deep in debt, forcing the sale of the mill to Knapp, Stout and Company. C.C. didn't ask for payment in cash, but took future payment in lumber. When the sale papers were signed, lumber was worth five dollars per thousand board feet. When C.C. collected his lumber it was twenty dollars per thousand board feet, so Washburn made quite a profit. Using the proceeds, Washburn purchased rights to portions of the Mississippi River and built flour mills in Minneapolis.

He and his partners built what became General Mills and made Minneapolis a major flouring mill location. General Mills has emerged as a premier company. Washburn's name is a legacy in Minneapolis and Minnesota. Not only was General Mills his creation, but there are streets, schools, and even a television station (WCCO) named using Washburn and his partner's initials.

Knapp, Stout and Company continued the mill in Waubeek. They built a general store and housing for the over one hundred employees of the mill. Waubeek was literally a company town, as everything in town depended on the mill. It did so until tragedy struck in 1870. In June of that year, the mill was destroyed by fire and marked the decline and demise of the village as well.

The Waubeek village may be gone, but the name lives on. Waubeek Mound is an area landmark.

Polk County

The Ubet Store, now at the New Richmond Heritage Center. (Author's Collection)

UBET

1897 – 1903 (1950s)

CLASS A

APPROXIMATE LOCATION:
County Road 4 East of Deronda

It seems I have an affinity for lost towns. Or maybe it is an "awareness." Most everywhere I go, most everything I read, I notice lost towns. On a recent trip to New Richmond, Wisconsin (my first visit, not my last), for a family reunion, we stayed at a wonderful hotel that was adjacent to the New Richmond Heritage Center. Even though it was off-season and the buildings weren't open, the grounds are always open for self-guided walking tours. Naturally I had to walk over and check it out. What I found was akin to walking through an old pioneer village. And best of all was the genuine general store, from a real Wisconsin lost town, sitting there waiting for me to discover it.

The heritage center is an eleven-acre historical park/respite in the heart of New Richmond. Several vintage buildings from the area include an 1884 farmhouse and barn, an 1887 log cabin, an 1891 church, a 1902 school, a new gazebo, green spaces, and a pond. There are informational signs on all of the buildings.

The Ubet store building is from nearby Ubet, now a lost town. In the 1910s, Ubet had a blacksmith shop, a warehouse, a creamery, a shoe repair shop, a post office, a stables, a feed mill, and the store. At its peak, the population was fifty. By 1960, the population was down to four, and two of them owned the store.

As the information plaque tells, the Ubet Store was built in 1933 by the bank in Dresser, Wisconsin, to replace the previous store building that had burned down. Al and Ruth Route operated the store for years. The building was later donated to the Heritage Society. The store stands as if it was still in business. The wainscot interior is original. The painted shelves hold stock that would have been carried in the store.

It's not often one is able to walk into an original general store (or a school, a church, or a farmhouse), but at the New Richmond Heritage Center, you can. Learn more at www.nrheritagecenter.org.

The grounds of the New Richmond Heritage Center. (Author's Collection)

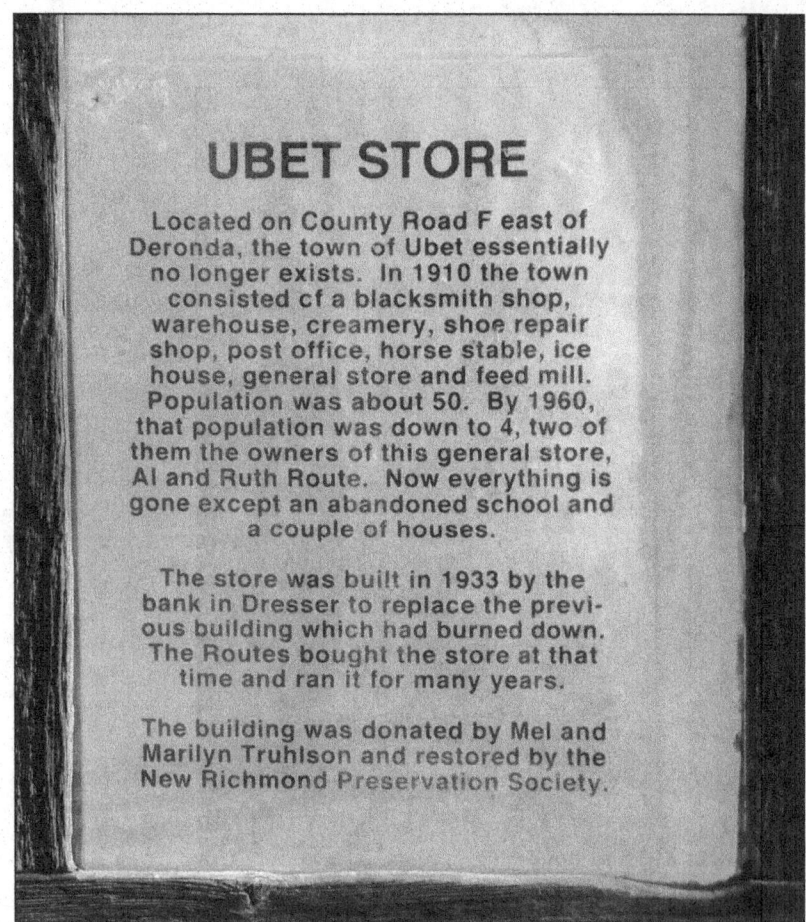

UBET STORE

Located on County Road F east of Deronda, the town of Ubet essentially no longer exists. In 1910 the town consisted of a blacksmith shop, warehouse, creamery, shoe repair shop, post office, horse stable, ice house, general store and feed mill. Population was about 50. By 1960, that population was down to 4, two of them the owners of this general store, Al and Ruth Route. Now everything is gone except an abandoned school and a couple of houses.

The store was built in 1933 by the bank in Dresser to replace the previous building which had burned down. The Routes bought the store at that time and ran it for many years.

The building was donated by Mel and Marilyn Truhlson and restored by the New Richmond Preservation Society.

Above: The Ubet store and another building at the New Richmond Heritage Center. (Author's Collection)
Left: An informational sign about the Ubet Store. (Author's Collection)

Portage County

The DVD cover for *Our Vines Have Tender Grapes*, which is set in Benson's Corner. (Author's Collection)

An early street scene in Benson's Corner. (Courtesy of the Portage County Historical Society)

BENSON'S CORNER (NEW HOPE)

1861 - 1904

CLASS A

APPROXIMATE LOCATION:
3 miles east of Nelsonville on Highway 161

Benson's Corner was the stuff of childhood, of memories and of stories. Back in the 1930s, George Victor Martin took the memories, the stories and the stuff of small towns from his wife, Selma's, childhood and wrote a book. The book, titled *Our Vines Have Tender Grapes*, depicted Selma's childhood from Benson's Corner in Portage County, Wisconsin. The World War II years in the small community were idyllic and ordinary. That book was later adapted to the big screen, and a movie starring Hollywood icons Edward G. Robinson and Margaret O'Brien was released in 1945. Extolling virtue and goodness, the moved was voted by *Parent's Magazine* as 1945's most wholesome family movie. Today it remains a classic and was recently released on DVD.

The inspirational location of the book and movie was Benson's Corner, or as it was officially known, New Hope. The popular name was most likely derived from Benson's store. The post office closed in 1904, but the community was quite active well into the mid to late twentieth century.

According to a 1992 *Stevens Point Journal* article, in recent years there was a handful of homes, the Lutheran church, and several abandoned buildings at the crossroads intersection. As the article summarized, Benson's Corner, the busy hamlet, may be gone, but the community lives on in literature and screen.

BLAINE

1876 - 1903

CLASS C

APPROXIMATE LOCATION:
4 miles northeast of Almond on County A & D

Most likely named for the defeated Republican presidential candidate in 1884, James Blaine, the bustling community had a post office for just over twenty-five years. The settlement also included a blacksmith shop, a general store, a creamery, a Methodist church, a Grange Hall, and several homes.

In later years the Grange Hall was used as the Belmont Town Hall. The church building, as well as other buildings and several homes, were still at the crossroads intersection.

Blaine Creamery. (Author's Collection)

Price County

Scenes from Reeds Mill in Clifford, Wisconsin. (Courtesy of Dale Heikkinen)

Top: Clifford's first co-op store. (Courtesy of Dale Heikkinen)
Middle: The co-op and post office. (Courtesy of Dale Heikkinen)
Bottom: The schoolhouse in Clifford. (Courtesy of Dale Heikkinen)

CLIFFORD

1904 – 1927

CLASS A

APPROXIMATE LOCATION:
Clifford Road between U.S. 8 and Old 8

The logging community once had two general stores, a post office, a blacksmith shop, a cheese factory, and a Finn Hall.

DANISH SETTLEMENT

Late 1880s – 1920s

CLASS A

APPROXIMATE LOCATION:
Southwest of Phillips

Farming in southern Minnesota wasn't working out, so the Danish settlers moved to Chicago. There they found others from their homeland. Most worked in the Pullman shop. Life was good enough and most were content with their lives in Chicago, until a land agent told them of the opportunities available in northern Wisconsin, where they could own their own land. According to Alice Jensen, an historian, the agent showed them photos and slides. Lured by the possibilities, they headed north to an area southwest of Phillips that became known as the Danish Settlement.

The Danish weren't the only ones lured by the possibilities. There were many Germans, as well. Both groups were lucky in that they arrived in the spring with time to establish their homesteads and get a crop planted by winter. Everyone chipped in and built log structures. Since the virgin land had never been tilled and farmed, it was back-breaking work to clear it and cultivate the farm plots. Thus, the first year's crops produced little yield. Many men worked the area's logging camps, some as far away as Duluth and Two Harbors, Minnesota, in the winter. Some packed up and moved back to Chicago.

When the settlers had children of school age, they built schools. Each of the schools were one-room. Teachers kept the fires going. There were no snowplows, so children made their own trails to school. Lunch buckets were kept near the stove to keep the contents from freezing.

The Danes, as were most early settlers, were a social people. Picnics, dances, the Fourth of July celebration, and other events were popular, year round. Folks from outside the settlement also joined in the festivities. Soon people saw a need for a community center. They built a dance hall on donated property. Building materials were purchased and labor was donated. The hall had one large room, a raised platform for a band, a stage, and a kitchen. Tables and benches were built on the grounds under the trees. A playground with swings, a teeter-totter, and a merry-go-round kept the children occupied. A lunch was always supplied.

After World War I, cars were becoming common. Young people traveled to other communities for entertainment and often jobs. No longer did people have to depend on their local communities to provide everything. As the young people left the community, there was no need for a dance hall. It was dismantled and the land given back to the original owners.

Today, many descendants of the original settlers live in the region. The road leading into the former Danish Settlement is named the Danish Settlement Road.

GERMAN SETTLEMENT (SPIRIT)

1880 – 1939

CLASS A/C

APPROXIMATE LOCATION:
Highways 86 & Highway 102

Early railroads found it too great of a risk and expense to build railroads into unsettled lands and wilderness. As incentives, railroads were given vast amounts of land. To offset costs and to make larger profits, the railroads needed people to settle on the lands. So the railroad, in turn, offered subsidies to anyone who would bring in settlers.

Siegfried Meier, in 1878, brought the first group of German settlers to the Spirit region. Siegfried had been a soldier in Germany and a farmer in Texas. According to a German Settlement history written by Roy Meier, Siegfried had been a good soldier and had farmed in Racine County. After the

Civil War he lived in Texas for a time and at some point moved back to Wisconsin, this time northern Wisconsin.

Eventually Siegfried made two trips to Germany, bringing homesteaders back. Those first settlers came by sailboat, which was an arduous six-week journey. Most were cousins or second cousins of Seigfried. They brought all of their belongings,

Above: Two views of Spirit, both looking east. (Courtesy of German Settlement History Inc.)
Right: Loggers near the German Settlement. (Courtesy of German Settlement History Inc.)

tools, and even potato eyes and apple seeds. According to Roy's history, Siegfried had told them just about anything could and would grow in the fertile soil of Wisconsin.

Certainly life and building homesteads in northern Wisconsin's wilderness were no easy tasks. In addition, they were strangers in a foreign land. But as Roy wrote, nothing could dampen their spirits.

In America they could get a piece of their own land, bigger than any they could have hoped to own in their homeland. They were free and could do as they pleased. They could build

The mill in the German Settlement. (Courtesy of German Settlement History Inc.)

their own homes, their children could go to school, and they could worship as they wanted. No, they didn't complain; they were grateful for their new lives and all it offered them. After all, the good things in life took hard work.

Traveling by way of Wausau, Jenny, and the tote road, they arrived at their new homesteads in the late spring. The first thing they did was plant their roots and seeds. They caught fish, bigger than any they had ever seen. Sure, as Roy wrote, the fish had lots of bones, but they were plentiful and tasted darn good. The woods were full of rabbits and other wildlife. Roy tells that never before had they had so much food to eat.

Siegfried had worked with the surveyor to plat out the homesteads, trying as hard as possible to make sure everyone was on running water. As it was, only one settler didn't get waterfront property.

Their first homes were shelters made of bark peeled from the large hemlock trees. They were primarily shelter from the elements. Later they built log homes, which were still crude. The Germans were used to working with stone and mortar and hadn't yet acquired the same skill with logs. Still, by winter, everyone had a warm home. Winter arrived much too soon, and many of the men worked in area logging camps.

After the logging season was over, Roy wrote that they took their pay and purchased farm animals. That was the beginning of the German Settlement.

The Knox Brothers later built a mill about ten miles north of Spirit. Later, the U.S. Leather Company of Maryland built tanneries in nearby locations, and this gave the settlers the option of selling peeled bark from the hemlock trees to the industries. Railroad ties made out of hemlock were another saleable product.

Education was important to the settlers so as soon as there were school-aged children, a school was built. The first things teachers taught was the English language. When the U.S. entered World War I, the school's name was changed to Liberty School. Roy's history tells that some days, especially rainy or inclement weather days, there were up to fifty students in school, with one teacher. The older boys only came to school when the weather was bad. They were quite a handful, as they weren't interested in "book learning."

Roy tells of one area settler, a Mrs. Scheller. She probably didn't weight 120 pounds wringing wet but she could outwork any man. One day she walked three miles with a tray of food in one hand and a coffee pot in the other.

In 1900, the Rib Lake Lumber Company built a rail line into the German Settlement and sawmills were quickly established. The logging companies provided work for anyone who wanted a job. The rail line also provided a handy market for farm products. With the added income, homes and barns could be improved and necessary items and supplies purchased.

Religion and church services were also important. As soon as they could afford it, they hired a pastor. A congregation was formed and was known as the German Lutheran Church. Area Norwegians also supported the church.

Norwegian Lutheran Church on Highway 86 in Spirit. (Courtesy of German Settlement History Inc.)

Kochs Hall and the Spirit Store, circa 1916. (Courtesy of German Settlement History Inc.)

Spirit Bridge. (Courtesy of German Settlement History Inc.)

Visitors can stop by the Yesterday House in the old German Settlement. (Courtesy of German Settlement History Inc.)

Liberty School as a school (top) and in its current state as a home (bottom). (Courtesy of German Settlement History Inc.)

In 1919, after World War I ended, a new school was built and is still standing. The last classes were held in 1953. The school closed in 1963, and students went to the Rib Lake schools.

That sense of community lived on. In 2003, residents, many of them descendants of the original settlers, including Siegfried Meier, organized the German Settlement History Inc. According to its mission statement, its goal was to "protect, conserve, and display buildings and artifacts and documents of historical value . . ." Annual events are hosted and a newsletter is published. The old Liberty School is now a home. The Yesterday House is a vintage building and allows a look back in time. Tours are also available. Plans are to continue the preservation of the German Settlement's history.

KAISER

1910 – 1939

CLASS A

APPROXIMATE LOCATION:
Along today's Tuscobia Trail

Kaiser was once dubbed the "village that never was" because the platted town site only had one home. Most of the actual settlement was adjacent to the cleared town site. The community once had a sawmill, a handful of homes, a state-graded school, a post office, and a store.

The Kaiser depot in 1911. (Photo by A.E. Kaiser, from *100 Years on the Flambeau*)

KENNEDY

1911 – 1938

CLASS A

APPROXIMATE LOCATION:
Pine Creek Road and County E

The saloon owner in Kennedy must have influenced the residents because when the settlement was platted in 1908, they most likely named the community after him. As logging grew, so did Kennedy. The logging attracted lumbermen and the cutover land attracted settlers. The first building constructed was a log schoolhouse. Soon a saloon, a general store, a hotel, a post office, and a boxcar depot were part of the settlement.

For two years the community was the terminus for the Omaha Railroad. In the late 1930s, the village was all but abandoned. Only four buildings remained and they were taken down, burned, or reclaimed by nature. The Pine Creek Trestle was removed in 1964.

Kennedy in 1910. (Photo by Willard Walther, from *100 Years on the Flambeau*)

Kaiser sawmill, 1911. (Photo by A.E. Kaiser, from *100 Years on the Flambeau*)

KNOX MILLS

1891 – 1909 (1930s)

CLASS A/C

APPROXIMATE LOCATION:
Halfway between Spirit and Brantwood

Old Mill Road runs east and west between County Road D and the West Knox Road, about halfway between Spirit and Brantwood (or north of Spirit and south of Brantwood).

Much has been written about Knox Mills, thanks to Joyce Bant and her historical perspective. Joyce was raised in Knox Mills and has offered us the chance to take a look not only at Knox Mills, but at all lost towns. In talking with Joyce, it is easy to be transported back in time and to see Knox Mills not only as a lost town but also as a home to the people who lived there.

In the beginning, it was all about the land and the money to be made from it. Frances Palms acquired the land shortly after it was surveyed. He knew that once the area was opened up to settlement, it would be valuable. Knox Mills was in a remote and isolated area with a wealth of pine. According to Joyce, Palms could afford to wait on his investment, and that he did, for twelve years. He then sold the property to the Knox brothers, William and Samuel. They, too, purchased the land strictly for the profit they would make on the timber. For ten years they logged the pines and shipped the product to Wausau.

In 1890, the mill in Wausau burned and the brothers dissolved their partnership. William stayed in Knox Mills and continued logging. He built his own mill along Meadow Creek. He dammed up the creek and created a mill pond. His early settlement was peopled with temporary transient workers. William also chose that location because the taxes were low. Since there were few permanent settlers they had no need

The mill in Knox Mills. (Courtesy of Joyce Bant)

Above: Knox Mills in its heydey. (Courtesy of Joyce Bant)
Below: Knutson dance hall and store. (Courtesy of Joyce Bant)

of roads, schools, and other services that would require tax dollars. After five years the timber was gone and William moved on to other places, other timber to cut.

Still, the cutover land had value. In 1897, William sold the mill property, including 27,000 acres of timber land, to E.H. Hobe, a real estate speculator. Hobe built a sawmill employing one hundred men with another sixty-five or so in the lumber camps. Knox Mills residents referred to sections of their town as Frog Town and Pig Town. Frog Town had two boarding houses (three stories high), the company office, the company store, and the post office. It was located near the mill pond, where the frogs were plentiful and noisy. Pig Town was the west side. There were no streets and perhaps a dozen homes, each with a pig.

With a new store and dance hall, Knox Mills was on its way to becoming a permanent town, a town families would call home.

In the early 1900s, the Norwegians started their own church congregation. Services were held in a company building. A cemetery was also established and by 1900, a resident preacher was hired. St. Joseph Catholic Church of Phillips established a mission church in Knox Mills. Other Protestants went to church in nearby Spirit.

A school district was established in 1891 and was the seventh district in the town of Brannan. It became District #1 in the town of Knox when that town was formed from sections of Brannan in 1895.

Tragedy struck the settlement in 1895, when the foreman was killed in a mill accident. His clothing caught on the machinery and he was pulled up into the narrow machine shaft.

Ignoring the negatives, Hobe saw the potential of the site. The cutover land would make it easier to farm. The land still had hemlock and hardwoods, which could be milled. Hobe planned to run the mill, buying the hardwood from the farmers, which would be a win/win for all. Hobe launched an ambitious and perhaps exaggerated advertising campaign. Many Norwegians were attracted to the area by the glowing ads. They also liked the region as the climate and terrain were similar to their homeland. Hobe sold the mill town as a package deal to Bradley and Collins.

Above: Pierson Murphy houses in 1897. (Courtesy of Joyce Bant)
Below: A map of early Knox Mills. (Courtesy of Joyce Bant)

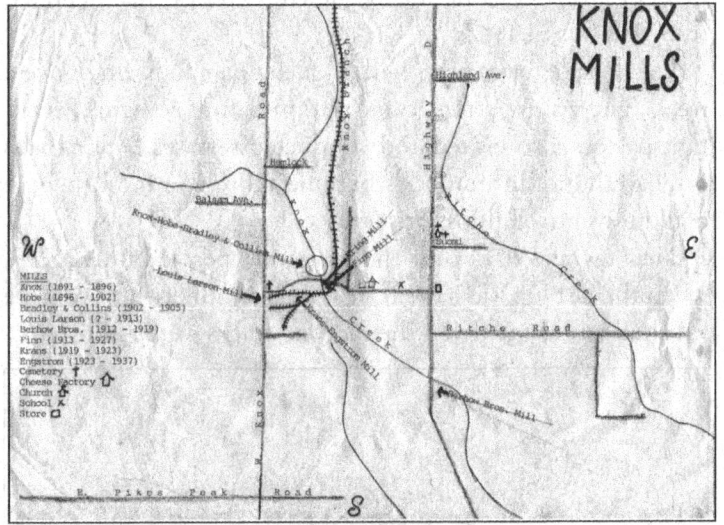

The last train out of Knox Mills. (Courtesy of Joyce Bant)

Bradley and Collins had other interests in the region. The managing partner died in 1903 and his heirs weren't interested in Knox Mills. So they sold Knox Mills. The planing mill, the boarding houses, the store, the dance hall, and other buildings were moved to nearby communities. As Joyce put it, "after the best of everything was gone," it was the end of Knox Mills as a company town.

New mill owners operated the small mills but they made Knox Mills their home, unlike the settlement's early "absentee" owners.

In 1926, a cheese factory opened and Joyce says that signaled the beginning of Knox Mills as a dairy community rather than a logging town.

A Sunday school was organized in 1901, as was a Ladies Aid Society. The society sponsored community dinners, basket and pie socials, and other events.

Recreational activities were simple but varied and often. Activities such as fishing, ice skating, picnics, sleigh rides, and other events were well attended and popular. But it was the

Fourth of July celebration that topped them all. The celebration began at sunrise. A noon dinner was attended by all. That was followed by a parade. Every farmer who had a wagon was said to have decorated it and participated. The afternoon consisted of races and other competitions such as sack races. As soon as it was dark, fireworks lit the sky over the mill pond. The evening festivities were capped off with a band and dancing. Hobe was said to have paid for it all.

Another popular activity, at least to some, was the Chirivai. Friends, neighbors, and relatives would call on newlyweds. They would bang pots and pans, ring bells, and make all kinds of noise until the couple relented and provided refreshments.

A Modern Woodmen of America chapter was active in the community. In 1901, there were twenty-three members and meetings were held twice a month. The MWA also hosted a wide variety of popular events and activities.

LUGERVILLE

1914 - 1943

CLASS C/D

APPROXIMATE LOCATION:
Northeast of Phillips on County F

A river runs through it—the Flambeau River, in Lugerville's case. Something else flows through the once-thriving settlement as well, that of community spirit and pride.

At the turn of the twentieth century, the Flambeau River spurred the idea for a sawmill. The Lugers, who owned a furniture company and store in Minneapolis, built a sawmill. That first sawmill's sole purpose was to make lumber to build a bigger

Above: An aerial view and map of Lugerville. (Courtesy of Gordon Stevenson, the Lugerville Project)
Below: An ad for the Lugers' furniture store. (Courtesy of Luger Furniture, www.lugerfurniture.com)

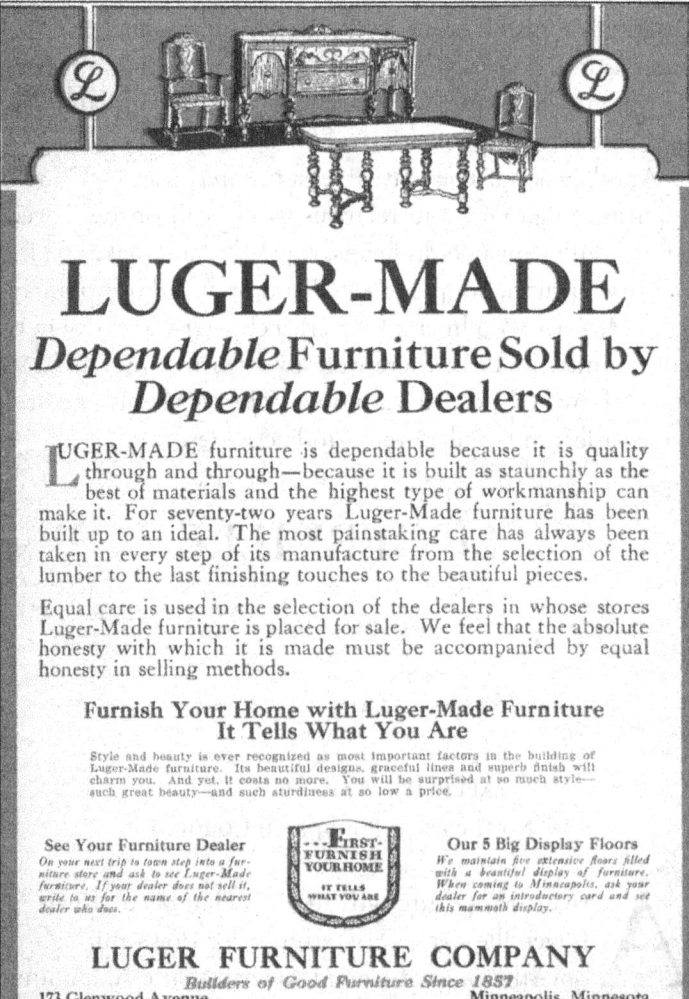

sawmill, which began operating in 1905. The company built eight frame homes in 1906, and logging began in earnest. Some of the lumber went to the Luger Enterprises in Minnesota. The company provided everything their employees needed, including a general store/post office with company offices in the rear. The upstairs of the building had temporary housing for men who lived elsewhere but needed short-term lodging. (In later years, the South Fork Tavern was on the old store's foundations.)

Workers were paid by company scrip, coupons that were redeemable in the company store. A narrow-gauge track, very rough, led to Phillips. Although there was a tote road, rail was the best way to get to Phillips.

Lugerville's peak was 1914 to 1919. By World War I, the population peaked at 450. There were fifty homes in the settlement and every one was occupied. A post office operated from 1914 until 1943.

Catholic services were held in a company building once a week. The visiting priest came out on Saturday night. Protestant pastors also visited and conducted services. After roads improved and automobiles became more common, people could travel to Phillips for services.

New owners took over the mill and operated until 1933, when the last log was sawed. In 1936, all mill operations were finished and done. Even the railroad tracks were removed.

Lugerville mill. (Courtesy of Gordon Stevenson, the Lugerville Project)

West Lumber Company administration building and store. (Courtesy of Gordon Stevenson, the Lugerville Project)

The school closed in 1971. For five years (1971 to 1976), the building was used as the Price County Achievement Center. The center helped adults and preschoolers with special education needs.

Gordon Stevenson's mother, Marie Averill, grew up on Lugerville. Gordon has, over the years, researched and documented the history of his mother's family and the history of Lugerville. His ongoing project, which he calls the Lugerville Project, is a wealth of information on the settlement. Gordon and his wife, Toni, manage and maintain a website, www.lugervilleproject.com.

The site is filled with photos, memoirs, history, and more. A companion website, www.averillproject.com, tells the story of the Averill family and their association with Lugerville. Both sites tell the personal side of life in a long-ago lost town. Gordon recently wrote up a brief summary of his family's involvement. It is as follows:

"In 1914, mill manager Herman Johannes asked Walter Averill, his wife Anna, and their three daughters, Margaret, Marie, and Dorothy, to move to Lugerville. Over the next twenty years Walter served as mill bookkeeper, postmaster, payroll manager, and he oversaw company store operations.

Above: Lugerville barracks for workers. (Courtesy of Gordon Stevenson, the Lugerville Project)
Below: Lugerville West Lumber Company dining hall. (Courtesy of Gordon Stevenson, the Lugerville Project)

"For the next eighteen years, Marie grew up in that small logging community, where the residents were more like a family than a town. All of the children, including Marie, attended the Lugerville School, which still exists today as a community center. The bonds created over this brief twenty-year span have lasted over 100 years. Marie and her sisters graduated high school in Merrill, and Captain Marie Averill served as a chief dietitian on the world's largest hospital ship during World War II. Until passing in 2002, her thoughts were never far

One of Lugerville's boarding houses. (Courtesy of Gordon Stevenson, the Lugerville Project)

A view of the Lugerville lumberyard. (Courtesy of Gordon Stevenson, the Lugerville Project)

from those childhood years, growing up with best friends, Elaine Bodenburg and Eileen Kenyon. Picnics at Rocky Carrie on the Flambeau River, and riding the cow catcher on the logging train engineered by Mr. Kenyon, loaded with residents of the town spending afternoons picking berries in the woods were two of her fondest memories. Marie remembers frantic knocks on their door in the night, summoning Walter to rush to unlock the company office so they could use the phone for various emergencies.

"With the last trees cut, in 1935 and 1936, Walter Averill was left with the task of liquidation of the mill. Walter's responsibility was to sell and oversee the disassembly of the mill, all of its equipment, and many of the company-owned residences. The railroad spurs were removed and shipped for use in other areas of the country. One might say that Walter had a rare opportunity to turn the lights on as the town entered its heyday, and turned them off in 1935 when the trees were gone. Even though Lugerville is a shadow of its former self, the stories and memories of the families who grew up here continue to be told today, with great fondness."

It is a fact that bears repeating. All of these lost and long-ago towns had a personal side to them. They were people's homes, their dreams, and their lives.

Today, the former school is a community center and is maintained by the community. It is truly a story of the history that lives on.

WORCESTER

1883 – 1913

CLASS A/C

APPROXIMATE LOCATION:
North of Prentice

Active in its day, Worcester was also known as Station 101, due to its distance from Stevens Point. It had a general store, a post office with daily mail, and several stores. During construction of the railroad it was a terminus for about a year. As the railroad was extended, settlers abandoned the Worcester site, taking everything with them.

Top: The rail line into the Lugerville camp.
Middle: Lugerville's school in 1976.
Bottom: Our Savior's Episcopal Church in Lugerville.
(All photos courtesy of Gordon Stevenson, the Lugerville Project)

216

Racine County

A marker commemorating Old Muskego, Wisconsin. (Courtesy of "McGhiever," Wikimedia Commons, http://commons.wikimedia.org/w/index.php?curid=25627857)

OLD MUSKEGO

EARLY 1800s

CLASS A/F

APPROXIMATE LOCATION:
Now part of Racine

Long before the Europeans first arrived in 1827, the area had been home to the Potawatomi. The name itself is a derivative of the Native American word for sunfish. The first European arrivals began a trading post and it was in 1836 that the first permanent settlers, Norwegians, made the area home. The settlement gave growth to the first organized Lutheran congregation in America, and they also published the first Norwegian-American newspaper. Old Muskego was also known as a mother colony to other settlements, as many settlers heading west first stopped in Old Muskego.

Outbreaks of cholera ravaged the community twice, in 1849 and 1851. Records tell that swamp fever or malaria outbreaks also occurred.

In 1904, the Norwegian Meeting House was moved to St. Paul, Minnesota, where it was reassembled on the campus of Luther Seminary. A highway marker was established at the town site in 1963.

Old Muskego's history does live on in the area. In 1976, a living museum began preserving the history of Old Muskego and the area. The center includes five structures as well as wetlands and woodlands. The Racine County Historical Society offers self-guided walking tours, and maps are available at the center and online. Annual "Halloween walks" are also hosted.

Old Muskego Church, now on the campus of Luther Seminary in St. Paul, Minnesota. (Courtesy of "McGhiever," Wikimedia Commons, http://commons.wikimedia.org/w/index.php?curid=25627857)

Richland County

Basswood's general store. (Author's Collection)

Early Byrd's Creek. (Author's Collection)

Gillingham today. (Courtesy of "Royalbroil," Wikimedia Commons, http://commons.wikimedia.org/w/index.php?curid=12206560)

BASSWOOD

1869 - 1911

CLASS A/C

APPROXIMATE LOCATION:
7½ miles southwest of Richland Center

BYRD'S (BIRD'S) CREEK

1890

CLASS C

APPROXIMATE LOCATION:
Northeast of Port Andrew on Highway 60

Today a cluster of homes (including a building that looks like a former store front) are all that mark Byrd's Creek. Postal records show the name spelled as Bird's Creek.

GILLINGHAM

1880 - 1983

CLASS D

APPROXIMATE LOCATION:
7 miles north/northwest of Richland Center

Reading through the old newspaper clippings, especially those from the 1950s, it's hard to imagine that Gillingham no longer has a school and is no longer the bustling community it once was. The center of the village seems to have been the school. There were always school activities going on with community-wide support. At one time Gillingham had to enlarge the school to a three-room building for its ninety students that included a gymnasium, two washrooms, and a kitchen with two full-time cooks.

A store, post office (that lasted over one hundred years), a welding shop, cheese factory, and three churches were part of the community. Today a few homes remain.

JIMTOWN

Late 1800s

CLASS A/C

APPROXIMATE LOCATION:
KK and Jimtown Drive

Not just one, but two Jims lived in Jimtown. One was the storekeeper and the other lived out by the spring. Busy in its heyday, Jimtown had a general store, which lasted into the late twentieth century, a stockyard, two garages, a cheese factory, a blacksmith, and a tavern (for one year the township voted "wet," which allowed the sale of alcohol.)

Folks recall that the store was run by "Bobby Dent," Robert Denton Smith. Regardless of the weather, Bobby wore a denim cap and a long denim coat. Kerosene lamps lit the store and a pot-bellied stove heated it.

For those who enjoy geocaching, the pastime of searching for hidden caches using GPS coordinates, there is a hidden cache—actually, two of them—in Jimtown. The caches were hidden by Randy, who in the 1980s and 1990s used to work on the nearby farms.

Top: Early Jimtown. (Author's Collection)
Bottom: An early photo of the Jimtown store. (Courtesy of Belleville Historical Society/Randy)

The Jimtown store today. (Courtesy of Belleville Historical Society/Randy)

Main Street in Tavera, Wisconsin. (Author's Collection)

LOYD

1855 – 1921

CLASS C/D

APPROXIMATE LOCATION:
Highway 58

Today's roadside hamlet was once a bustling place. Three stores, two blacksmiths, a post office, a barber, the mill, a cheese factory, and a school were all busy and active. In later years there was an auto body shop and a consignment sales business that operated in the cheese factory building. Today, Loyd is a handful of homes and a cemetery.

TAVERA

1893 – 1940

CLASS A/B

APPROXIMATE LOCATION:
County U

It is amazing how fast nature can reclaim a site. Tavera had a post office until 1940. Today only one house and the cemetery remain.

TWIN BLUFFS

1883 – 1954

CLASS C/D

APPROXIMATE LOCATION:
County TB and Twin Bluffs Drive

Today Twin Bluffs is a cluster of homes, but their post office lasted until 1954. The town also once had a school that was the heart of the community.

A vintage photo of a Loyd building. (Photographer unknown)

Twin Bluff's general store in the town's earlier days. (Author's Collection)

WEST LIMA

1860 – 1973

CLASS D

APPROXIMATE LOCATION:
County D & A

Folks still call West Lima home. Today the formerly bustling city is a cluster of homes. As one resident put it, a lot of farmers are in the area and Amish are self-employed. Everyone drives somewhere to work, as only one small business remains. In the 1950s, the village was home to over 350 residents and many small businesses.

Above: A bird's eye view of West Lima. (Author's Collection)
Below: An early street scene in West Lima. (Author's Collection))

225

WOODSTOCK

1855 – 1919

CLASS C/D

APPROXIMATE LOCATION:
Near Woodstock Drive and County D

One of West Lima's storefronts. (Author's Collection)

oodstock's first business, a general store, began in 1855. A rather long-lived post office operated from 1855 to 1919. An 1881 history tells that by 1883, the community included four stores, two blacksmith shops, a tannery, a wash and dry house for drying ginseng, a mill or two, a Methodist church, and a Disciple church.

A view of Woodstock, Wisconsin, in 1910. (Author's Collection)

Rock County

The marker at the site of the former Jefferson Prairie Settlement. (Courtesy of Creative Commons)

JEFFERSON PRAIRIE SETTLEMENT

1830s – 1860s

CLASS A/F

APPROXIMATE LOCATION:
4 miles south of Clinton on Wisconsin Highway 140,
near the Wisconsin/Iowa state line in the town of Clinton

Situated about as far south as one can get and still be in Wisconsin, Jefferson Prairie Settlement is considered a pioneer colony. It was a center for Norwegian immigration and for the development of the Evangelical Lutheran Church of America (ELCA).

Two brothers, Ole and Ansten Nattestad, came to the area in 1837. They played a key role in Norwegian immigration. The first organizational meeting of the ELCA was held in the settlement in 1860.

Today a historical marker is located at the site.

LEYDEN

1850 – 1903

CLASS A/C

APPROXIMATE LOCATION:
Northwest of Janesville at County H and Highway 14,
halfway between Janesville and Evansville

Settled by the Irish, Leyden at its peak included a general store, a railroad depot, a creamery, a tavern, the Leyden House, and about a dozen homes. A daily train made stops in the community. The store is closed, though in recent times it was still standing.

TURTLEVILLE

Mid-1800s

CLASS A

APPROXIMATE LOCATION:
8 miles northeast of Beloit

Not the first to settle in the region, or in Turtle Township, Pennsylvania brothers John and Abel Lewis knew the area was ideal for a sawmill. Soon they also opened and operated a store. By 1860, with the addition of a stone schoolhouse and a Baptist church, Turtleville was an up-and-coming trade center.

Wealthy Englishman William Hodson settled in Turtleville in 1850. He built a flour mill, a distillery, and a large and very grand home. Only the finest materials were used in the house, including walnut from the area. Built in the Greek Revival style, the house had seventeen rooms and twelve-foot ceilings, and the grounds included lush gardens.

When the Civil War broke out in 1861, Hodson, like most Englishmen, sympathized with the South, so much so that Hodson refused to put federally mandated stamps on his whiskey. He ordered his men to hide the bottles under potatoes. Unbeknownst to him, one of his employees was a federal agent. Hodson was arrested and ordered to pay fines totaling nearly $100,000. To avoid paying, Hodson tried to transfer the titles to his many properties to other names. It didn't work. In 1872, his properties were confiscated and sold at public auction. Hodson's house, the mill, and the distillery were all sold to the highest bidder, which was the First National Bank of Dresser. The winning bid was at the bargain, rock-bottom price of $3,000 for all.

Hodson was ruined. He drank heavily and frequented Janesville's bars playing his fiddle for coins. He died penniless in 1889.

Turtleville, the village, faded into history.

Rusk County

Left: The marker in front of the Apollonia Congregational Church. (Courtesy of www.schoepski.com)
Right: Apollonia Congregational Church today. (Courtesy of www.schoepski.com)

APOLLONIA

1891 - 1933

CLASS D

APPROXIMATE LOCATION:
Highway 8 and Apollonia Road

During the 1890s, Apollonia was the busiest community in Rusk County. Located at the juncture of two railroads, the CR&M and the Soo Line, it was originally called Verona Junction.

Lumber baron Frederick Weyerhauser visited the settlement often as he had substantial timber interests in the region. Verona Junction was renamed Apollonia, in honor of Weyerhauser's daughter.

Peaking in 1895, Apollonia included two large stores, two hotels, a church, an opera house, a saloon, a school, a drug store, a creamery, a doctor's office, and a population of three hundred. Apollonia was also home to Rusk County's first newspaper, *The Weekly Budget*.

As with most towns and settlements dependent on timber, once the resource was gone, so went the community. For years the only remnant of the village was the white-frame Apollonia Congregational Church. In 1978, the congregation donated the building to Rusk County, asking that it be maintained as a historical site. Today the church still stands and a historical marker has been erected.

CRANE

1910 - 1933

CLASS A/C

APPROXIMATE LOCATION:
8 miles north of Ladysmith

Crane was a family affair. The three Crane brothers, Lou, Ed, and Bill, arrived in the area in 1908. Attracted by the area's rich timber supply, they set up logging operations. They also played a major role in the Crane settlement.

The community's first school and church were in private homes. Later, when enrollment reached forty-nine students,

a two-room school building was constructed. Presbyterian services were the first offered and later a Catholic church was built.

Early residents recalled that you could get "anything you needed" at the Crane Store, even fresh meat. A Ladysmith meat market shipped fresh meat by train everyday and it was stored in a hole dug in the north corner of the store.

The train also played an important part in the community, so much so that the locomotives were named. There was "Old Rosy," later "Maude," "The Dinky," and "Scoot." It was common for Crane residents to walk the eight miles to Ladysmith to shop and return home by train.

A diphtheria epidemic brought tragedy to the area, with many members of families falling victim. A bit of scandal was also in Crane. According to a Rusk County history, a woman was reading postcards and spreading gossip and rumors. She was sued for slander. The trial was in Ladysmith and both parties, plaintiff and defendant, rode to the courthouse on the same wagon.

When timber resources dwindled, Crane faded into history.

PORT ARTHUR

1907 - 1912

CLASS A/C

APPROXIMATE LOCATION:
Port Arthur Road

Current events often played a role in naming early communities. Port Arthur supposedly received its name from Port Arthur in Manchuria, half a world away. Most of the news in the papers at the time talked of Port Arthur and the Russo-Japanese War (1904–1905), and early residents adopted the name.

Port Arthur's first residents arrived in 1904 and soon after, a dam was built. A mill was constructed at the same time, as was the railroad. Soon Port Arthur was in the business of pulp. In its earliest days, the mill employees worked eleven-hour day shifts and thirteen-hour night shifts. Sunday's swing shift worked around the clock, a twenty-four-hour shift. Pay was thirteen cents an hour. Around 1922, the mill changed to an eight-hour shift.

A school was built in 1907, and six other frame buildings were also constructed at the time. Before long, Port Arthur had twenty-six buildings and included a blacksmith, a store, a boarding house, and a dance hall. The store closed in 1939, after twenty-eight years in business.

In 1968, official permission to abandon the dam and to restore the river to its original state was granted. By 1969, all traces of the dam were gone.

THORNAPPLE

1880s – 1930s

CLASS A/C

APPROXIMATE LOCATION:
Walrath Road, south of Glen Flora

Highway 8 between Bruce and Ladysmith

A rriving in the late 1880s, the first pioneers came to Bruce by rail from Chippewa Falls. The settlement was the site of an early logging camp.

The arrival of more settlers soon necessitated a school. With no available building for the school to operate, one of the families moved their sitting room furniture into a bedroom and converted the now-empty space to a classroom, supplying the desks, blackboards, and other necessities. The first teacher was a daughter of that family, Mary Jane, who was only fifteen years old at the time. In 1904, a new schoolhouse was built and a teacher hired.

WALRATH

1916 – 1933

CLASS A/C

APPROXIMATE LOCATION:
Walrath Road, south of Glen Flora

R ather than ending definitively, Walrath gradually declined and eventually faded into history. First called Valley View and established in the early 1900s, the settlement later took on the name of its founder, who also built all of the houses, owned most of the land, and operated the mill: A.E. Walrath.

By the 1920s, the town of Walrath included a box factory, a chair factory, and a large store with an upper floor dance hall. A post office operated in the store. A large hotel and a school (built in 1919) completed the community. Sunday school classes were held in the school.

The community also organized a community club that met once a month. Several events were hosted. According to a Rusk County history, one of the first events hosted was the 1922 Thanksgiving dinner. The meal was cooked by the men and all parts of the meal came from the land, even the meat. The men used the boarding house kitchen. Memorial Day and the Fourth of July were big, community-wide events.

Also according to the Rusk history, the school had two horse-drawn buses/sleds. They were long and narrow with two doors and windows that could be lowered. Children sat on benches facing each other. The wheels were iron rims with wood spokes and could be swapped out for runners when the weather or conditions necessitated. The school later merged with the Glen Flora schools in about 1953. After consolidation, the Walrath school building was used as the town hall.

The entire Walrath village was threatened by a 1936 fire. All area men and boys, from as far away as Ladysmith and Glen Flora, as well as the men from the local Civilian Conservation Corps (CCC) camp, helped fight the flames. Not a single building was lost.

The hotel burned in the 1940s. In 1940 electricity via the REA came to the area. After that, the village slowly faded away. The depot was torn down, the railroad tracks pulled up, and the houses were moved or torn down.

Sauk County

Above: La Rue's Illinois Mine. (Courtesy of www.miningartifacts.org)

Right and below: Images from the mines in La Rue. (Courtesy of the Don Ginter Collection/Mid-Continent Railway Museum)

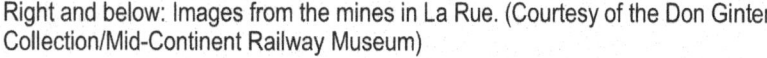

LA RUE

1840s – 1950s

CLASS C/D

APPROXIMATE LOCATION:
County PF

Twice the settlement of La Rue was a mining boom town, and twice it experienced a mining bust. The first time, it was iron ore, the second quartzite.

The first boom-and-bust cycle was in the mid-1840s. Iron ore was discovered half a mile from La Rue and soon things boomed. The Chicago, Northwestern Railroad built a spur line and the population swelled to over five hundred. Shafts were dug and mining crews (primarily Germans, Swedes, and Norwegians) worked two and three shifts. The settlement soon had two taverns, a hotel, a general store, and a multi-denominational church adjacent to the village. A "suburb," Owen, was platted and included over five hundred lots.

La Rue's mines did have one serious issue—water. Pumps had to run continuously to keep the mineshafts dry. When Minnesota's Mesabi Range open-pit mines opened in 1906, most of La Rue's mines shut down. In all, the iron ore mining boom lasted less than ten years.

After the mines closed, the settlement of La Rue reverted to its former quiet hamlet life. In 1917, the hustle and bustle started all over again when quartzite was discovered nearby. Quartzite was used to line the Eastern steel mill blast furnaces. The rail spur was extended to the quarry, known as the Rattlesnake. When a better grade of quartzite was found in Ohio, the La Rue site shut down. The last load was shipped out in 1957.

Since 1965, the Mid-Continent Railway Museum and Historical Society has called North Freedom home. The society members restore, maintain, and operate vintage rail equipment. A steam train excursion operates during the summer and fall and at events throughout the year. Especially fun is the Santa Express during the Christmas holidays and the Snow Train in February. The old steam train makes a nine-mile round trip out to the Rattlesnake Quarry. On the way, the train passes through the old settlement of La Rue at about the halfway point. Passengers experience a true "step back in time," and the scenery is a beauty to behold. Learn more at www.midcontinent.org.

A photo of early La Rue (below) shows two taverns. According to Jeffrey Lentz of the Mid-Continent Railway Museum, the white building in the foreground (Ruhland's) no longer exists. The dark-colored building (with the Effinger Beer sign) is the same structure standing today, with a dance hall added on at some point. It operated as the La Rue tavern up until a few years ago. The building in the background to the right was the LaRue General Store.

Above: Main Street in La Rue. (Courtesy of the Don Ginter Collection, www.midcontinent.org)
Below: La Rue in 2016. (Courtesy of the Mid-Continent Railway Museum)

A 2011 aerial photo of La Rue, Wisconsin. (Courtesy of the Mid-Continent Railway Museum)

LORETO

1900 - 1907

CLASS A/C

APPROXIMATE LOCATION:
County G & GG

Lots of debate went into the choice of a name for the settlement. Deciding that Loreto was short and easy to remember, Loreto it was. Spelled a number of ways—Loreto, Loretto, Loreta—the village was short-lived. To add to the confusion, there could have been two communities with the name.

According to the Sauk County Historical Society, the church is also confusing, sometimes referred to as Our Lady of Loretto, Our Lady of the Fields, and St. Patricks. The cemetery goes by St. Patrick's. Some records show the church's name as the Loretto Church, but records don't clear up the confusion.

St. Patrick's Cemetery is well-maintained and located adjacent to the white frame church building.

Our Lady of Loretto Catholic Church. (Courtesy of "Jeff the Quiet," Wikimedia Commons, http://commons.wikimedia.org/w/index.php?curid=20584521)

VALTON

1868 - 1915

CLASS C/D

APPROXIMATE LOCATION:
County EE

Nearly every settlement, village, or community had a Modern Woodmen's Hall. All kinds of activities were sponsored by the MWA, including dances, programs, celebrations, and more. The halls were usually the community social center. Even though I'd seen MWA references countless times, I never knew just what the MWA, Modern Woodmen of America, were until recently. The Sauk County Historical Society sent me a brochure published by the MWA telling the history of the "Painted Forest," but also telling the organization's history and purpose. The organization is still active today.

Established by Joseph Cullen Root in 1883, the MWA was a fraternal life insurance organization. Chapters were built across the country. Local chapters offered life insurance policies to assist in the case of tragedy. They also provided wholesome activities and character building. The group wanted to eliminate the financial burden families faced when a man died, leaving behind a wife and children.

Sauk County's Valton chapter was just one of the many chapters and halls all over America. But what a hall it was and is. The white frame building was sixty by thirty-three by twenty-four feet, and included a foyer and two rooms. But it is what is on the walls of those rooms that is remarkable. The walls

St. Patrick's Cemetery in Loreto. (Courtesy of B. Gardener)

and ceiling are completely covered with murals painted by an itinerant painter from Germany, Ernest Hupeden, also known as the "bum painter."

The scenes depict a literal and symbolic version of MWA camp activities at the time the paintings were done. Frightening scenes symbolizing death, family, and home are depicted almost as peaceful scenes. The murals were intended to get people "thinking about" leaving a wife and children behind.

Hupeden traveled the area trading his artwork for room and board. It took him two years to paint the Valton MWA hall. He is also credited with painting outside barn walls and buildings as well as painting portraits on plates and bottles. He was found dead in a snowbank near Hillsboro in the early 1900s.

The Valton chapter was disbanded in 1915. The Valton post office was also discontinued that year. Valton itself began to fade as well. As one resource put it, "As America became more urban, Valton got smaller." Seems that happened to lots of small communities.

In the 1960s, the MWA hall was purchased by local residents Ronald and Delores Nast. They maintained the building and allowed area residents to use it for special events. They named the hall the "Painted Forest."

In 1978, efforts began to preserve artistic and historic folk art. The Wisconsin Kohler Foundation purchased the hall in 1980, and a major restoration project was undertaken. Hupeden had painted nearly every inch of the building including the ceiling, which sadly did not survive the years. After the restoration was completed, the Kohler Foundation gifted the deed to the building to the Sauk County Historical Society. The hall is open for viewing on select summer days and by appointment. Learn more at www.saukcountyhistory.org/areaattractions/paintedforest.html.

Above: Volton's Modern Woodmen of America hall today. (Courtesy of www.wisconsinosity.com)
Below: Examples of the murals inside Volton's Modern Woodmen of America hall. (Courtesy of www.wisconsinosity.com)

Sawyer County

Hauer's general store. (Author's Collection)

HAUER

1922 – 1956

CLASS A/C

APPROXIMATE LOCATION:
Highway F near Strand and Hauer Road

Wisconsin's northwoods are known for their beauty, their serenity, and their peace and quiet. On November 18, 1966, that tranquility was shattered. That evening a supersonic B-52 bomber was hurled to the earth just a few miles from Hauer. The plane was on a training mission, which required a bomb run over Stone Lake at an altitude of 2,900 feet, then on to Grantsburg, Wisconsin, and eventually to St. Cloud, Minnesota, at an altitude of just 800 feet. Something went tragically wrong, and the plane and its crew of nine were lost. The crash cut a swath one hundred yards wide and a half mile long. An area history tells that many witnessed the crash, and the impact could be heard for miles.

Hauer was, in its heyday, a busy center. In 1907, The Wisconsin Central Railroad routed a line through the region. Soon a general store and post office were established. According to a local history, when the post office petition was approved, they asked for the name of the community and the postmaster replied, "Hauer," which was a derivative of his last name, Howard.

An early school was established. In order to warrant a teacher, little four-year-old Viola Howard was enrolled so as to meet the minimum number of students. A later school was built and it operated until 1946, when it burned to the ground. An unused school building was then moved to Hauer, where it was remodeled. It was used until the Hauer schools closed in 1958 upon consolidation with Birchwood.

OXBO

1900s

CLASS A

APPROXIMATE LOCATION:
20 miles west of Winter on Highway 70

Once a busy burg of fifty residents, by 1980, only five people lived in the vicinity of Oxbo.

The community had a church/school and was at one time home to a resort. The Flambeau River flows nearby.

An early scene near Oxbo, Wisconsin. (Author's Collection)

Shawano County

HAYMAN FALLS

1856 – 1917

CLASS A

APPROXIMATE LOCATION:
Between Pella and Leopis on the Embarrass River

Remote would be an apt word to describe the area in 1856, when the first settlers arrived. From Holland, Gerhardt and Bertha Hehman settled a homestead fourteen miles from the nearest neighbor. Gerhardt had to cut a road to the village of Embarrass, where the area's closest flour mill was located. He also cut a road from near Buckbee to Pella.

Somewhere along the way, the spelling of the settlement changed from Hehman to Hayman, and the area was known as Hayman Falls. Not only did the name change, but so did the area's primary land use. Originally a farming settlement, it became an electric power producing region. In 1917, the Topp Stewart Tractor Company needed more electricity for their plant in Clintonville, so they build a dam. The dam was later taken over by the Wisconsin Power and Light Company. Afterward, the region quickly became a recreational destination and today the site is a county park.

HUNTING

1880 – 1934

CLASS A

APPROXIMATE LOCATION:
Near County SS and Hunting Road

Hunting's first settlers arrived at the same time as the railroad did, in 1882. Soon a store, a Methodist church, a school, a dance hall, a creamery/cheese factory, a gravel pit, coal kilns, and several other businesses were up and running. Of all the activities, it is said the coal kilns were the most important.

Farmers from miles around sold two-foot lengths of maple, birch, and elm for $1.25 per cord. The kilns would heat to a high intensity and then be shut down. This process changed the wood into charcoal, which was then shipped to blacksmiths and foundries, especially those in Fond du Lac.

The establishment of a post office often meant that a settlement was growing. So when Hunting opened its post office, folks thought things were looking good. The post office was housed in the two-story general store/tavern combination.

Trains stopped in Hunting twice a day, bringing mail and passengers along the route between Big Falls and Hunting. By 1898, the station was so busy there were two agents—one for days, the other for nights. For unknown reasons, the depot closed between 1903 and 1905.

By 1898, Hunting's population was fifty, and several new businesses had been established. A school was built in 1899, and in 1905, enrollment was fifty-one students. The school quickly became the region's social center. Basket socials and Christmas programs were popular events. When the creamery burned in 1905, a dance hall was built on the site. The area was also home to a ginseng farm.

Several train derailments occurred near Hunting between 1909 and 1915. One of the largest was in 1909. Fourteen cars jumped the tracks. No one was hurt, but clearing the tracks took several days.

Hunting remained prosperous and growing well into the 1910s. A new saloon was built in 1912, followed by a cheese factory in 1914. Operating until 1923, the building stood vacant for many years until it was moved to Marion in the 1940s. By that time, Hunting, as a village, had ceased to exist. The depot had closed in 1930 and was demolished a few years later. The tracks were also removed. The area's timber resources had been logged off and the area became primarily agricultural. The post office was discontinued in 1934.

Dismantling of the village was ongoing. The dance hall was torn down. The general store collapsed in the 1950s. The school was razed and passenger service was discontinued in the 1950s, as well.

SPLIT ROCK

1889 - 1935

CLASS A/C

APPROXIMATE LOCATION:
State Highway 45 and County SS,
between Marion and Tigerton

Originally developing around the Aschiner Mill, the settlement was also originally called Aschinerville. The arrival of the railroad a short distance away caused the settlement's shift to the railside location.

The first settlers arrived at about the same time as the Milwaukee, Lake Shore and West Railroad arrived. The relocated settlement took on the name of Split Rock, so named because of nearby large bedrock outcropping with a substantial crack. By 1898, Split Rock's population was fifty and the village included all the staples a small village wanted or needed. The Wisconsin Coal Company operated coal kilns in the area. The kilns produced charcoal that was used in powering engines.

The Peace Lutheran Church was established in 1890, with a new building constructed in 1917. A cross was built out of logs from the first church. Services were in German until 1948. The church is still active and is now part of a two-church parish.

The original mill was sold in 1895, and a new one built in the Split Rock location. Two eleven-hour shifts were running and men earned twelve cents an hour.

A newspaper, the *Split Rock Review*, started publication in October of 1897. Annual subscriptions were one dollar.

In 1900, the blacksmith shop was destroyed by fire and was rebuilt as a wagon shop/blacksmith.

The village had several active organizations, including the Split Rock Engagement Club (which sponsored an annual masquerade ball) and Split Rock Jubilee Club. A chapter of the Modern Woodmen of America owned a meeting hall and events were hosted at least twice a month, on the second and fourth Sundays.

Making headlines in the 1970s, a group of area residents strongly opposed to state, local, and county taxes formed the Posse Comitatus. The posse formed their own church, called the Basic Bible Church. Several members deeded their lands to the church to avoid real estate taxes. Several trailer houses were moved in. In 1985, Shawano County condemned them due to code violations. In the 1990s, they were removed.

Peace Lutheran Church today. (Author's Collection)

Peace Lutheran Church's early days. (Author's Collection)

Sheboygan County

A calendar plate from Dacada. (Author's Collection)

St. Nicholas's mailbox. (Courtesy of Galen Frysinger)

St. Nicholas Church (left), located in Sheboygan County, and St. Nicholas Cemetery (right), located in Ozaukee County. (Courtesy of Galen Frysinger)

AMSTERDAM

1850s – 1940s

CLASS A

APPROXIMATE LOCATION:

Town of Holland along Lake Michigan

It was always about the fishing. Once the summer site of Ohio fisherman Gilbert Smith in the 1850s, the settlement grew to depend on fishing as its livelihood. Smith platted the settlement and constructed a 600-foot pier into Lake Michigan. The American Fish Company was established and the most common method of fishing was "pound netting."

In "pound netting," thirty- to forty-pound nets are set and positioned in thirty-foot water. The nets stretched out to form a wall of net from the bottom of the lake to the surface of the water. A lead ran from shallow water to the pound net. Fish swimming along couldn't go over or under the net, so they followed the lead. Once in the enclosure, they were trapped. Fishing continued in the area until the 1940s.

There are no post office records shown for the village, which was, after all, primarily a fishing village. Amsterdam's history has always been tied to that of Cedar Grove, just one mile inland. Some records indicate the two were one community, while other stress that the two were separate communities.

In recent years, Sheboygan County purchased a stretch of lakeshore, the last stretch of undeveloped shoreline. The shoreline is known as Amsterdam Dunes.

DACADA

1866 – 1903

CLASS D

APPROXIMATE LOCATION:

County K

Area residents like to say that Dacada was too big for one county, so it was located in two counties, Ozaukee and Sheboygan. St. Nicholas Church and cemetery stand across the street from each other, yet the church is in Sheboygan County and the cemetery in Ozaukee County. The entire village of Dacada straddles the county line. However, the post office was in Sheboygan County, thus its designation in Sheboygan County.

Settled by immigrants from Luxembourg in the 1840s and 1850s, the new arrivals believed that the area was inhabited by the Dakota, thus the name. The community was also known as St. Nicholas, in honor of one of Luxembourg's favorite saints.

A log church was one of the first buildings they constructed, and it was later replaced (in 1863) with a stone church. The present church was built in 1911 and had major renovations in 1941. A large, two-story school operated until the 1960s.

FIVE CORNERS

1876 – 1903

CLASS A

APPROXIMATE LOCATION:

County V & I, Town of Lima

Knowing travelers and stage coach passengers along the busy route would need refreshments, John Kennedy built a tavern in the 1870s. Travelers also needed lodging, so a hotel was built. Soon a post office, a cheese factory, a Catholic Church (St. Rose), and a school were part of the community. First called Kennedy's Corner, the settlement took on the name Five Corners due to its location at the intersection of five roads.

The church was organized in the 1860s. It was permanently closed in 2006, and torn down in 2015.

Five Corners is still offering food and refreshment to travelers. Recently reviewed the by the *Sheboygan Press* food editor, Kim's Five Corners Tavern and Eatery is the place to go for good food and good times.

Five Corners, Lima Center, in 1909 (the hotel on the left is now Kim's Five Corners Tavern and Eatery). (Courtesy of Kim's Five Corners)

Top: Early days in Five Corners. (Courtesy of the Sheboygan County Historical Society)
Middle: Present day Five Corners. (Courtesy of the Sheboygan County Historical Society)
Bottom: St. Rose of Lima Catholic Church. (Courtesy of www.loopnet.com)

HAVEN

1897 – 1984

CLASS A

APPROXIMATE LOCATION:
County FF near Lakeshore Road

After World War II, the world was in the grips of the Cold War. Building military might and weaponry to protect the country from the might and power of other countries (such as the communists) was the priority.

Haven, with its two miles of shoreland and nearly perfectly level land, was the ideal military training ground. So the United States government leased the 160-acre parcel and set about building a training camp, called Camp Haven, near the old town site. From 1949 to 1959, the former town site and its area was an anti-aircraft testing range. After 1959, the land was sold to Wisconsin Power and Light for their planned nuclear power plant. Local government opposition nixed those plans. For years the property sat vacant and became a dumping ground and youth hangout.

In 1998, a premier golf resort opened on the former camp site. Whistling Straits is a lush, picturesque, and world-class golf facility. Its rolling green grounds convey nothing of its past. In its seventeen years, Whistling Straits has hosted five major tournaments and will host the 2020 Ryder Cup.

Haven's post office lasted nearly one hundred years. Today the settlement is home to the Haven Bar and Grill, which is a popular destination, and a handful of homes.

Haven today. (Courtesy of Andrew Turnbull)

Above: The view from the eleventh fairway at Whistling Straits in Haven, Wisconsin. (Courtesy of "KevinTR," Wikimedia Commons, http://commons.wikimedia.org/wiki/File:WhistlingStraits11Fairway.JPG)
Below: The Onion River dam. (Vintage Post Card)

Onion River's flouring/grist mill. (Courtesy of National Register of Historic Places, Onion River Flouring/Grist Mill, Waldo, Sheboygan, Wisconsin, #84000679)

ONION RIVER

1850 – 1877

CLASS A/C

APPROXIMATE LOCATION:
Along the Onion River

Coursing its way through the heart of Sheboygan County, the Onion River travels thirty-six miles until it joins the Sheboygan River in Sheboygan Falls. At one time long its route, seven settlements had been established. Most no longer exist as villages.

Onion River was established in 1849, and was first known as Olio. With successive postmasters it was also known as Mitchell and Joppa. Later, the post office/settlement moved one mile west and became Waldo.

In those days, post offices based the continuance on postal receipts. For the year 1851, Onion River's receipts were only $9.30.

PARNELL

1883 – 1903

CLASS C/D

APPROXIMATE LOCATION:
County A & V, and Parnell Road

Irish patriot Charles Stewart Parnell was a hero to his countrymen. He believed in and fought for Irish Home Rule. When his countrymen settled in Wisconsin in the 1870s, they named the community in his honor.

A blacksmith was the sole business until 1891, when a store and a cheese factory were established. Over the course of its livelihood, Parnell had two stores, two hotels (an east and a west, and across the street from each other), a meat market, a school, and a baseball team. The store was later a fixit shop and is today home to the Parnell Tavern. Peaking early in the twentieth century, by the 1920s Parnell had run its course.

The collapse of the farm economy after World War I, the coming of Rural Free Delivery (RFD), and changes in transportation from a horse-and-buggy era to the automobile era combined to hasten Parnell's demise.

Today, it is a quiet crossroads settlement.

Parnell in 1914. (Author's Collection)

Parnell today looking east (top) and north (bottom). (Courtesy of "Royalbroil," Wikimedia Commons, https://en.wikipedia.org/wiki/File:Parnell_Wisconsin_Looking_East.jpg, https://en.wikipedia.org/wiki/File:Parnell_Wisconsin_Sign.jpg

SIX CORNERS (ST. GEORGE)

1879 – 1901

CLASS D

APPROXIMATE LOCATION:
County A, O, and V

Early settlements were often located at crossroads of busy travel routes, as was Six Corners. The community was also known as St. George. A general store, a hotel with a post office, and a school were part of the settlement. The school operated until consolidations with nearby towns. In recent years the Six Corners Tap was at the location.

WINOOSKI

1853 – 1903

CLASS A/C

APPROXIMATE LOCATION:
South of Plymouth, near County U

One of America's first anti-slavery crusaders was an early settler in Winooski. Jonathan Walker was in fact the only man in United States history to be branded a "slave stealer." The letters "SS" were branded into the palm of his right hand. Walker was the owner of twenty acres of land and moved to Wisconsin in the early 1860s.

Walker was believed to be helping slaves escape by offering them free passage on his ships. Government steamboats overtook Walker's ship. Upon inspection, they found slaves. Walker was arrested, placed in irons, and returned to Florida to stand trial. He was found guilty, was assessed a huge fine, was sentenced to a year in solitary confinement and was branded.

After serving his sentence, he lectured in the northern states. Poet John Greenleaf Whittier based his "Man with the Branded Hand" on Walker. While definite proof is lacking, it is surmised that Walker, while in Winooski, was a link in the Underground Railroad, and that other locations in the state also assisted with the effort.

Winooski was also home to an early Sheboygan County insane asylum, as they were called in those early days. Approximately twenty patients were at the facility. The owners were paid four dollars a week per patient. Tragedy struck in 1878, when a fire broke out. Four patients and a night watchman were killed.

Winooski reached its peak in 1881, boasting a population of eighty-eight, thirteen homes, two mills, a post office/store, and a dance hall. The dance hall was on the top floor of the store and was said to be large enough for six sets of square dancers.

A popular Fourth of July activity was "firing the anvil." According to an early twentieth-century news article, at midnight on the Fourth, and every hour on the hour throughout the day, gunpowder was poured into a hole bored into a heavy block. An anvil was put on top and a line of gunpowder was poured out and at a safe distance was lit. Sounds a mite dangerous.

Plans were made for the railroad to route through the region, running to Green Bay. Hopes were that the line would run through Winooski. But it was not to be. It ran through Waldo and sealed Winooski's fate.

The area 4-H club built a historical marker in 1970 and erected it at the former site of Winooski. A Wisconsin historical marker was also placed at the site.

Today the area is home to a long-standing and very popular maple syrup farm. Drewry's Maple Syrup offers the best-tasting maple syrup, tours of their facility, and more.

A bird's eye view of early Winooski. (Courtesy of the Sheboygan County Historical Society)

St. Croix County

ERIN CORNERS

1862 - 1902

CLASS A/C

APPROXIMATE LOCATION:
5½ miles southeast of New Richmond

Erin Corners was located at the geographic center of Erin Prairie. With the name of Erin, it is apparent that the area was settled by Irish immigrants.

Today, Mary's Erin Corners Bar and a ballpark are at the site.

JEWETT

1865 - 1944

CLASS A/C

APPROXIMATE LOCATION:
County T five miles east of New Richmond

Touted as a booming village in a scenic setting, complete with streets and parks and more, the lots sold quickly, many of them sight unseen. The advertisements were a bit exaggerated. When the buyers arrived and saw what the settlement really looked like, they were not happy. They searched for the German immigrant who had sold them the lots. He was eventually found and arrested. However, the buyers never saw a penny of the supposedly $275,000 the seller was said to have made.

Jewett did develop and for a time was a busy and bustling village. There were several stores, a sawmill, a grist mill, and an abundance of saloons.

Today the Roosters Roadhouse, with great food and fun events, is a popular Jewett area spot.

Trempealeau County

Above: A view of Russell's school and store in 1908. (Courtesy of the Trempealeau County Historical Society)

Left: Russell's school and store in 1960. (Courtesy of the Trempealeau County Historical Society)

HAMLIN

1862 – 1892

CLASS A

APPROXIMATE LOCATION:
County V

Legend has it that famed outlaw Jesse James once stayed in Hamlin's hotel after a nearby robbery. Some say the buried treasure has still not been found.

The pioneer village had a post office that operated for thirty years and a hotel. The settlement was also an early stage stop.

RUSSELL

1882 – 1906

CLASS A/C

APPROXIMATE LOCATION:
8 miles northwest of Independence,
Highway 121 and County V

Mortally wounded in 1863 while serving during the Civil War, Russell's founder didn't live long in the settlement. The community was named for another early settler from Scotland. The village included a post office, a general store, a cheese factory, and a school. The Russell school held classes until consolidation with Independence schools in 1962. Both the store and school buildings are still standing. The store has been converted to a private home and the school building is used for storage.

Russell school and store in 2014. (Courtesy of the Trempealeau County Historical Society)

Vernon County

Above: Early Avalanche. (Author's Collection)
Below: An aerial view of early Bloomingdale. (Author's Collection)

![Aerial view of early Bloomingdale]

AVALANCHE

1854 - 1905

CLASS A

APPROXIMATE LOCATION:
Junction of County S and County Y

What a sight it must have been. Two men, one the buttermaker, clinging to the roof of the cheese factory building as it careened down the surging waters toward the bridge. The 1907 flood waters pushed it helter skelter. Once the structure hit the bridge, the two men jumped to safety. The building itself was demolished.

The cheese factory was rebuilt, and it operated until the mid-1940s, when it was financially unable to compete with larger, consolidated and corporate dairies. Bankruptcy was filed in 1947 and the building and lot were put up for sale.

The timing couldn't have been better. The Ladies Aid Society and the Sunday school had just been notified that church-related activities could no longer be held in the schoolhouse. The two groups pooled their resources and bought the cheese factory building and lot for $1,500.00. The entire town pitched in to remodel the building. The Ladies Aid meetings and Sunday school classes were held in the refurbished building until 1986, when they were discontinued due to lack of participants and students.

Founded in the 1850s with the establishment of a sawmill, Avalanche reached its peak population as a village in the 1870s. Merchants in the village (named for the prominent land formation which resembled an avalanche—some old timers say an avalanche did occur) included the sawmill, a flour and grist mill, a cooper shop, a school, a store, the creamery and cheese factory, and a wool carding and knitting mill. At one time the community had its own band, the Avalanche Cornet Band.

BLOOMINGDALE

1858 - 1905

CLASS D

APPROXIMATE LOCATION:
3 miles east of Westby on County S

The pioneer village of Bloomingdale could be described as "bustling." Growing from an early trading port to a village of nearly one hundred by 1883, Bloomingdale included three general stores, a grist/flour mill, a doctor's office, a tanner shop, a shoemaker shop, a wagon maker shop, a blacksmith shop, a school, a post office (1858 to 1905), a sawmill, a dance hall, and a furniture factory. The 1883 business directory listed more than ten merchants, some of great skill and local renown.

Andrew Bakken, the furniture maker, won several state fair blue ribbons as well as winning one at the Chicago World Fair. He used native woods and had a factory where he kiln-dried his own lumber. On an as-needed basis, he crafted many a coffin.

Bloomingdale was supposedly named by early Norwegian immigrants after they saw the hillside covered in blooming wildflowers. "Blom" is Norwegian for flower and "dalen" for valley, thus Bloomingdale.

The village was platted in 1857. The mill ran day and night until it was destroyed by a flood in the early 1900s. It was never rebuilt. Another busy business was the Bloomingdale Co-op Creamery. Established in 1905, it later merged with Westby's creamery in the 1940s.

Bloomingdale was considered the social center for the entire region. People rode sleighs, drove wagons, or walked, some

A bird's eye view of Bloomingdale. (Author's Collection)

as far as seven miles, to attend dances at the hall. Unescorted females could attend free of charge. However, if an oyster supper was served at midnight, the cost was fifty cents per couple. During summer dances, refreshments and donuts were served at midnight. Skating and skiing in the winter and croquet in the summer were popular events. There was a swimming hole down by the mill, but it was said to be strictly a man's sport. The Fourth of July was an annual and much anticipated event. The first Independence Day celebration was held in 1879, with more than five hundred attending.

BROOKVILLE (NEW BROOKVILLE)

1856 - 1860

CLASS A

APPROXIMATE LOCATION:
3 miles south of Viroqua on Highway 14

Several Vernon County firsts took place in the short-lived Brookville, including the first church in the county, the first school in the county, and the first practicing physician in Vernon County.

Before 1860, Brookville included a post office (1856 to 1860), a store, a blacksmith shop, a hotel, a Templar's Lodge (with twenty-seven members), a school, and a church. The community also hosted many camp meetings over the early years. Historical records tell that by 1955, there were no remains of the pioneer village.

BUD (BUDD)

1894 - 1901

CLASS C

APPROXIMATE LOCATION:
7 miles west of Viroqua on Highway 56

Folklore has it that the small fledgling community wasn't quite "blooming" yet, so they named it Bud. Depending on where you look it could be spelled Bud or Budd. If you look at a Wisconsin state map, you won't find it at all. However you spell it, it was a "budding" community.

In the early days the settlement included a steam-powered sawmill. A post office operated just seven years, from 1894 to 1901. However, the demise of the post office did not mean the end of the community. A general store opened in 1907. It included an upstairs dance hall where several events were held. A late twentieth-century news article featured the community.

DILLY

1895 - 1920

CLASS A/C

APPROXIMATE LOCATION:
Near intersection of Highway 82 and County P

Life in Dilly can be defined as "before the fire" and "after the fire." In the early days, Dilly was bustling. After the fire, Dilly went into decline. Before the 1928 fire, Dilly sported a general store, a sawmill, a stockyard, a hotel, a hardware store, a creamery, a blacksmith shop, a post office, a doctor's office, and a population nearing one hundred. After the fire destroyed the Dilly Mercantile Company (Dilly's largest business), people began moving away, taking their homes with them. One house was said to have been cut in half, by hand. One half moved to Hillsboro, the other to a nearby farm.

The fire was believed to have started by a smoldering cigarette left behind by one of the older men who frequently sat and visited around the potbellied stove. All accounts say that the fire was the beginning of the end for Dilly. With the store gone, area residents were forced to shop elsewhere, especially in nearby Hillsboro. The increasing use of automobile travel aided in the ability to go further to shop.

A valentine bearing a Dilly postmark. (Author's Collection)

In its day, the dance hall attracted people from far and wide. Dances would last well into the wee hours of the morning. Not as risqué as it sounds, the women of Dilly often hosted "stripping bees," where fowl feathers were stripped for use in pillows and ticks.

ESOFEA

1868 – 1905

CLASS A

APPROXIMATE LOCATION:
County B near Park Road

Automobile accidents were often and common on the stretch of County 11 (B) through the village of Esofea. The highway department had long wanted to rework the highway. With several homes standing near the roadway, "how" was the question. Some were occupied, the others vacant. When the last resident moved, the county placed an ad in the newspaper offering the homes free of charge to anyone who would move them out. No one stepped up or offered to take them. A perfect solution to get rid of the homes and to provide a training event for area fire departments was agreed upon. The homes were scheduled to be burned in a controlled burn, and all area fire departments took part in the training opportunity. Fires were started in each of the four structures (two houses, an old store/post office, and the Templar Hall/school). It was a win-win: the houses were safely removed, the local fire departments participated in a valuable training event, and the roadway was upgraded. The former townsite serves the area as a recreational park.

Rentz Memorial Park is a popular place. Activities abound with the park's two ponds, which provide fishing and swimming, a picnic shelter, and a lighted ballfield.

Esofea was a thriving place in its heyday. The community got its start when, in 1870, Norwegian settlers Michael Rentz and his brother started a tannery. A bustling community developed and soon a store and cheese factory were operating. There was also a post office. According to a Vernon County history summary, Rentzville was suggested as the name of the new settlement but the Rentz brothers declined. So the owner of the cheese factory took his first initial "E" and added his wife, Sophia's, name to it. Thus, Esofea. A blacksmith and pool hall, with a dance hall on the top floor, also called Esofea home. As the population increased a school was established and the Bethany Lutheran Church was founded.

Bethany Lutheran Church in Esofea. (Courtesy of Kari Venden Waterbury)

A calendar plate from Esofea. (Author's Collection)

KICKAPOO CENTER

1854 – 1900

CLASS A

APPROXIMATE LOCATION:
3 miles south of Viola on Highway 131

From its earliest days, Kickapoo Center was home to a cast of colorful characters, starting with one of the region's first settlers, Samuel Estes. Estes was said to be floating down the river on a raft, in 1850, with a group of men he had met an encampment. The men decided to travel together but it wasn't long before an argument broke out. Estes thought it best that he disembark. He built a primitive cabin, hunted, and trapped in the Kickapoo Center area. Soon other settlers came to the region and before long a settlement developed.

Just north of Kickapoo Center, early physician Daniel Hill resided. Practicing medicine wasn't his only source of income; he also practiced horse thievery. Hill's homestead was said to be the headquarters of an interstate crime operation, specializing in stealing horses in Illinois and then selling them in Wisconsin, Iowa, and Minnesota. After the Civil War, the crime of choice was robbing local travelers. The change in operation led to Hill's men's capture. Hill was convicted and was sentenced to three years in Waupaca.

Vernon County's most notorious murderer also called Kickapoo Center home. According to a Vernon County history, in May of 1888, Andrew Grandstaff murdered a man, the man's wife, and two of the couple's grandchildren. After his arrest in June of the same year, he was lynched by an angry mob.

Platted in 1854, Kickapoo Center included a log school, which burned and was replaced with a frame building. A store also operated in the small settlement, as did a post office. For years Kickapoo Center was home to a large dancing and amusement center, which was destroyed by fire in 1945.

In the mid-1960s, a new bridge was built over the Kickapoo River. Kickapoo Center had always been located along river bottomland and floods plagued the settlement. With the new bridge, the road was routed around Kickapoo Center. The settlement's former Main Street was reclaimed by nature. Most traces of the early village were moved or are under river silt.

LIBERTY POLE

1869 – 1901

CLASS C

APPROXIMATE LOCATION:
6 miles southwest of Viroqua, Highways 27/82

People—both the people living in the towns and the people you meet while researching the towns—and their stories are what makes lost towns so special and so fascinating. Liberty Pole has both.

Today, just as it had been since 1845, the store offers an inviting respite. The creaking wood floors, the wonderful aromas, and the eclectic mix of handcrafted items all convey a true old-fashioned welcoming.

Recently I had the opportunity to visit with Nora Soltau, who, with her husband, Mike, purchased the long-vacant historic store building in 2000. From the beginning it was easy to tell how much Nora loved the old store, the old town, and all of its history. As Nora told me, the community was originally known as Hogtown because it was common for the farmers to march their pigs down Main Street to be slaughtered. Area folks didn't take to being called Hogtown, so the name was officially changed to Liberty Pole. Nora says that the name came from a flag-raising ceremony during the presidential campaign of John Fremont.

The Liberty Pole Store has a special area set aside to showcase local history. The post office, Vernon County's first, used to be in the rear of the store. Original Black Hawk Trail signs are on the wall. The road in front of the store used to be part of the historic Black Hawk Trail. Local history artifacts abound.

The Liberty Pole Store today. (Courtesy of Bruce Wicks)

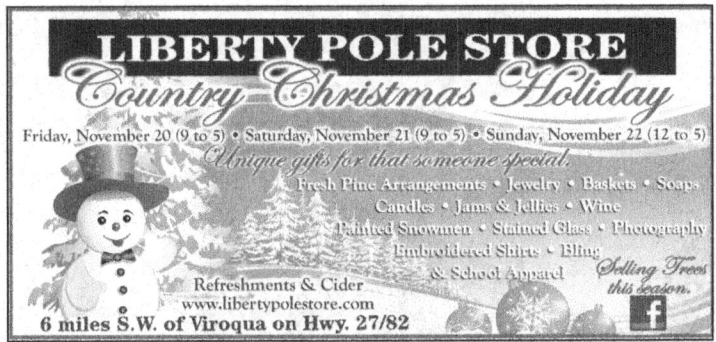

Above: The store in Liberty Pole hosts special hours during the Christmas season. (Courtesy of the Liberty Pole Store)
Below: The Liberty Pole Store decorated and ready for Christmas. (Courtesy of the Liberty Pole Store)

Nora says there is speculation that Liberty Pole was once a station on the Underground Railroad, a series of safe houses that fleeing slaves used along their route to Canada. There is good reason to believe the speculation to be true.

There aren't many general stores still standing, let alone open for business. There also aren't many stores that offer a wide range of unique items, many Wisconsin-made and many

St. Joseph's Catholic Church in Mount Tabor and a partial street view. (Author's Collection)

handcrafted. Special Christmas hours are hosted. Give yourself a treat, pick up a few Christmas gifts (even for yourself) and visit the Liberty Pole Store. You'll pick up some history as well. Learn more at www.libertypolestore.com.

MOUNT TABOR

1856 – 1939

CLASS A/C

APPROXIMATE LOCATION:
Town of Forest

Established by Bohemian settlers, the one-street community was named for the settlement's first postmaster. A creamery, a blacksmith shop, a school, and St. Joseph's Catholic Church made up the community. The post office was discontinued in 1939, and the creamery closed in 1962. In 1999, a grocery store, a garage, a general store, and a feed mill were still in existence.

NEWTON

1864 – 1905

CLASS A/B

APPROXIMATE LOCATION:
9 miles east of Viroqua on County D

Dubbed the cultural center of the county, Newton was known for its exceptional teachers and its academic pursuits and activities. Spelling bees, debates, essay contests, orators, and guest speakers were often hosted in the two-story school house.

Social events were also popular and included basket socials, sleigh rides, skating parties with bonfires providing light and warmth, and fierce hockey games.

Located on the Bad Axe River, Newton had a population, at its peak, of approximately one hundred. The settlement also had a sawmill, a flour/grist mill, a wagon shop, two churches, a blacksmith, a physician, other stores, and several residences.

A 1916 flood washed out the mill and the bridge. A new road and bridge were constructed just east of Newton. A 1951 flood also flooded the area.

A bird's eye view of Newton, Wisconsin, in 1908. (Author's Collection)

Retreat's Methodist church. (Author's Collection)

RETREAT

1855 – 1905

CLASS D

APPROXIMATE LOCATION:
9 miles east of the Mississippi River

Nearly one hundred years after its debut, the "Retreat World's Fair" is still going strong. In 1919, there were exhibits, dairy, food, games, contests, and a parade. A community hall to house some of the events was constructed in 1928.

The settlement was named for a decisive battle in the Black Hawk War. General Atkinson and his troops came upon the Native American forces near the confluence of the Bad Axe and Mississippi rivers in 1832. After the Natives' defeat, the developing community became known as Retreat. (Note there is also a Victory in Vernon County.)

The settlement's first school was a mortar, stone, and wood building. It was constructed in 1855, but was later replaced with a frame building. As was common at the time, female teachers were hired for the fall and summer terms. Male teachers were hired for the winter term as that was when the older, more unruly boys attended school. The school closed in 1960. The building was later used as an artist's studio and lastly as a private home.

Three churches were active in the community: a Disciple of Christian church, a Congregational church and a Methodist church. The Methodist church celebrated its 120th anniversary in 1994. Area women formed a Ladies Aid group and the group hosted many events, including an annual Memorial Day dinner and pie and ice cream socials.

Retreat was honored and proud to have a Medal of Honor recipient in their community. Frances (Frank) Wallar was awarded the Medal of Honor for courage in the Battle of Gettysburg during the Civil War. During heavy fighting, Wallar jumped into the ranks of the Second Mississippi and captured their colors. Wallar also saw service in the Battle of Antietam, Bull Run, and others. His Medal of Honor was on display at the Vernon County Historical Society, but, sadly, it was stolen. Fourteen years later it was found in the estate of a Civil War collector in Pennsylvania. It has since been returned to the Vernon County Historical Museum.

ROCKTON

1869 – 1936

CLASS C/D

APPROXIMATE LOCATION:
Highway 131 halfway between La Farge and Ontario

As a former teacher, I can certainly relate to Rockton's first school teacher. Records tell that she taught three days, then ran away! She never returned. It is said the first school was crude, but running away sounds a bit drastic.

Built on solid rock seventy-five feet above the surrounding area, the countryside was rich dairy and farmland. Platted in 1873, the eight-block early community included a post office, a blacksmith shop, a doctor's office, and a grist mill. Rockton was a mail center located on four different mail routes.

Above: A bird's eye view of Rockton. (Author's Collection)
Below: Rockton Bar today. (Author's Collection)

Below: Rockton's rich farmland. (Author's Collection)

As Rockton grew, a new two-story school was built, complete with two staircases, one for the boys and one for the girls.

In later years and to this day, other establishments still call Rockton home. Rich in scenic beauty, the Kickapoo Yacht Club offers scenic canoe rides, canoe rentals, and more. The Rockton Bar, by all accounts, is a treat for the tastebuds. Wild Fur Things offers custom, handmade fur items (mittens, hats, etc).

ROMANCE

1855 - 1898

CLASS C

APPROXIMATE LOCATION:
5 miles east of Genoa on Highway 56

Much conjecture has been raised about the origin of the settlement's name—Romance. Theories range from the ordinary to the fanciful and outlandish.

Top: The first post office in Romance. (Courtesy of Thomas Schmidt, www.romancewisconsin.com)
Middle: Downtown Romance. (Courtesy of A.K. Lallas, www.romancewisconsin.com)
Bottom: Inside the Romance Store. (Courtesy of A.K. Lallas, www.romancewisconsin.com)

Top: Romance road sign. (Courtesy of A.K. Lallas, www.romancewisconsin.com)
Middle: Romance's cemetery. (Courtesy of Thomas Schmidt, www.romancewisconsin.com)
Bottom: Another view of the Romance Store. (Courtesy of A.K. Lallas, www.romancewisconsin.com)

Still no consensus has been reached. No one knows why the small community was named Romance.

One indisputable name for the community is that of Turkey Capital of Wisconsin. Recently bestowed (1983), the distinction came just seven years after twenty hens and nine toms were released in the area. In those seven years, turkeys thrived, and the area is now known for its premier turkey hunting.

A post office operated from 1854 until at least 1883, and some records indicate until 1898. The school was longer-lived, operating from the 1880s until 1962. In 1965, the village had a tavern, a store, and a stockyard. According to A.K. Lallas, a resident of Romance since 1969, the store is gone, the tavern is gone, and so are the highway signs. Today Romance is home to a handful of enterprises including a photographer, a woodworker, and an organic farm.

Romance also has its own website. You'll find information about Romance: where it is located, day trips, its history, information on current businesses, trivia, a fanciful tale, and many photos. Check it out at www.romancewisconsin.com.

SEELEYBURG (STAR)

1858 - 1902

CLASS A

APPROXIMATE LOCATION:
North Seeleyburg Road near intersection with Lawton

Water power was of prime importance in the establishment of early pioneer villages. At that time, rivers and creeks were the only available source of power, so many a settlement was located along the banks of a waterway. Seeleyburg (first known as Star) was one of them.

Platted in the mid 1850s and dubbed Star, the settlement was located on the Kickapoo River. When native New Yorker Dempsey Seeley purchased government land at $1.25 an acre, he planned to harness the water power and establish a sawmill at the point where the Kickapoo River took a sharp turn to the west. High bluffs lined the west bank, but the east bank was the valley floor. Seeley also purchased several acres to the north. That land was rich in virgin timber, perfect for a budding sawmill owner. As the timber began to be cut and the sawmill began operating, other settlers came to the region. Soon a bustling community developed around the mill.

Early resident Ray Nixon recalled in 1977, that "Seeleyburg soon had a north/south main street with an intersecting eastern road." Quickly more than a dozen businesses lined Main Street, including a general store, a shoemaker shop, a doctor's office, and several homes. Growth was steady during the Civil War. After the war, the village boomed and was officially platted. A church and a school were constructed and many more merchants established businesses.

Ray Nixon also recalled the Seeley had quite an enterprise going. He had crews running the mill, harvesting timber, building bridges, and rafting logs. Population of the community was nearly one hundred. In 1870, Seeleyburg was said to be at its peak, and it lasted until the early 1890s.

Often what brings a community to life can also be its demise. Seeleyburg's location on the river gave it life. Since Seeleyburg's buildings were barely above the water, the river's frequent flooding ravaged the community again and again. In the spring, great chunks of ice would come hurtling down the river. Nixon recalled that the ice could—and often did—crash right through a house or building. Disgruntled residents soon moved to the newly created community just south of Seeleyburg, La Farge.

Seeleyburg's death knell was in 1897. In October of that year, the first train pulled into La Farge, sealing Seeleyburg's demise. Nearly all the remnants of Seeleyburg are gone.

VICTORY

1854 - 1972

CLASS C/D

APPROXIMATE LOCATION:
5 miles north of DeSota off Highway 35, overlooking the Mississippi River

Considered a "river town," and a scenic one at that, Victory was built into a steep hillside. The area had been witness to significant history. The vicinity had early been a river landing and a rendezvous point for Native Americans and French fur traders. It was also the site of the last battle of the Black Hawk War. The town site was named in memory of that last battle, a "victory."

In 1852, three houses were standing when Victory was platted. One was used as a hotel for a short time. Two general stores, a blacksmith shop, a steam sawmill, and a school called Victory home. The first school was a log building. Desks were placed around the wall. Basswood logs were split in half and served as seats. Parents supplied the heating wood, which students were responsible for splitting and chopping.

Farming was a mainstay of the region and bumper crops were often reported.

A newspaper report stated that in 1970, the general store and post office were still operating and approximately seventy people lived in the village. The post office closed two years later.

The area is still picturesque and blessed with scenic river views.

WEST PRAIRIE

1862 - 1935

CLASS C/D

APPROXIMATE LOCATION:
Highway 82 and County N

The West Prairie Lutheran Church was built in 1874, with significant additions in 1928 and 1958. The church is still serving the surrounding area.

From the earliest days until the waning days, the West Prairie store (Halverson's) was the center of the community. Built in 1894, the store operated until 1997, nearly 104 years. For all of those 104 years, it is said the coffee pot was always on.

The two-story building had two staircases outside on the eastern side of the building. An implement dealer was in a building to the east, sharing it with the blacksmith. At one point, Titan tractors and Overland automobiles were sold in the town.

A post office operated from 1862 until 1935, forty of those years in the store building. In 1965, the West Prairie Cheese Factory, a well driller, and a county maintenance shop were located in the village. Some original buildings still stand.

West Prairie Lutheran Church. (Courtesy of West Prairie Lutheran Church congregation)

Halverson's Store in West Prairie. (Author's Collection)

Walworth County

Early Millard. (Author's Collection)

Left: Millard's taxidermied "dinosaur." (Courtesy of www.wisconsin-osity.com)
Below: Voree's church. (Creative Commons)

MILLARD

1851 – 1906

CLASS C

APPROXIMATE LOCATION:
County A and Millard Road

It's not often you see a dinosaur sticking its head out of the old store building, but in Millard you will. The store now houses a taxidermy shop and while the owner probably doesn't get many dinosaurs to work on, they can do most any other critter.

VOREE

1845 – 1847

CLASS C

APPROXIMATE LOCATION:
2 miles east of Burlington

Strictly a religious settlement, little is known about the village independent of its founder, James Jessie Strang. The community's story is his story, and the two are impossible to separate.

Voree, which Strang translated as "Garden of Peace," was established by Strang in 1845. He was thirty-two years of age at the time. Strang was short, with copper hair and a full red beard. As Wisconsin historian William Stark wrote, Strang didn't attend school much in his childhood but was a voracious reader and obsessed with fame. He was by all accounts charismatic and an eloquent speaker. He passed the New York bar exam at age twenty-three. Married by twenty-three as well, his wife, Mary Perce, was related to Moses Smith, one of the founders of the Mormon Church. Strang and his wife followed her family to Burlington, Wisconsin, where Strang fell under the influence of Mormonism, quickly becoming a convert. Strang, who believed he had been given the authority to found a Mormon settlement, acquired 105 acres just two miles west of Burlington. From the beginning, Voree prospered. Roads were constructed and houses built. Strang offered free room and board to any incoming converts so that they had time to adjust to life as Mormons and had time to build their own homes. The settlement even had a regularly published newspaper, *The Voree Herald*. The editor was, of course, Strang, who by now went by the name "The Prophet."

Strang often had divine visions. After one such vision, Strang told four of his followers that they must go to what he called the Hill of Promise. Strang then instructed them to dig at the base of a large oak tree. They did so and unearthed three metallic plates with hieroglyphics engraved on them. Strang then received a vision that told him the translation of the plates. They said that Strang was the "mighty prophet." He told his followers they must build a Temple of Zion, which would cover two and a half acres of land on an abandoned island in Michigan. Strang visited the island in 1847, and in 1849, he and his followers moved to the island. Strang's latest vision told him that the island was to be his "Kingdom" and he the king, and as such he was coronated in a bizarre ceremony. In June of 1850, Strang would be the first and only human in the history of the United States to be crowned king.

Strang now embraced polygamy, having five wives, four of whom were pregnant. Things continued to get even more bizarre. Strang became a dictator and often subjected his followers to a whipping post. In 1856, Strang was mortally wounded by two of his followers. He returned to Voree to die and is buried in the area. A stone and brass marker marks Old Voree and a stone church building still stands.

A marker at the Voree settlement. (Courtesy of Creative Commons)

Washburn County

Top: A marker at the school in Chittamo. (Courtesy of Wanda Johansen)
Bottom: The old school in Chittamo. (Courtesy of Wanda Johansen)

CHITTAMO

1908 - 1910

CLASS A/C

APPROXIMATE LOCATION:
Frog Creek Road and Wozny Road
(Trunk Highway G, north of Highway 77)

Ojibwe chief Chittamo and his people were not happy that the encroaching white settlement—and especially the railroad—were in the center of his land. But, as Vince Plesko wrote in a 1974 article, the settlers needed the railroad, so the chief and his people were rounded up and shipped to a reservation near Hayward, Wisconsin. Hoping to soothe the chief's anger, the village was named in his honor.

At the peak of Chittamo's existence, it held a general store (the only one in the township), a school (with sixty students), a town hall that had a dance every Saturday night, and a church. Even though the post office lasted just two years, the general store operated until 1951 and the school was used until 1952, when it consolidated with the Minong School District.

Plesko writes that the town of Chittamo died during the World War II years. The war siphoned young men into the armed forces, and after the war they did not return to their hometown. The larger cities had better jobs, better pay, and more opportunities.

As for the chief, folklore legends tell that one day the elderly chief walked back to see the village named for him. Others say he never saw the town.

Today the old school building and a marker note the location.

VEAZIE

1880s

CLASS A

APPROXIMATE LOCATION:
Near Trego along the railroad tracks
and the Namekogan River

The Namekogan River is truly a national (and natural) treasure. Part of the St. Croix Scenic Riverway, the river affords scenic beauty, nature, wildlife, and, as Park Ranger Joan Jacobowski tells it, history.

Jacobowski wrote that Veazie was the first white settlement on the Namekogan. Not a true village in the beginning, the region's remoteness played a significant role in its development.

The remote logging camps of the region had to be supplied. The nearest settlement, Trego, was a good four days' walk away. So in 1871–1872, the region's oldest logging company established Namekogan Farm. The farm grew crops to feed the animals for winter logging operations and provided housing for them in the summer. Its location made it a popular stopover (and the only one) for loggers and businessmen visiting the remote logging camps. The farm store was the only store within a four-day walk.

The farm was a big operation. It housed dozens of draft animals as well as twenty-five lumberjacks working the farm. The complex included two one-hundred-foot barns. Jacobowski wrote that the barns were side by side with a connecting roof, which allowed a hay wagon to pull between the two to fill both haylofts.

In 1880, the town was laid out on both sides of the track. A post office operated just two years. Things didn't go well after the settlement was platted. Log jams on the St. Croix River in 1883 and low water in 1884 caused financial stress to the Walker, Judd and Veazie lumber company. The financial concerns caused the firm to go bankrupt. That caused the closing of the farm. The Veazie House burned in 1898, and the dam washed out in 1902. Veazie was, for all accounts, done as well.

Decades later, in 1955, an area farmer cleared the land removing most traces of the former village.

Jacobowski writes that a few visible remains can be found. She tells that about one and a half miles from Earl Landing on the river, around the bend, is a flat-topped hill that marks the site. The old rail tracks, a few telegraph poles in the woods, and the cleared land mark the site as well. Watch for trains, as the Spooner Railroad uses the tracks on its scenic jaunts along the Namekogan. Learn more about the train rides at www.spoonertrainride.com, There are summer rides, dinner rides, fall color rides, and even a Christmas holiday ride.

Waupaca County

Baldwin Mill's school. (Author's Collection)

BALDWIN'S MILL

1875 - 1900

CLASS C

APPROXIMATE LOCATION:
Baldwin's Road and Big Lake Road

Asa and Horace, the Baldwin brothers, knew the location was the right place to build their sawmill. Constructing a dam on the Little Wolf River, they harnessed enough water power for their venture. As usually was the case in early settlements, a small community grew up around the mill.

In 1855, a half-acre of land was purchased and a school was built. The school year had two terms of three months each, one beginning in May, the other starting in December. A new school building was constructed in 1882. The old building was moved to the rear of the new building, where it was used as a woodshed. An especially large enrollment in 1908 required the school be remodeled, creating two rooms and becoming a state-graded school. In the 1920s, enrollment dwindled and the school was back to just one room. The school closed in 1965, upon consolidation with the Weyauwega-Fremont School District. The building was later used for social events.

The late 1890s saw a store, a creamery/cheese factory, a sawmill, a post office, and several homes as part of the settlement. The cheese factory operated until the 1950s. After sitting vacant for a time, the structure was purchased by the Waupaca County Highway Department. In deteriorating condition, the county burned it down in 1987.

A Lutheran church began in 1884. Church services were sporadic in the early years. The pastor had to travel great distances and would visit Baldwin's Mill about every three weeks. When a new church was constructed in 1906, a resident pastor was appointed.

A post office operated for twenty-five years, from 1875 until 1900. Records tell that the mail was delivered by a team of horses pulling a mini post office, complete with rows of pigeonhole boxes along the inside.

White Lake on the southern edge of the village was Waupaca County's largest lake and a popular picnic spot. Rising water levels in 1866 necessitated the digging of ditches. In 1881, water levels were too low, and at that point, a low-water level guide was established. The area, then and now, is a dairy farming region.

BUCKBEE

1884 - 1898

CLASS A

APPROXIMATE LOCATION:
Southeast of Highway 45 near Buckbee Road

Home to not only one but two sawmills, Buckbee was also home to a saloon/dance hall, two boarding houses, a meat market, a general store, a blacksmith shop, a railroad depot, a post office, a school, and a Methodist church, among others. The two sawmills had different purposes. One made lumber, the other broom handles. Over one thousand handles were made in one day. The National Furnace Company operated nine kilns in the area.

Dry conditions in early May of 1893 sparked a tragic forest fire. Started in a nearby swamp, high winds fanned the flames. Reaching first a pile of sawdust and then a stack of two hundred cords of wood, the flames intensified. People ran for cover and for their lives. Historians report that if not for the Pigeon River running through the center of town, the entire settlement would have gone up in flames. After all was said and done, twenty-four buildings were destroyed and ten families were homeless.

That same day, a train wreck occurred. The train was carrying railroad officials and even though they could see the destruction of Buckbee, they chose to continue on. They were also warned that the hot rails could be dangerous, but did not heed the warning. After all, it was a Saturday and they wanted to get home to Milwaukee by nightfall. Once the train hit the hot rails, they expanded, dumping the cars into a ditch. The passengers and crew had to walk a mile to a nearby farm.

By 1903, the broom factory was nearing its demise. The owner moved to Michigan, where he purchased all new machinery, and set up shop there.

Three hundred people once called Buckbee home. After the 1893 fire, the village quickly declined. There was no motivation to rebuild. The closure of the post office marked the end of Buckbee. A few buildings remained in the 1990s.

CANARY

1900 - 1902

CLASS A

APPROXIMATE LOCATION:
North of present Highway 22, one mile east of County O

Two small churches were in the community, each with its own cemetery. The Danish church was moved and the marble church was converted to a home. The post office was in existence only two years. The former post office building was an unused barn in the 1990s.

CARMEL

1894 - 1902

CLASS C

APPROXIMATE LOCATION:
Area of County T and St. Patrick's Catholic Church

Religion and faith were important to the Carmel-area settlers. In 1860, land was donated for a church. Other families donated the building materials. Things were progressing and construction was going well with the forty-by-sixty-foot church until 1861, the Civil War.

Education was also important to the community. An academy was built on an acre-sized site. The academy included two large classrooms, dormitories, and living quarters for three Catholic sisters. Tuition was fifty cents per child, per month, and it was charged to cover expenses. Since there were no other schools in the immediate vicinity, children of all denominations attended the academy. Teachers were supplied by the St. Agnes of Fond du Lac order. With decreasing enrollment, the academy closed in 1890. A nearby public school was then constructed, and it sat a quarter mile from today's church.

The academy building was rented out as a home, with one room converted to a store and post office. The settlement became known as Carmel. The post office closed in the early 1900s, when the postmaster resigned. The building was demolished in 1909.

The next year, land was donated for a new church and a two-story rectory. In 1933, the church burned to the ground. Area neighbors began hauling stones from their farm fields to be used in the construction of a new church building. The first Mass in the new fieldstone building was in 1934. That same year, the rectory burned to the ground, so a fieldstone rectory was constructed adjacent to the church.

The stone church, parish hall, rectory, and the school (which now serves as the town hall) were all that remained in the 1990s.

EVANSWOOD

1854 - 1886

CLASS A/D

APPROXIMATE LOCATION:
South of Weyauwega on Highway 10

Shoppers love today's village of Evanswood. Though no longer a true village, the eclectic shops at Evanswood attract shoppers from far and wide. With shop names such as the Brass Butterfly, Lucky's, Sweet Pickle Gramma's, and Wild Grape Wine Shop, the stores offer a bit of everything and then some.

In 1982, the Brass Butterfly stood solo on the old town site. When Highway 10 was improved and widened, it took the land

St. Patrick's of Lebanon Church in Carmel. (Courtesy of St. Patrick's of Lebanon Church, www.newdublin.com)

Evanswood today. (Courtesy of www.wisconsinosity.com)

Top: Shops in Evanswood. (Courtesy of www.wisconsinosity.com)
Bottom: The Brass Butterfly. (Courtesy of the Brass Butterfly)

upon which the original store stood. Undeterred, the shop moved west and added other buildings, making Evanswood home to a unique shopping experience not to be missed.

Back in its day, Evanswood included a basket factory, a cheese factory, a brickyard, and a stagecoach way station. A Methodist church was later moved to Weyauwega and was converted to a home. The school operated until consolidation with Fremont. The building was used as an extra classroom until an addition to Weyauwega Elementary School could be completed. The school building was later sold and remodeled into a garage. In later years, the cheese factory became a tavern for a time.

GILL'S LANDING

1859 – 1925

CLASS A/G

APPROXIMATE LOCATION:
4 miles east of Waupaca on County F

Primarily a river settlement, Gill's Landing was named for John Gill. Gill built a small structure and landing for steamboats to dock, and to load and unload passengers and freight. In 1853, Gill and other businessmen paid for a plank road to be built to points leading to Wausau, Plover, and Stevens Point. A stage operated in 1854. With the coming of the Wisconsin Central Railroad through the region, any hope of the plank road becoming a reality fell through.

The property was later deeded to Waupaca County with the stipulation that the land be used for the general public's recreational purposes. It is now a park (Decker Memorial Park). The county began development plans for an aquatic park in the 1980s.

Left, below: A river scene in Gill's Landing. (Author's Collection)
Below: Hannah's Hotel in Gill's Landing. (Author's Collection))

GRANITE CITY

1876 - 1903

CLASS A

APPROXIMATE LOCATION:
Southeast corner of the town of Wyoming,
just northeast of today's Big Falls

For decades after the fading away of Granite City, the old derrick stood rusting away. If you looked close enough you could still see the village layout, ten blocks wide by ten blocks long.

Originally based on a timber economy, the nearby granite quarry was developing. Granite would dictate the growth and the demise of Granite City. By 1857, Granite City was a thriving settlement. A large log boarding house was built to house the workers. It is said that the likes of these boarding houses were never seen in Wisconsin backwoods before. Each room had its own matching water pitcher, washbasin, and hurricane lamp. Other necessary establishments, such as a grocery store, a saloon, and a company office were also part of the community.

With time, good, solid granite began to run out. Many of the blocks had seams running through them, which caused breakage and the corners to chip off. The dwindling granite supply coupled with a tragic incident sealed Granite City's fate. A foreman was shot and killed. The murderer was caught, convicted, and sentenced to prison. Amidst the turmoil, workers drifted away and Granite City was reclaimed by nature.

GRANITE QUARRY

1886 - 1920s

CLASS A

APPROXIMATE LOCATION:
5 miles north of Waupaca

It is possible to find Waupaca Granite quarried from Granite Quarry all over the United States. It's been used in some impressive places, including in a monument to Wisconsin soldiers at Orchard Knob, Chickamauga, Tennessee; the gateway to the Lakewood Cemetery in Minneapolis,

Minnesota; and the capitol building in Madison, Wisconsin, has 276 pieces of Waupaca Granite in its interior decorations.

Strictly a company town, most of the buildings were constructed for the use of employees and the quarry company. At one point, over one hundred workers were employed at the quarry. Structures included machinery buildings, a blacksmith shop, a two-story office building, an ice house, a store (later remodeled into a home), and a boarding house.

The boarding house had a large kitchen and dining room with the rest of the house being all bedrooms. Opened in 1886, the quarry shut down in the 1920s.

LIND CENTER

1885 - 1902

CLASS A/C

APPROXIMATE LOCATION:
5½ miles south/southeast of Waupaca on County A

Aptly named, Lind Center was located at the geographical center of the town of Lind. Lind Center also has the distinction of being the first town to be organized in Waupaca County.

A post office was established in 1850. The community was named Lind because the postmaster was an admirer of Swedish singer Jenny Lind. A Methodist church, the settlement's first church, was built in 1865. It was later torn down and the sale proceeds were donated to the hospital being built in Waupaca.

Other merchants included a photographer's shop, a couple of general stores, a creamery built of fieldstone, and a blacksmith shop with the top floor being used for meetings, rollerskating and dances. It later housed a garage and repair shop.

The Lind Center school, now the town hall. (Courtesy of Reunhasie)

Built of logs, the first school was replaced by a two-room building. That structure burned in 1941, and was replaced by a two-classroom brick building. After consolidation in 1964, the school became the Lind Town Hall.

Elwyn West, a former World War I pilot and known as "the Pioneer Aviator of the Fox Valley," retired in Lind Center. For many years he had a game preserve that included buffalo, elk, and llamas.

When the railroad bypassed Lind Center, the village declined. In 1991, the former post office/house was still standing. The original owner's great-great-granddaughter still lived in the building.

LITTLE WOLF

1853 - 1903

CLASS C

APPROXIMATE LOCATION:
Highway B & BB

Primarily a lumber town, Little Wolf had a sawmill in the 1850s. By 1857, a two-revolving-stone flour and grist mill stood next to the sawmill. A nearby barrel factory supplied the mill with all the barrels it needed. Fire destroyed the flour/grist mill in 1916.

A school was built in 1857. Two terms of classes were held. The fall term ran from October to December and the spring term ran from May to July.

Mail was carried by foot on a route that ran from Green Bay to Plover.

A county poor farm was built in 1874. In the days before welfare and social programs, poor farms were instituted. After its use as a poor farm, the majestic building was later used as a rest home, then the New Life Retreat Center. Most recently, the farm was sold to a non-profit group and serves as an artistic center. Art exhibits, programming, artists' programs, and more are hosted at the building. Learn more at www.poorfarm-experiment.org.

Obtaining rail service was a big boon to a community and could mean the life or death of a village. Railroad officials told Little Wolf residents that if two thousand dollars could be raised, the new line would route through their community. Area businesses advanced one thousand dollars, but residents were unable to raise the remaining one thousand dollars. The railroad routed through Manawa instead. The loss of the railroad was the death knell for the village.

MARBLE

1863 - 1901

CLASS A/C

APPROXIMATE LOCATION:
12 miles southwest of Clintonville

To say the first Marble School was crude would be an understatement. The log school was built in 1890, when the settlement's population reached six families. The floor was dirt, the windows and doorways open, and student seats were logs split in half. The area's first church services were also held in the school.

Top: Little Wolf's school. (Author's Collection)
Bottom: Waupaca Poor Farm, now the New Life Retreat Center. (Courtesy of Michelle Grabner, www.poorfarmexperiment.org)

291

The first mail route was established in 1862 and was thirty miles long. Oftentimes the mail carrier, on foot, could not complete the route in one day. When darkness fell, he overnighted in houses along the route. An official post office was established in 1863 and operated until 1901.

Most of Marble was built between 1857 and 1900. For some reason, things went downhill for the settlement after the turn of the century. Many buildings were moved to new locations, burned, or torn down.

One building did remain and operated until the 1950s. It was later remodeled into a tavern, and in later years it was the only remaining remnant of Marble. It was known as the Triple D Supper Club, and closed in the 1990s.

MUKWA

1850 – 1860

CLASS A

APPROXIMATE LOCATION:
Town of Mukwa

Settlers knew that a county seat designation could not be awarded unless the village was surveyed and platted. So that was the first priority in establishing Mukwa. Originally a post office/tavern/store combo was located at the crossing of the Wolf River at the crossing of the Little Wolf River. Mukwa declared its intentions to pursue county seat designation, which it garnered for a short time. With the designation, the community grew both in population and in number of

The Mukwa Motel (area residents have a sense of humor). (Courtesy of www.wisconsinosity.com)

Mukwa shuttle bus. (Courtesy of www.wisconsinosity.com)

businesses established, which included a hotel, a large warehouse, a sawmill, and several homes.

In 1856, a ferry across the Wolf River was established. Fees were on a sliding scale and ranged from one cent for people on foot to ten cents for a single horse and vehicle, up to twenty cents for a team of horses or oxen.

A new community was established just a short distance from Mukwa—New London. Closer to the forests and the head of navigation for larger steamboats, New London attracted Mukwa business. Adding a county seat battle to the mix (between Mukwa, Waupaca, and for a time Manawa and Weyauwega), which Waupaca won, put Mukwa in decline. It is said that a mass exodus from Mukwa to Waupaca occurred. Building after building moved to Waupaca or were simply abandoned. Former village lots became farmland, so much so that in 1871, a vote passed to vacate Mukwa. Mukwa the village was no more.

NICHOLSON

1890 – 1902

CLASS A/C

APPROXIMATE LOCATION:
Near intersection of Highway 22 and County T

Early missionaries had visited the area as early as 1854. It took many years for a settlement to develop. The community included a general store (1894 to 1927), a garage, two sawmills (one operated until 1940), and a cheese factory (operated until 1970), and is on the National Register

Nicholson's Kasper, Philip H. Cheese Factory. (Courtesy of the National Register of Historic Places, Bear Creek, Waupaca, Wisconsin, #76000081)

of Historic Places. The factory, also known as Kasper, Philip H. Cheese Factory was added to the National Register of Historic Places in 1976. An early cheesemaker won nearly every competition he entered, national or international.

Early mail was carried by foot, later by horseback. When RFD routes were instituted, each resident had a box, which was kept padlocked. The mail carrier had a different key for each box. Needless to say, that system didn't last long, as it was too difficult to carry around a string of keys, especially in the cold weather.

NORSKE

1900 – 1907

CLASS A/C

APPROXIMATE LOCATION:
County P

Norske's carpenter was known for his "Kubblestols." Just what is a Kubblestol, you ask? So did I. Turns out Kubblestols are Scandinavian (Norwegian) chairs carved out of wooden stumps. There are often "flat relief" etchings and engravings on the stools. Designs range from ordinary

to exquisite, depending on the skill of the carver. They can often be works of art, each a masterpiece. In fact, the Vesterheim Museum in Decorah, Iowa, has a display of Kubblestols. A true master is today's Phillip Odden of Norke Wood Works in Baronette, Wisconsin. You can learn more and even purchase carved items at www.norskewoodworks.com.

The village of Norske was a former logging camp and included a blacksmith shop, a hotel, a warehouse, a post office, and a store. Under a succession of owners, the store lasted until the 1950s.

Examples of Kubblestols. (Courtesy of Phillip Odden, Norske Wood Works)

NORTHLAND

1890 - 1938

CLASS C

APPROXIMATE LOCATION:
Highway 49 near Lund Road

Ole Wrolstad wanted to get into the logging business, so he built a sawmill and did just that. Later, Ole's son John operated the mill, but by the 1920s, the vast timber resources were nearly depleted, so the mill was closed down and dismantled. Highway 49 crosses the old mill site.

After the sawmill closed, a feed mill was built. The mills even generated enough electricity to power four homes, the store, the church, and a couple of street lamps.

Northland, named simply because it was to the north of nearby Iola and Scandinavia, had a post office from 1890 to 1938. A creamery was established in 1902 and was later a cheese factory. Soon Northland included a hardware store, a blacksmith shop, a grocery store, and a general store. One store sold farm machinery and later Ford automobiles. Insurance policies were written by the Modern Woodmen of America. The store closed in 1978.

A Norwegian Lutheran Church was established in 1907. For many years, services were conducted in the Norwegian language.

Northland was home to many skilled residents. John Barikimo was a skilled carpenter and carved beautiful items, including the church altar.

John Gill was a community dentist for over twenty years. He was especially skilled at making dentures and had customers from as far away as Chicago. Sadly, Gill never had a state license. An Iola dentist turned him in, and Gill was sentenced to jail. Gill died in 1936, some say from a broken heart.

A school operated from 1887 until 1946, at which time it merged with Iola. Northland's baseball team, which played from 1912 to 1918, was said to be exceptional.

Said "to never forget a face," an early resident, Harold Bergstein, was purported to have a photographic memory. Supposedly he memorized 40,000 photos, which he could identify by seeing only a tiny portion of the facial image. Ripley's Believe it or Not traveled to Northland to interview Harold.

The last remnant of Northland, the store, was torn down in 1985.

NORTHPORT

1859 - 1911

CLASS D

APPROXIMATE LOCATION:
Highway 54 and near Ferry and Broadway Street

Known by a variety of names, including New Boston, when the village was platted in 1855 the name was officially Northport. At that time the village was the northernmost port of navigation on the Wolf River.

The region was dense woods and land had to be cleared before farming could commence. While clearing the land was hard work, the timber was valuable, and the deep woods provided wildlife to supplement food stocks.

A store was established in 1859. In its earliest days, daily receipts totaled three to four dollars a day. Once lumbering activity began, sales were six hundred dollars per day. The stave factory and steam-powered sawmill employed over one hundred men. Workers worked from 7:00 A.M. until 6:00 P.M. for three dollars per day.

An early photo of Northport's Methodist church. (Author's Collection)

The timber activity required a large lumber warehouse and a dock on the river, as much of the product was shipped to Oshkosh and beyond. In 1881, six million board feet of lumber were made into wheels, frames for wagons, harvesters, reapers, cultivators, and more.

Waupaca County's first Catholic church, in fact the first Catholic church north of Oshkosh, was built in 1857. Struck by lightning in 1861, it burned to the ground but was rebuilt in 1866 (St. Bridget's). A 1877 cyclone blew off the steeple and in 1922, it was struck by lightning and burned to the ground. It was rebuilt in Royalton.

A Methodist church was built in 1864, and soon had two hundred members. By 1979, the remaining sixteen members closed its doors. The building was later torn down. The school closed in 1966.

Bustling in 1890, Northport had a population of 350 whites and 400 Native Americans. It had a general store, two saloons, two blacksmiths, a sawmill, a lumber yard, a planing mill, two churches, and a hotel.

Northport continued along, slowly dwindling away. Much business was lost to the new settlement along the railroad, New London. In recent years, three taverns, a garage, and a few small businesses and homes were in the village.

NOWELL

1889 - 1902

CLASS A

APPROXIMATE LOCATION:
4½ miles southwest of Bear Creek, County N and County T

Irish settlers first arrived in the Nowell area in 1857, yet it would be the late 1800s before the village developed. A sawmill and stave factory were among the first businesses up and running. Both would later be destroyed by fire.

One of the first orders of business was the establishment and construction of a school. The first classes were held in a building located on the Gorman farm. But then, the only students were Gorman children, so it made things easier. A designated frame building was constructed in 1870, at a cost of five hundred dollars. All frame school buildings were condemned by the state in 1917, so a brick building was constructed. Built in 1920, it was a two-room structure. With consolidation in 1969, students attended school in Manawa and the school closed. It was repurposed as a home and later was totally destroyed by fire.

Looking north up Main Street from the bridge in Northport (Author's Collection)

A post office was established in 1889 or 1890 and first operated out of a home. Later, it was moved to the store building. The top story of the store housed a dance hall. At one time a dance platform was erected at the edge of the woods. Area men congregated at the store for years, until the store closed in 1953. By 1991, all traces of Nowell had faded with time.

OSTRANDER

1882 - 1898

CLASS A

APPROXIMATE LOCATION:
5 miles west of New London

The year 1900 seems to mark the demise of Ostrander. In May of 1900, the New London newspaper carried a story describing the moving and razing of the village of Ostrander. Many buildings were moved to New London.

Records tell that New London held fifty to sixty homes, a general store, a blacksmith, a saloon, a post office, a hotel, and three boarding houses. Two sawmills operated during the settlement's earliest days. The two stood across the river from each other (just south of today's Ostrander Bridge). The one on the east side of the river produced common building materials such as lumber, shingles, and laths. The mill on the west side of the river produced wheel hubs and spokes. The west mill later converted to the manufacture of chairs and was then named the Wisconsin Manufacturing Company. With financial difficulties and a succession of owners, the west mill was sold to the Wausau Furniture Company. Most of the manufacturing machinery was later moved to Wausau.

By 1991, the only evidence remaining of Ostrander were the cemetery and some depressions in the ground.

PARFREYVILLE

1894 - 1897

CLASS C/D

APPROXIMATE LOCATION:
4 miles southwest of Waupaca

Established in the 1850s, Parfreyville had a grist mill, several blacksmith shops, a school, and a church that is still active today, the Parfreyville United Methodist Church. The church has long been a cornerstone of the community. First organized in 1856, the present building was constructed in 1905. Since that time the building has had extensive renovations. In 1995, a second-story addition was completed and in 1997, the old church hall was sold.

Below, left: Former Parfreyville church hall. (Courtesy of "Royalbroil," Wikimedia Commons, http://commons.wikimedia.org/w/index.php?curid=14030843)
Below: Parfreyville United Methodist Church. (Courtesy of Parfreyville United Methodist Church)

PETERSVILLE (PETERSONVILLE, SURAT)

1882 – 1896

CLASS A

APPROXIMATE LOCATION:
3½ miles northwest of Iola on Highway 49 and County M

When the post office was established in 1882, the settlement was known as Petersville. In 1891, it was renamed Surat. The post office was discontinued in 1896. Petersville was a stopping place for travelers. The store was still standing in the late 1990s.

REAMS (REAMER)

1893 – 1904

CLASS A

APPROXIMATE LOCATION:
Town of Harrison

Box elder trees abounded in the area. The seeds for those trees were brought by an early settler.

Reams Store was exactly what one envisions when imagining a country store: kindly owners, penny candy treats for the kids, a barrel of peanuts by the door with a sleepy cat on top.

When the post office closed in 1904, so did the store.

In later years, the community became known as Newman's Corner and Schmidt's Corner, which had a garage, a tavern, and Schmidt's Snack Bar.

Early teachers rode horses to school.

SHERIDAN (SHERIDAN MILLS, COBBTOWN)

1865 – 1974

CLASS C/D

APPROXIMATE LOCATION:
5 miles west of Waupaca on U.S. Highway 10

Called Cobbtown, the settlement was first known as Sheridan Mills. When the post office was established, it was called Sheridan. The village answered to all. That post office was extremely long-lived, lasting over one hundred years.

Begun as many settlements were, located next to a water-powered mill, Cobbtown also had a flour mill, which for years ground wheat, rye, buckwheat, corn, oats, and cornmeal. Corn cobs piled up like haystacks right to the eaves, thus the name "Cobbtown." An early brand was Star and Crescent. Wisconsin Power and Light purchased the mill in 1925, and seven years later it was destroyed by fire.

A millinery shop was across from the mill. The owner was also the postmistress and she ran the post office from her store. RFD routes were instituted in 1906. Later, the millinery shop became a grocery store. A parcel of land near the store was donated for the construction of the Sherman Co-op Cheese Factory. The cheese factory operated under many owners, closing in 1962.

Sheridan's little red schoolhouse was the first school in the town of Farmington. The cracks in the school walls were so large it was said you could see outside through them. During very cold weather, students wore overshoes, coats, and mittens all day. The school also served as a church. A frame building later replaced the little red schoolhouse and later the frame building was replaced by a brick building. The school closed in 1962 and was converted into a private home.

The millinery shop was later destroyed by fire. The cheese factory was demolished in the 1960s. Today a carnival, the Tip Top Rides and Attractions, has its home base in the area.

Above: A house in Sheridan, Wisconsin. (Author's Collection)
Left: A train wreck in Sheridan. (Author's Collection)

Winnebago County

A postcard from Mikesville featuring an early street scene in the town. (Author's Collection)

DELHI

1850 - 1893

CLASS A

APPROXIMATE LOCATION:
County E between Omro and Eureka

A trading post was established in 1836. Twelve years later, Luke LaBorde purchased the post and moved it across the river. The Menomonee Indians controlled the west side of the river and moving the post across the river allowed trade with the white population. He called the new site LaBorde's Landing. The settlers petitioned for a post office in 1850. The U.S. Postal Service was swamped with names with "Landing" in them so they did not allow any new "Landing" communities. So Delhi was chosen, for reasons unknown. The next year Delhi was platted with thirteen streets and designated lots. The community included a twenty-two-room hotel (the American House), a school, three stores, many houses, and a population of 150.

During the 1850s, Delhi was known for its crops of hops, used in beer. The hops would be shipped by boat to Oshkosh breweries and beyond. Rather high prices were paid for hops in the beginning, so many farmers converted their farmland to producing more of the crop. However, the market became glutted and the price dropped. During harvest time, one report tells that the community was flooded with people, so many that folks staying in the American House had to sleep in the attic and in the halls.

Delhi also had a ferry that operated until a floating bridge was installed. However, the nearby communities of Omro and Eureka were a source of competition for Delhi. When both communities built sturdy bridges, Delhi's floating bridge was insufficient. The railroads arrival in Omro finished Delhi.

Today, the old cemetery, a few homes, and a road named for the village are all that remain.

KORO

1850 - 1903

CLASS A

APPROXIMATE LOCATION:
County E and Highway 91

K oro grew up in the heart of the farming community. A multitude of activities and events were hosted in the settlement, including an area-wide Fourth of July celebration, Christmas programs, concerts by the Koro band, and competitions hosted by the Koro Calf Club. The community business district included a post office, a blacksmith shop, the Koro Evangelical Church, a school, and a creamery. The church building was sold in 1932. Though the creamery closed, the building stands.

MIKESVILLE

1896 - 1901

CLASS A

APPROXIMATE LOCATION:
County T and Oakridge Road

M ikesville was originally known as Thompson Corners, named for the area's first settlers, the Thompson Brothers. A busy trade center for a short time, Mikesville had a blacksmith shop, a church, a school, a cheese factory, a general store, and a saloon.

When the petition for a post office was submitted, it turned out there were already four Thompson Corners in Wisconsin. The postal service notified the community they had to have a new name. Since the postmaster's first name was Michael, it was decided to name the new post office Mikesville as a way to thank him for his service.

When the hoped-for railroad never materialized, the town faded away.

ZOAR (BOOM)

1871 - 1883

CLASS A

APPROXIMATE LOCATION:
Town of Wolf River

As the name implies, Zoar, or Boom, as it was often referred to, existed because of and only as long as the logging boom lasted. The Wolf River Boom Company gathered logs coming down the river from the northern logging camps, lashed them together, and floated them down to such locations as Oshkosh, Neenah, and Menasha.

Housing was needed for the workers, so the company established Zoar/Boom on the river's shoreline. Estimates tell that, at its peak, the population was over 200. With the decline of the lumber supply, workers abandoned the site.

Today there are few remains in the area, other than a few homes and the Boom Bay Bar and Grill. The area is also a recreational destination.

OTHER WISCONSIN LOST TOWNS

Finding lost towns is difficult at best and requires the help and assistance of many people. Listed below are lost towns on which I could find little to no information. If you have any information on any of the lost towns featured in the book, or the following list of towns, or any others we missed, please contact me at www.rhondafochs.weebly.com or at www.facebook.com/MinnesotasLostTowns.

BROWN COUNTY
Preble: 1859 – 1964, consolidated with Green Bay.

BUFFALO COUNTY
Anchorage: 1868 – 1907.
Bohri: 1890 – 1901.
Savoy: No postal records.
Springdale: No postal records.

BURNETT COUNTY
Ekdall: 1891 – 1917, Swedish for "oak gale" or "oak slope."

CALUMENT COUNTY
Gravesville: 1860 – 1904, annexed by Chilton in the late twentieth century.
Harrison: No postal records.

CHIPPEWA COUNTY
Nothing found at this time.

DUNN COUNTY
Fall City: 1858 – 1900.

EAU CLAIRE COUNTY
Oak Grove: No postal records.
Nelsonville: No postal records.

GREEN COUNTY
Dayton: 1854 – 1918, a store in business until the 1950s.
Dutch Hollow: No postal records.
Exeter: 1843 – 1901, the school stood until the 1950s.

Moscow: No postal records.
Schultz: 1889 – 1905.

GREEN LAKE COUNTY
Nothing found at this time.

IRON COUNTY
Carson: No postal records.
Curry: 1890 – 1903.
De Fer: 1912 – 1929.
Fouche: No postal records.
Germania: No postal records.
Hamilton: No postal records.
House: No postal records.
Hoyt: No postal records.
Iron Center: No postal records.
Ironton: No postal records.
Magnetic Center: No postal records.
Meadville: No postal records.
Moore: 1901 – 1925.
Orva: No postal records.
Osborne: No postal records.
Pine Lake: No postal records.
Plummer: 1888 – 1910.
Potato Junction: No postal records.
River Branch: No postal records.
Sandrock: 1904 – 1914.
Tyler Forks: No postal records.

KENOSHA COUNTY
Ranney: 1885 – 1907, the last house was demolished in 2006, nothing remains of the former rail town.

KEWAUNEE COUNTY
Foscoro: 1871 – 1902.
Rosiere: 1871 – 1904.
Rostok: 1899 – 1904.
Tonet: 1887 – 1904, petitioned as Jonet, the postal service misread the J for a T.

LANGLADE COUNTY
Bavaria: 1905 – 1921.
Bryant/Hoxie: No postal records.
Irwin: 1915 – 1922.
Koepenick: No postal records.
Mayking: 1894 – 1902.
Post Lake: 1884 –– 1913.

LINCOLN COUNTY
Nothing found at this time.

MARATHON COUNTY
Corinth: 1895 – 1934, along the rail line from Athens to Abbotsford, it had a number of businesses and disappeared when logging was done in the 1920s.
Gad: Lumber mill.
Little Rose: area still known as Little Rose, near Highway 153 and County E. Had a store and tavern that later burned down.
Mannville: 1875 – 1892, along the Wisconsin Central Railroad line between Marshfield and Spencer.
McMillan: 1818 – 1919, the only residents were the mill owners and employees—once a population of 200, which declined after mill closed in 1911. The population left and the buildings were sold and moved to other locations.
Moon: 1891 – 1908, Highway O and Moon Road. It had a Seventh Day Adventist Church in 1899 and a sawmill 1899, and a local land agent and woodsman called "Man in the Moon."
Mylrea: 1900 – 1905.
Naugart: 1866 – 1940, there was a long-lasting post office, but little else known.
Rib Falls: 1908 – 1911.
Shantytown: 1888 – 1909.
Staadt: 1894 – 1914.
Taegesville: 1891 – 1901, known for Schmidt's Ballroom, which dates back to the 1930s and is all that is left of the once-thriving village at Highway A and Highway 153.
Wuertsburg: 1887 – 1904, had a post office, saloon, grocery store/ice cream parlor, and St. John's Catholic Church.

MARQUETTE COUNTY
Nothing found at this time.

MENOMONIE COUNTY
Perote: No postal records, said to be 5 miles south/southwest of White Lake.

ONEIDA COUNTY
Manson: 1923 – 1924.

OUTAGAMIE COUNTY
Grand Chute: No postal records, now part of Appleton.
Lawesburg: No postal records, now part of Appleton.
Lime Rock: 1865 – 1878.
Wakefield: 1852 – 1879.

PIERCE COUNTY
Olivet: 1870 – 1907, South of Spring Valley, the town had a number of businesses, a large school, and a church, though only houses remain.
Waverly: 1878 – 1904, Highway 72 and CC, south of Spring Valley, today only a few homes remain.

PORTAGE COUNTY
Lake Emily: 1858 – 1860.

RACINE COUNTY
Raymond Center: 1846 – 1902, post office and early trading point.

RICHLAND COUNTY
Balmoral: 1889 – 1902.
Excelsior: 1858 – 1958, mill town.
Henrietta: 1857 – 1904, halfway between Hub City and Yuba City on Wisconsin 80.
Mill Creek: 1857 – 1901, had two blacksmiths, general store, a grist mill, and two churches.
Richland City: 1850 – 1904, swept away by Wisconsin River.

TAYLOR COUNTY
Nothing found at this time.

VILAS COUNTY
Nothing found at this time.

WASHINGTON COUNTY
Nothing found at this time.

WAUKESHA COUNTY
Calhoun: 1882 – 1918.
Dodget's Corners: 1855 – 1903.
DeNoon: 1851 – 1903, In 1853, the town had a population of 100. Cholera epidemic in 1850s.

WAUSHARA COUNTY

Rodney: 1891 – 1906.

Sacramento: 1850 – 1851, 2 miles east of Berlin, a steamboat
port on the Fox River, it had a hotel and a saloon.

WINNEBAGO COUNTY

Perrysburg: No postal records.

Snells: 1876 – 1886.

WOOD COUNTY

Saratoga: 1855 – 1915, located on Highway 13 and settled by
the Irish, the community had two stores, a boarding house,
a blacksmith, a dam and sawmill, and approximately twenty
home.

BIBLIOGRAPHY

Abitz, Jerry. "A Tale of Two Places." Kewaunee County Historical Notes. October 2012.

Acheson, Dean. "Stovewood Stacks Made Walls for the Ages." *Our Wisconsin*. June/July 2016

Adams County Historical Society. "Adams County and the Grand Army of the Republic: County Civil War veterans formed two Successful GAR posts." *The Quatrefoil*. Spring 2003.

—— "They Called the New Village Cascade: What is now White Creek was once the most promising village in the county." *The Quatrefoil*. Fall 2005.

—— "The Cottons Called It 'Roche a Cri' but 'Cottonville' Was the Name That Stuck: The promising 1850s Cottonville community lost its promise but kept the name." *The Quatrefoil*. Summer 2006.

—— "New Rome," unpublished manuscript. N.d.

—— "Notes from Town of Leola Meeting." September 12, 2007.

—— "The Neibull Schoolhouse." Winter 2002.

American History Class of DeSoto Union Free High School. "Episodes in the History of Bloomingdale." January 6, 1958.

Aztalan Historical Society. "Ancient and Pioneer Aztalan." www.orgsites.com/wi/aztalan.

Bant, Joyce. "Knox Mills." Phone. Emails, Februrary 2016.

—— "Culture and Continuity of Knox Mills, Wisconsin, 1864–1931." 1985.

Bednar-Clemens, Jodie. Phone. "Manitowish." December 30, 2015.

Bednar-Young, Joyce. Phone. "Manitowish." February 24, 2016.

—— Phone. "Manitowish." May 26, 2016

Belleau, Dawn Jax. "New Life for Old Cemetery." *Sheboygan Press*. December 3, 1995.

"Benson's Corners made a name for itself." *Stevens Point Journal*. May 19, 1992.

Bernierm, Brian. "Historic Sheboygan County Tavern Serves Delicious Food." *Sheboygan Press*. July 8, 2015.

Bie, Michael. *It Happened in Wisconsin*. Guilford. 2007.

Bird, Miriam. *A History of Granville Township*. 1996.

Birmingham, Robert A. & Goldstein, Lynne G. *Aztalan: Mysteries of an Ancient Indian Town*. Madison. 2005.

Bohren, Lucille, G. "Pokerville, the Vanished Village, Is Dane County's Earliest Town." *The Wisconsin State Journal*. December 6, 1925.

Bothwell, Ian. Email. "Holliday Mills."

Brevvaxling, Royal. "Kaszube's Park marks an interesting past." www.onwisconsin.com. November 23, 2011.

Brown, Betty W. "Brookville was Pioneer Settlement." *Vernon County Censor*. June 23, 1955.

Buege, Bob. *Pine Bluff: A Crossroads in Wisconsin*. Milwaukee. 2004.

Bunde, Judge Herbert A. *Shanagolden, a Personal Account*.

Burke, E.C. *I Lived at Peshtigo Harbor*. Peshtigo. 1971.

Burnett County Homemakers Club. *Pioneer Tales of Burnett County*. Danbury. 2002.

Carter, Jim. Ed. *Historic Leadmine School and Village*. Monroe. 200?

Carter, Margaret S. *New Diggings on the Fever: 1824–1860*. Benton. 1959.

Centennial Committee of the County of Shawano. *The Shawano Story: 100 Years of History 1874–1974*. Shawano. 1974.

Chappelle, Ethel Elliot. *A Pioneer History of Washburn, Sawyer, Barron and Rusk Counties*. Rice Lake, 1990.

—— "Around the Four Corners."

Clark County Historical Internet Library. www.wiclarkcounty.org.

Clark, Myrtle (Aldrich). *Leola: Adams County, Wisconsin*. 1948.

Columbia County Historical Society. *Columbia County History*. Dallas.

Curtiss-Wedge, Franklin. *Biographical History of Clark County, Wisconsin*. Chicago. 1918.

"The Day They Burned Esofea Down." *Westby Times*. June 1992.

Degner, Martha. "Cooksville Farmhouse Inn." Email. July 30, 2015.

Derrick, Beatrice Durand. *Great Scott! A History of Northern Wisconsin's Earlier Days*. Webster. 1965

Dixon, R.C. "Newport, the Rise and Fall." *Wisconsin Magazine of History*. Vol. 25, no. 4. June 1942.

Dunn County Historical Society. *Dunn County History*. Dallas. 1984.

Edson, Milan. "Breaking Ground in Plainville, Settling Adams County's First Platted Village." *The Quatrefoil*. Winter 2001.

Emerson, Hugh. *The Emerson Legend*. 1966.

Engel, Dave. *Shanagolden: An Industrial Romance*.

Evanson, Richard. *Cayuga, Personal Memoirs*. Mellon Area Chamber of Commerce. January 2016.

Falkenstein, Linda. "A Sauk County folk art site makes a great Saturday trip." www.lsthumus.com. May 24, 2012.

Farrey, Loren. *A Tour Guide to the Mines of Lafayette County, Wisconsin*. Pardeeville. 2001.

"Fatal Fire." *Sheboygan Herald*. December 31, 1892.

Feldner, Emmitt. "Lost Places of Sheboygan County." *The Review*. July 1988.

Fisher, Leland. "Ghost Towns, Langlade County." www.rootsweb.ancestry.com.

Foley, Crystal. "Richland County." Email. February 15, 2016.

Folkedahl, Beulah. "Forgotten Villages, Helena." *Wisconsin Magazine of History*. Vol. 42, No. 4. Summer 1959.

Fredrick, J.L. *Ghostville: Remembering Wisconsin Ghost Towns*.

Frenz, Robert W. "Inquiry into Northwoods Country Schools." www.countryschooljournal.com.

"Hoppin' Along in Frog Station." *Our Wisconsin*. October/November 2013

Gehl, Robert. "Bud or Budd. That's the Question." *La Crosse Tribune*. 1971.

—— "It's Neat and Clean, West Prairie People Proud of Community." *La Crosse Tribune*. 1965.

—— "Victory store established in 1854 is one of four left of country post offices." *La Crosse Tribune*. February 8, 1979.

—— "Origin of Romance's Name Lost, But It Had a Post Office in 1854." *La Crosse Tribune*. November 21, 1965.

"Ghost Town was Birthplace of Governors." *Milwaukee Journal*. 1929.

Goe, Michael. *A Sesquincentennial History*. Friendship. 2004.

—— *From Past to Present: The History of Adams County*. Friendship. 1999.

—— *100 Years on the Flambeau: Park Falls and Eisenstein 1889–1989*. Friendship. 1989.

Greene, HelenMary. *Lugerville, Town of Flambeau. 1904–1954*. Park Falls. 1954/1992.

Grke, Barb and John. "Moquah." Phone. June 2, 2016.

Gurda, John. *Bay View, Wisconsin: Centennial Edition*. Milwaukee. 1979.

—— *The Making of Milwaukee*. Milwaukee.

Hengel, Genevieve. *Gillingham, Wisconsin, Or a little bit of Heaven*. 1955.

Hildebrand, Janice. *Sheboygan County: 150 Years of Progress: An Illustrated History*. Northridge. 1988.

Hollister, Mary Bormann. "After 104 Years of Business West Prairie Store Closing Its Doors Friday." *Vernon County Broadcaster*. November 13, 1997.

Holman, Earle. "Shortest logging railroad built to serve Ormsby." *Antigo Daily Journal*. September 4, 1969.

Hughes, Jim. "Graves tell of peace, pain." August 5, 1971.

Jacobowski, Joan. "Veazie: Ghost Town of the Namekagon." www.nps.gov. May 29, 2013.

Jensen, Alice. "The Danish Settlement." www.rootsweb.ancestry.com. 1982.

Johnson, Virginia Feld, Carl Kannerwerf. *Here Comes the Mail: Post Offices of Kewaunee County*. Sturgeon Bay. 2010.

Jolma, Charles. "Marenga Valley History Association." June 2016.

Jorgenson, Hans. "Historically Yours." *Westby Times*. March 21, 2002.

Joslyn, Bob. "Winooski: A Memory Preserved." *Sheboygan Press*. February 16, 1970.

"Kent is gone in all but fleeting memories." *Antigo Daily Journal*. November 25, 2006.

"Keyeser". www.deforesthistory.org. July 12, 2016.

Klueter, Howard R., James J. Lorence. *Woodlot and Ballot Box: Marathon County in the Twentieth Century*. Wausau. 1977.

Kriehn, Ruth. *The Fisherfolk of Jones Island*. Milwaukee. 1988.

Kronenwetter, Michael. *Wisconsin Heartland: The Story of Wausau and Marathon County: An Illustrated History*. Midland. 1984.

Kropp, Margaret. Phone. July 11, 2016.

Laaser, Jennifer. "Archeologists seek to understand mysteries of Aztalan State Park." *Milwaukee Journal*. June 29, 2013.

Lallensack, Rachael. "Championship Golf Course Fashioned from Old Army Base." *Sheboygan Press*. July 21, 2015.

Lundeen, Thomas. B. "Ghost Towns in Grant County, Wisconsin." 1981 Arts and Sciences Address.

Marple, Eldon M. *A History of the Hayward Lakes Region: The Visitor Who Came and Stayed*. Hayward. 1976.

McDevitt, Robert. Ed. *From Sawmills to Villages: The Early History of Caroline, Leopolis, Pell and Buckbee, Granite City, Hunting and Split Rock*. 1992.

Meier, Roy. R. *German Settlement History*. 1977.

Meyer, Mrs. Alfred. *History of Oak Creek Township*.

Minnham, William B. *The History of Calumet County*. Kenosha. 1984.

Modern Woodmen of America. "A Proud Reminder of Yesteryear." Brochure.

Moltzan, Mary. Marathon County Historical Society website.

Morrill, Charlotte Holbrook. "Reflections of Powell and Springstead."

"Niebull One-Room School Days: An Interview with Rena Murphy: Niebull School Student and Teacher." *The Quatrefoil*. Spring 2002.

Neuenschwander, John A. *Kenosha County in the 20th Century*. 1976.

Noltz, Kathy. *Ulaa: Footsteps on the Bluff*. Arizona. 2011.

Norris, Tim. "St. Martin's Street Fair and Tattersall History Keep It on the Map." *The Milwaukee Journal*. April 2, 1987.

Old Brule Heritage Society. *Wisconsin's Far Northwest: Brief Histories of the Rural Communities in Northern Douglas County*. Superior. 2004.

Plesco, Vince. "Twilight Era for Wisconsin Town." *Evening Telegram*. Superior. July 1974.

"Pokerville died when bypassed by railroad." www.madison.com. May 3, 2006.

Portage County Historical Society. "Benson's Corners." www.pchswi.org.

Pripps, Norman. *Memories of Springstead*. Park Falls. 1999.

Rasmussen, LaVerne. "A Look at the History of Strassburg." *Antigo Daily Journal Primetime*. January 5, 1998,

Reed, Larry. "Cooksville." Phone. July 31, 2015.

Richland County Historical Society. *Richland, Wisconsin*. Dallas. 1986.

Ritterbush, Cory. "Driftless Territory: A Landscape of Human Choices and Changes." *Voice of the River Valley*. February 2016. www.voiceofthevalley.com.

Rohe, Randall. *Ghosts of the Forest: Vanished Lumber Towns of Wisconsin, Volume I*. Wisconsin Rapids. 2002.

Rosholt, Malcolm. *Lumbermen on the Chippewa*. Rosholt. 1982.

Ruff, Allen & Will, Tracy. *Forward! A History of Dane: The Capital County*. Cambridge. 2000.

Rundio, Steve. "Jackson County home to three former logging communities." *Jackson County Chronicler*. January 2, 2013.

St. Martin of Tours. "History of St. Martins." www.stmoftours.org. January 11, 2016.

Sander, Phyliss Baugh. *Of Days Gone By*. Minneapolis. 1985.

Scharfnagel, Marion. "Bayfield County." Phone. June 1, 2016.

Scott, Margaret Helen. *The Place Names of Richland County, Wisconsin*. Richland Center. 1973.

"The Search for Perch . . . It leads to Mill Center, where Fish Fry Fans Love Kropp's Supper Club." *Our Wisconsin*. April/May 2014.

Sime, John H. "There was once a town at Kickapoo Center." Vernon County Historical Society. 1999.

Simonar, Carol Jean. *A History of Luxemburg Township and Village: 1855–1983*.

Skaaland, Monica W. "Newton." Vernon County Historical Society files. N.d.

Stark, William F. *Wisconsin Ghost Towns*. 1977.

Stevenson, Gordon. Email. Phone. February 2016.

—— "Lugerville Project." www.lugervilleproject.com.

Tlachae, Math S. *The History of the Belgian Settlements in Door, Kewaunee and Brown Counties: A Legacy in 10 Parts*. Algoma. 1974.

Town of Cato. "History of Cato." www.townofcato.com.

"Town of Lima 1846, St. Rose of Lima Chapel torn down last week." *Sheboygan Press*. August 18, 2015.

Trechtmann, Catherine. *Rooted in Resources: Iron County, Wisconsin 1893–1993*. Friendship. 1993.

—— Phone. Email. February 25, 2016.

Tschudy, Kim D. *Green County*. Charleston. 2010.

Tucker, M.G. *Adams, Wisconsin*. 1880.

Valle, Joel. "Nasbro." www.ghosttowns.com.

Van Alstine, Charlotte. *Town of Rome 1854–1982*. N.d.

Vilas County Chamber of Commerce. *Vilas County Headwaters to Wisconsin: Historical Reflection of the Towns in Vilas County, Wisconsin*. 1998.

Vissers, Norbert. "Powell." Phone. January 19, 2016.

Walter, Dave. "Moquah." Phone. June 2, 2016.

Waupaca County Historical Society. *Ghost Towns of Waupaca County*. Royalton. 1991.

Westerhead, Harold. *Westward to the St. Croix: The Story of St. Croix County, Wisconsin*. Hudson. 1977.

"Whatever happened to Bibon?" *Eau Claire Leader*. June 2, 1907.

"Winooski." *The Sheboygan Press*. April 29,, 1927.

Wisherd, Nan. *Pathways: The Earliest History of Northern Wisconsin's Brule Region*. Brule. 2005.

York, James. *History of Franklin Village (later St. Martins)*. March 1975.

Zechner, David. *The History of Dale and Medina, Wisconsin*. 1989.

Zillier, Carl. "History of the Asylum prepared by Trustee Zillier." *Sheboygan Press*. November 16, 1911.

Zuhorik, Joseph. *The Max Boehm Mill Site at Taus*. 1950/1960.

INDEX